GENDER IN HISTORY

Series editors:
Lynn Abrams, Cordelia Beattie, Pam Sharpe and Penny Summerfield

The expansion of research into the history of women and gender since the 1970s has changed the face of history. Using the insights of feminist theory and of historians of women, gender historians have explored the configuration in the past of gender identities and relations between the sexes. They have also investigated the history of sexuality and family relations, and analysed ideas and ideals of masculinity and femininity. Yet gender history has not abandoned the original, inspirational project of women's history: to recover and reveal the lived experience of women in the past and the present.

The series Gender in History provides a forum for these developments. Its historical coverage extends from the medieval to the modern periods, and its geographical scope encompasses not only Europe and North America but all corners of the globe. The series aims to investigate the social and cultural constructions of gender in historical sources, as well as the gendering of historical discourse itself. It embraces both detailed case studies of specific regions or periods and broader treatments of major themes. Gender in History books are designed to meet the needs of both scholars and students working in this dynamic area of historical research.

Modern motherhood

MANCHESTER
1824
Manchester University Press

MODERN MOTHERHOOD

WOMEN AND FAMILY IN ENGLAND, c. 1945–2000

+== Angela Davis ==+

Manchester University Press

Manchester and New York

distributed in the USA exclusively by Palgrave Macmillan

Published by Manchester University Press
Oxford Road, Manchester M13 9NR, UK
and Room 400, 175 Fifth Avenue, New York, NY 10010, USA
www.manchesteruniversitypress.co.uk

Distributed exclusively in the USA by Palgrave
175 Fifth Avenue, New York,
NY 10010, USA

Distributed exclusively in Canada by UBC Press
University of British Columbia, 2029 West Mall,
Vancouver, BC, Canada V6T 1Z2

British Library Cataloguing-in-Publication Data
A catalogue record for this book is available from the British Library

Library of Congress Cataloging-in-Publication Data applied for

ISBN 978 0 7190 8455 3 *hardback*

First published 2012

Typeset in Minion with Scala Sans display
by Koinonia, Manchester
Printed in Great Britain
by CPI Group (UK) Ltd, Croydon, CR0 4YY

Contents

Acknowledgements

I would first like to thank the women who shared their recollections and thoughts with me. I hope they will feel I have done justice to their memories.

I would like to express my gratitude to the Bodleian Library, Oxford; the British Library; the Centre for Oxfordshire Studies; the Elizabeth Roberts Archive at the Centre for North-West Regional Studies, Lancaster University; the Trustees of the Mass Observation Archive, University of Sussex; the Wellcome Library; and the Women's Library.

I began the research on which the book is based as a DPhil student at the University of Oxford (2003–2007). I am grateful to the Department for Continuing Education and St Cross College for the research grants they provided. I completed the book while a Leverhulme Early Career Fellow at the University of Warwick (2008–2010). I am indebted to the Leverhulme Trust for their generous support.

I would like to thank the many colleagues who have offered advice and constructive criticisms. Special thanks go to my DPhil supervisors, Janet Howarth and Kate Tiller; my DPhil examiners, Sally Alexander and John Davis; and my colleagues at the University of Warwick.

Final thanks go to my family and friends who have all helped with the writing of this book.

List of Abbreviations

AIMS	Association for Improvements in the Maternity Services
BBC	British Broadcasting Corporation
BLISS	Baby Life Support Systems
ERA	Elizabeth Roberts Archive
GP	general practitioner
MOA	Mass Observation Archive
MOH	Medical Officer of Health
NCT	National Childbirth Trust
NHS	National Health Service
OWL	Oxford Women's Liberation
PPA	Pre-school Playgroups Association
SANDS	Stillbirth and Neonatal Death Society
WHO	World Health Organization

I

Introduction

The years following 1945 were marked by significant social developments. Yet, the post-war era remains greatly neglected by historians.[1] Perspectives on the period also tend to be over-generalised. For example, the 1950s are often seen as a golden age of prosperity and consensus before the upheavals of the 1960s. In reality, as has been increasingly demonstrated, the picture is more nuanced. Many of the social changes believed to have occurred after the war had already commenced beforehand and there was a great deal of continuity as well as change in the years that followed. In recent years historians have shown how these developments were also mediated by factors such as gender, class, region and ethnicity. This book builds upon such existing scholarship but offers new insights through its focus on motherhood. Looking through the prism of motherhood provides a way of understanding the complex social changes taking place during this time. Motherhood is an area where a number of discourses and practices meet, such as education, health care, psychology, labour market trends and state intervention. In consequence the experience of motherhood has a wide resonance, demonstrating change in: women's lives, gender relations, culture and society, family and community patterns, health and welfare, and the relationship between the family and the state. Drawing on the themes of continuity and change I will examine the legacies of these developments and will consider what they indicate about both the past and future of motherhood in England.

While motherhood is both a biological and cultural state there is, as Ellen Ross argues, little that is truly 'natural' about an institution which is so embedded in social and cultural practices.[2] Ideas about motherhood have accordingly changed over the centuries. Indeed the term 'motherhood' itself seems to be a relatively recent invention. Ann Dally cites 1597 as the first entry for 'motherhood' in the *Oxford English Dictionary*, and then only as a fact rather than an ideology. She argues it was not until the Victorian era that the word emerged as a concept, when many elements of motherhood as it was conceived in the post-1945 decades, such as its association with sex, cohabitation, and capitalist consumption became established.[3] However, understandings of motherhood in the years after 1945 were also influenced by some theoretical developments specific to this period, such as mother-centred psychoanalysis, structural-functionalist sociology and second-wave feminism.

Indeed motherhood in the second half of the twentieth century is a particularly interesting subject due to the dramatic changes in conceptions of the role of women that occurred at this time. As Carol Dyhouse points out, the years after World War Two were a time of contra-dictions for women. There was 'a growing ideology of home-centeredness reflected in the proliferation and phenomenal growth of the women's magazines spreading the gospel of salvation through consumption during the period'; but this was accompanied by 'a steady significant rise in the number of women leaving their homes, particularly when children were old enough to go to school, and returning to paid employment.'[4] However, while married women were increasingly present in the workforce they were not conceived of as workers on the same terms as men. Instead, after the war, there was a redescription of the housewife as worker. Women as mothers or potential mothers were, in the words of Denise Riley, 'the true target of postwar social philosophy'.[5] Dennis Dean argues that the consequence of this emphasis on women's domestic role was that: 'Other demands, even those for equality of pay or career opportunities, were regarded as preoccupations of a minority of women who had rejected either marriage or motherhood. They came far down the list of priorities of a reforming government.'[6] The Birmingham Feminist History Group stress that post-war ideologies about women were 'underpinned by the notion of "equal but different". This notion of separate spheres was not new, but they note that the conditions prevailing in the 1950s gave it new connotations. This was a generation of women who were expected to successfully combine the loving and caring role of the mother 'with an ability to run their own homes probably without domestic help and to work in the public sphere as well.'[7]

Moreover there were additional social, cultural and demographic changes taking place from the late 1960s, encouraged by new legislation, which further complicated the role of mothers. The introduction of the contraceptive pill to Britain in 1961 made contraception easier to obtain, easier to use and more reliable. The National Health Service (NHS) Family Planning Act of 1967 allowed doctors to give family planning advice and to prescribe free contraceptives, though initially only to married women.

The Abortion Act of the same year allowed the termination of pregnancy if two independent medical practitioners agreed that continuance would cause physical or mental risk to the health of the woman or her existing children. And the 1969 Divorce Reform Act made the 'irretrievable break-down' of the marriage the sole grounds for divorce, although it was neces-sary to prove this in one of five ways (unreasonable behaviour, desertion, adultery, two years of separation with consent, five years of separation without consent). Growing feminist activism from the late 1960s in the form of the Women's Liberation Movement further encouraged a reassess-ment of the place of women in the family and society. However many of the developments ascribed to the 1960s, such as the growth of never-married motherhood,[8] were not fully realised until later decades. In addition, change had, in fact, been occurring throughout the late nineteenth and twentieth centuries. Writing in the late 1990s, Susan McRae thought, 'Much of what we are seeing in Britain today is the continuation of trends briefly interrupted by the 'ideal family of the 1950s and 1960s.'[9] Nonethe-less a great deal was new. The 1970s and 1980s witnessed rising rates of cohabitation and divorce. While marriage remained popular at the end of the twentieth century, non-marriage and singleness were becoming increasingly common, and those marriages that took place often ended in divorce. This collapse of the assumption that childbirth would take place inside marriage was a profound change. Reviewing the twentieth century Jane Lewis has concluded: 'At the beginning of the century the vast majority of people married before they had sex, had their children inside marriage and stayed married. At the end of the century people's family arrangements looked increasingly messy.'[10]

The years following 1945 are also fascinating because of the changing expectations of women who were reaching adulthood at this time. Judy Giles believes that girls growing up in the 1920s and 1930s 'experienced a widening of their cultural horizons that had not been possible for their mothers.' The department store, the cinema, the dance hall, and the mass production of newspapers, magazines and cheap books offered 'a kalei-doscope of images, commodities, and experiences, representing a world beyond the family, home, and the locality.' At the same time the growth of public and private transport systems allowed women to extend the geographical boundaries of their worlds.[11] Developing this theme Sally Alexander argues it was above all an era of new aspirations:

> advertising and the cinema, playing on fantasy and desire enabled women to *imagine* an end to domestic drudgery and chronic want ... Few women replaced the copper with the washing-machine or the outside lavatory with the bathroom during the 1930s. But the dream was there.[12]

In this book I will therefore examine: how powerful these new desires were in women's accounts of their attitudes and experiences of motherhood over the second half of the century; whether it is possible to discern differences in how women articulated their hopes over time; and how far women in differing circumstances were able to realise their dreams.

Sources and methods

The book is based on oral history interviews with 166 women living in the following rural, urban and suburban locations of Oxfordshire: the villages of Benson and Ewelme in south Oxfordshire; the Wychwood villages in west Oxfordshire; the twenty-four square miles near Banbury in north Oxfordshire covered by the *Country Planning* (1944) survey;[13] the market town of Thame, which lies in the east of the county; Oxford city centre; and the contrasting suburbs of industrial, working-class Cowley and Florence Park in east Oxford, and professional, middle-class North Oxford and Summertown in north Oxford. In addition two villages in the neighbouring county of Berkshire – Crowthorne and Sandhurst – were included.[14] The book examines the impact of locality on the health and welfare provision available to mothers. Incorporating the Berkshire villages into the book's sample enables the comparison of provision between the local authorities of Oxford city, Oxfordshire and Berkshire, as well as the influence of local practices and personalities. A group of graduates of Somerville College, Oxford, who lived in Oxfordshire, were also interviewed to enable the experience of highly educated women to be considered. The interviewees all lived in Berkshire or Oxfordshire when their children were growing up, but the range of communities they lived in was specifically chosen to enable a comparison of local experiences. As many women as logistically possible were interviewed. While the numbers are significantly lower than for social survey and sampling methods, as Kate Fisher argues, 'Oral history provides the historian with dense and rich qualitative material rather than strength in numbers.'[15] Interviewees were principally found through community groups, social clubs and by women referring other women to be interviewed.[16] The Somervillians were found through the college's alumni association. The sample was self-selecting in that all the women had volunteered to be interviewed. However the aim was to construct a sample that ranged in age from late fifties to nineties, that represented both middle and working classes,[17] and that demonstrated a variety of educational backgrounds (from minimum-age school leavers to graduates) to see how locality, education and class influenced women's experiences.[18] A case study was selected rather than a national survey to enable an in-depth analysis of how living in different types of localities and communities affected women's experiences of motherhood. However, the experience of the Oxfordshire interviewees will be analysed in the context of a range of existing primary and secondary material, such as Elizabeth Roberts' oral histories of women in Lancashire and the correspondents to Mass Observation, in order to enable a national perspective to be gained. Similarly, while the Oxfordshire sample was largely homogenous in terms of ethnicity, reference to studies which have focused more specifically on the experience of non-indigenous women will be made. There are also significant variations between the different parts of the United Kingdom. However it would not be possible to do justice to these differences (for example in medical care, welfare provision, educational and legal systems) in a book of this length and scope; therefore it will focus on the English experience.[19]

The strength of using oral history combined with a case study approach is that it allows the cross-generational experience of motherhood to be examined through an analysis of different cohorts of women from within the same communities. It has long been known that memories are formed collectively. Maurice Halbwachs established that, 'The individual calls recollections to mind by relying on the frameworks of social memory'.[20] The family plays a crucial role in this construction of memory. Memories are transmitted through the stories family members tell.[21] Children learn to remember in the family environment, guided by parental intervention and shared reminiscence. We rely on the memories of older members of our family, with the result that many of our earliest memories are actually recollections of stories we heard from adults about our childhood.[22] Attitudes, values and taboos, as well as linguistic, perceptual, cognitive, educational, communicational, and emotional resources (or handicaps), and economic and patrimonial resources are all transmitted through the generations.[23] In their study of the transmission of fathering practices Julia Brannen and Ann Nilsen found that intergenerational transmission occurs in complex ways though, so that a resource passed on by one generation may be used in a different way by the next. For example, one of the fathers they interviewed said that what was transmitted from his family was the freedom to choose to live his life in a different way to his parents' generation.[24] Cultural transmission within the family is therefore a subtle process, but examining the ways in which both material and emotional resources were passed down through the families of the women interviewed enables a fuller consideration of the notions and practices that guide people's lives in different family and historical contexts. Interviews were therefore based upon the life cycle, and interviewees were encouraged to reflect upon their own lives in comparison with those of their parents' and children's generations. The life-cycle model was also employed because it mirrors the way women tend to construct and articulate their narratives.[25] The model allowed the women interviewed to tell their own stories with as little intervention from the interviewer as possible. However it also enabled some comparability between the interviews as they all covered the same key themes.[26] Moreover, as Marie-Françoise Chanfrault-Duchet proposes, such an approach 'makes it possible to go beyond the preconstituted discourses and "surface assertions" collected through survey research. It highlights the complexity, the ambiguities, and even the contradictions of the relations between the subject and the ideological image of woman.'[27]

Oral history allows women to be the central figures of this book. They were involved in creating the history through the oral history interview and are the principal focus of the study. Because oral history is reliant on memories, usually of older people, it has faced criticism. However, oral historians have offered many convincing defences for the practice while reflecting on its methodological challenges.[28] There are some particular difficulties (although also benefits) in the use of oral data due to the ways in which people remember and the methods of storytelling that interviewees employ. People use narrative genres as a way of structuring their accounts.[29] But in the context of a range of other sources, oral history can reveal the complex ways in which women compose their narratives in order to reconcile ideals of femininity with the reality of their own lives.[30] Much can be learnt about the expectations of and constraints upon women in the second half of the twentieth century through analysing the silences, uncertainties and contradictions within the oral history interviews.[31] Hence oral history is a methodology that can provide objective information about women's lives, but also reveals their thoughts and feelings through the subjectivity of their accounts. To quote Alessandro Portelli, 'oral sources tell us not just what people did, but what they wanted to do, what they believed they were doing, and what they now think they did'.[32] Oral history enables the relationship between the ideal and reality of motherhood to be examined. A further advantage of oral history is that, unlike other sources, it makes it possible to examine how women review their experiences in light of later developments in their own lives and the changing attitudes towards women that occurred over the course of the century.[33]

This book is a study in gender history and women's history. Sally Alexander has commented that: 'Women's history in the early 1970s sprang from that utopian and romantic disposition – 200 years old –

which sought to tell women's stories in their own words, to unveil new vocabularies for women, and to re-map the division between the personal and the political.'[34] Oral history seems an ideal methodology to meet these aims, encouraging as it does the study of subjectivity within historical accounts of women's lives. As Alexander argues, subjectivity need be neither universal nor ahistorical, and 'structured through relations of absence and loss, pleasure and unpleasure, difference and division, these are simultaneous with the social naming and placing among kin, community, school, class which are always historically specific.'[35] Psychoanalysis offers a way of analysing this subjectivity and construction of identity. Indeed Alexander believes that the first wish of feminist history, 'to fill the gaps and silences of written history, to uncover new meanings for femininity and women, to project sexuality to the forefront of the political mind', shares some of the intentions of psychoanalysis. The 'discovery of a subjective history through image, symbol and language' is central to both.[36] Judy Giles believes psychoanalytic theory's recent emphasis on symbolic and linguistic structures has provided gender historians with new approaches to the historical construction of gendered subjectivities.[37] Graham Dawson, for example, has developed an analysis linking Melanie Klein's theory of psychic composure with cultural theories of narrative, coining the term 'cultural imaginaries' to describe the 'vast networks of interlinking discursive themes, images, motifs and narrative forms that are publicly available within a culture at any one time, and articulate its psychic and social dimensions.'[38] The use of oral history in this book enables an exploration of the 'cultural imaginaries' which shaped women's experiences of motherhood in the second half of the twentieth century.

The local context

Through examining how women's experiences of being a mother were affected by where they lived and the type of community in which they lived, this book demonstrates the importance of locality in shaping lived experience. Using Oxfordshire as a case study it is possible to examine a range of communities: rural, urban and suburban. Within these categories there are further differences such as those between the middle-class suburbs of north Oxford and the lower-middle and working-class suburbs of east Oxford, and between expanding villages and static villages. Oxfordshire is also a suitable place for testing other variables which could influence women's attitudes towards motherhood. The county has a population with a variety of educational experiences amongst its female inhabitants, from those who attended rural elementary schools where a range of ages were taught in one or two rooms by one or two teachers, to women who were Oxford University graduates. There were also many significant differences in the maternity care women received in Oxford, Oxfordshire and Berkshire and there is an interesting comparison to be made between the three authorities and in the provision of care in urban and rural areas. For example, while in the city of Oxford antenatal clinics were available in the 1930s these were not on offer in rural areas until the late 1960s.[39] In terms of antenatal education Oxfordshire also lagged behind the city. Antenatal classes were not started in Oxfordshire until 1961, and then only two classes were in operation.[40] In the city of Oxford mothercraft classes were on offer by 1947.[41] Perhaps the most striking difference was in the provision of family planning advice. In the city of Oxford a birth control clinic was started in May 1935 by the Assistant Medical Officer of Health (MOH), Dr Mary Fisher, to give birth control advice on medical grounds.[42] With regard to the county, however, it was not until the Family Planning Act 1967 came into force that the first clinic was set up.[43] Oxford's advanced position in relation to birth control was also seen in comparison with Reading, the county town of neighbouring Berkshire. It was not until 1964 that the term family planning appeared in the report of Reading's MOH and the first clinic was set up in 1966, thirty-one years after Oxford.[44] There were significant variations in the services available to urban and rural dwellers. The authors of the 1944 survey of north Oxfordshire, *Country Planning*, argued: 'Both in his purchasing power and in the physical and social conditions of his life – housing, the public services, education, leisure and the opportunities for using it – the countryman was at a disadvantage with almost any urban dweller.'[45] The quality of housing and provision of facilities for many of Oxfordshire's rural residents were inferior to those for their urban counterparts. For instance, until the 1960s there were still many rural areas without mains water or sewerage.

There were also differences in employment opportunities. At the start of the twentieth century Oxfordshire was predominantly a rural county. However the nineteenth century had seen a decline in the power of agriculture, as in the country at large, and it continued to decrease in the twentieth century. The opening of the Morris Motor Company in Cowley in 1913 was a significant development. Morris' factory inevitably attracted workers from the rural regions around Oxford. Over the period 1911 to 1931 the number of agricultural workers in the county fell by roughly half.[46] In sum it was estimated that around 3,000 ex-agricultural workers were in the Cowley motor industry by 1936.[47] The expanding car industry also lured workers from further afield. In the 1930s 43 percent of all male insured workers in Oxford were recent immigrants. Of these immigrants the largest proportion, 36.7 percent, came from south-west England; 10.8 percent came from Wales (for the most part south Wales); 10.7 percent came from London; the south-eastern region contributed 9 percent, and the midlands 8.2 percent.[48] Migrants from outside the home nations did not settle in Oxford in significant numbers until after World War Two. It was estimated that in early 1959 there were about 400 to 500 non-white workers in Oxford, about 60 to 70 percent of them being West Indian and the rest Indian and Pakistani. Most migrants at this time were men, and the number of women was relatively small.[49] However, South Asian women started to arrive in larger numbers from the end of the 1960s after the Commonwealth Immigrants Acts of 1962 and 1968 introduced tighter controls on immigration. Men who originally intended to work in Britain and move home at some later date, were anxious to bring their wives and children over to Britain, fearful that further immigration controls would prevent a later family reunion.[50] By 1981 there were 3,500 people of South Asian origin in Oxford, of a total resident population of 93,500.[51]

The second half of the twentieth century was therefore a period of transformation for Oxfordshire. Employment opportunities, population size and service provision were all undergoing change. There were important differences between the experiences of women living in urban and rural localities, especially early on in the period, but they also shared some significant similarities. The decline in agriculture and domestic service affected employment opportunities for men and women. More stable male employment in both rural and urban areas meant that women's (and children's) employment was not so necessary to keep families afloat. The growth of industry, which ran parallel to this transition, created many new jobs for the population of the towns in which these industries were located, but also for the surrounding countryside. The motor industry, the nexus of which was the works at Cowley, was perhaps the most significant of these industries but there were others, such as the aluminium factory at Banbury which opened in 1931. Linked to changes brought about by these new employment patterns was that of population mobility. Jobs in the locality where people had traditionally lived, such as in agriculture, were declining, and improved transport and communications meant people no longer needed to live where they worked, resulting in many of the old communities, both urban and rural, breaking down, and new ones being created. Government planning policy, at both local and national levels, exacerbated these trends. Some communities were judged suitable for development, such as Benson, which was classified as an expanding village in the late 1950s; others shared the fate of St Ebbe's, demolished as a slum clearance area in the 1960s. There were some positive changes. Services such as water, sewerage, gas and electricity became universal; the better wages available in the new industries, and the improved living conditions that new housing brought, benefited many people. The new communities that developed could never replicate the old, but after initial periods of dislocation they did mature and began to provide support for their members. These alterations were not without their consequences. As populations became more mobile family members lived further apart which could lead to loneliness and isolation, especially for women. While transport brought improved access to facilities outside the local area, those services on offer within a village or district often declined. For example, the growth in car ownership meant that local bus services were severely reduced and local shops closed. The latter half of the twentieth century brought substantial change to Oxfordshire. Although the pace of these developments did vary across the county none of its inhabitants were unaffected. Moreover, as the book will demonstrate, it was often women, and particularly mothers of young children, who felt the consequences of this change most keenly.

Throughout the second half of the twentieth century, motherhood was a role characterised by ambivalence and complexity. In this book I will demonstrate the joy and pain, improvements and regressions, and the achievements and disappointments that women as mothers have experienced. In order to do this, the book will form a thematic study looking at six aspects of motherhood. Each chapter will begin with an introduction giving the context of the debate and then will focus on the experiences of women themselves through an analysis of the personal testimonies gathered. To start, chapter 2 examines the place of the mother in the family. It investigates the ideas of motherhood and family life that were in vogue through an analysis of contemporary texts, such as social surveys and community studies, and considers them in the light of the oral history interviews. Chapter 3 addresses the process of educating women to be mothers and asks how far commentators, and women themselves, felt they needed to be taught how to mother or whether it came naturally to them. Furthermore, if women did need to be educated about motherhood, where was it assumed that this education should take place? Chapter 4 then develops these debates by looking at maternity provision and the changing relationship between mothers and medical professionals in the spheres of antenatal care, childbirth and postnatal care. Next, chapter 5 examines how ideas of what made 'good' and 'bad' mothers were conveyed to women through the works of childcare experts. It considers women's attitudes towards these theories, and the consequences of trying to follow 'expert' advice. Following on from this, chapter 6 explores mothers' feelings about work inside and outside the home, how women combined paid labour and motherhood in the course of their lives, and how society perceived the working mother. Chapter 7 then looks at cultural conceptions of the family and the relationship between these public understandings of motherhood and women's accounts of their personal experiences. Taken together, these analyses present a picture of the dilemmas and contradictions that existed for women as mothers of young children during the second half of the twentieth century, and how they tried to reconcile them.

Notes

1 Selina Todd, *Young Women, Work and Family in England 1918–1950* (Oxford: Oxford University Press, 2005), p. 11.

2 Ellen Ross, *Love and Toil: Motherhood in Outcast London 1870–1918* (New York: Oxford University Press, 1993), p. 4.

3 Ann Dally, *Inventing Motherhood: The Consequences of an Ideal* (New York: Schocken, 1983), p. 17.

4 Carol Dyhouse, 'Towards a "feminine" curriculum for English schoolgirls: the demands of an ideology', *Women's Studies International Quarterly*, 1 (1978), 291–311, p. 308.

5 Denise Riley, *War in the Nursery: Theories of Child and Mother* (London: Virago, 1983), p. 171.

6 D.W. Dean, 'Education for moral improvement, domesticity and social cohesion: the Labour government, 1945–1951', in Liz Dawtrey, Janet Holland and Merril Hammer, with Sue Sheldon, *Equality and Inequality in Education Policy* (Clevedon: Multilingual Matters, 1995), 18–30, p. 18.

7 Birmingham Feminist History Group, 'Feminism as femininity in the nineteen-fifties?', *Feminist Review*, 3 (1979), 48–65, p. 50.

8 Jane Lewis and John Welshman, *The Issue of Never-Married Motherhood in Britain, 1920–70, Social History of Medicine*, 10 (1997), 401–18.

9 Susan McRae, 'Introduction: family and household change in Britain', in Susan McRae (ed.), *Changing Britain: Families and Households in the 1990s* (Oxford: Oxford University Press, 1999), 1–34, p. 2.

10 Jane Lewis, 'Marriage', in Ina Zweiniger-Bargielowska (ed.), *Women in Twentieth-Century Britain* (Harlow: Pearson Education Limited, 2001), 69–85, p. 74.

11 Judy Giles, 'Narratives of gender, class, and modernity in women's memories of mid-twentieth century Britain, *Signs*, 28 (2002), 21–41, pp. 34–5.

12 Sally Alexander, *Becoming a Woman, and Other Essays in 19th and 20th Century Feminist History* (London: Virago, 1994), p. 205. Emphasis in original.

13 The Agricultural Economics Research Institute Oxford, *Country Planning: A Study of Rural Problems* (London: Oxford University Press, 1944).

14 In the book the sample will be referred to as the Oxfordshire interviewees rather than Berkshire and Oxfordshire interviewees for brevity.

15 Kate Fisher, 'An Oral History of Birth Control Practice c. 1925–50: A Study of Oxford and South Wales' (DPhil dissertation, University of Oxford, 1997), p. 40.

16 Kate Field argues this 'snowballing', where each respondent gives the name of another person to participate, is a particularly appropriate method for finding elderly respondents to a local study because it helps secure the trust of interviewees through being 'recommended' to them by their friends. Katherine Field, 'Children of the Nation? A Study of the Health and Well-being of Oxfordshire Children, 1891–1939' (DPhil dissertation, University of Oxford, 2001), p. 103.

17 Interviewees were asked to give their class of origin.

18 The interviews were semi-structured, following the model described by Penny Summerfield, and were typically between one and two hours long. Penny Summerfield, *Reconstructing Women's Wartime Lives* (Manchester: Manchester University Press, 1998), pp. 1–42. To enable informed consent the aims of the research were explained to potential respondents in advance of the interview. Interviewees were also given the chance to specify any restrictions they wished to make on their contributions. To preserve the anonymity of the interviewees pseudonyms have been used. Interviewees are referenced by identifying codes. The codes are formed of the first two letters of the locality from which the interviewee came and an identifying number: BA = 24 square miles of north Oxfordshire near Banbury covered by the 1944 Country Planning survey; BE = Benson; CO = Cowley and Florence Park; CR = Crowthorne; EW = Ewelme; NO = North Oxford and Summertown; OX = Oxford city centre; SA = Sandhurst; SO = graduates of Somerville College, Oxford; TH = Thame; WY = Wychwood villages. Recordings and transcripts are held by the author.

19 For the experiences of women from different parts of the United Kingdom, see, for example, Jane Aaron, Teresa Rees, Sandra Betts and Moira Vincentelli (eds), *Our Sisters' Land: The Changing Identities of Women in Wales* (Cardiff: University of Wales Press, 1994); Lynn Abrams, *Myth and Materiality in a Woman's World: Shetland 1800–2000* (Manchester: Manchester University Press, 2005); Lynn Abrams, Eleanor Gordon, Deborah Simonton and Eileen Yeo (eds), *Gender in Scottish History since 1700* (Edinburgh: Edinburgh University Press, 2006); Deirdre Beddoe, *Out of the Shadows: A History of Women in Twentieth-Century Wales* (Cardiff: University of Wales Press, 2000); Leanne McCormick, *Regulating Sexuality: Women in Twentieth-Century Northern Ireland* (Manchester: Manchester University Press, 2009).

20 Maurice Halbwachs as cited in Barbara Misztal, *Theories of Social Remembering* (Maidenhead: Open University Press, 2003), p. 51.

21 Michael G. Kenny, 'A place for memory: the interface between individual and collective history', *Comparative Studies in Society and History*, 41 (1999), 420–37, p. 421.

22 Misztal, *Theories of Social Remembering*, p. 19.

23 Daniel Bertaux and Isabelle Bertaux-Wiame, 'Heritage and its lineage: a case history of transmission and social mobility over five generations', in Daniel Bertaux and Paul Thompson (eds), *Pathways to Social Class: A Qualitative Approach to Social Mobility* (Oxford: Clarendon Press, 1997), 62–97, pp. 65–6.

24 Julia Brannen and Ann Nilsen, 'From fatherhood to fathering: transmission and change among British fathers in four-generation families', *Sociology*, 40 (2006), 335–52, pp. 340–1.

25 Isabelle Bertaux-Wiame, 'The life history approach to internal migration: how men and women came to Paris between the wars', in Paul Thompson (ed.), *Our Common*

History: The Transformations of Europe (London: Polity Press, 1982), 186–200; Susan Geiger, 'Women's life histories', *Signs*, 11 (1986), 334–51.

26 See Appendix 1.

27 Marie-Françoise Chanfrault-Duchet, 'Narrative structures, social models and symbolic representation in the life story', in Sherna Berger Gluck and Daphne Patai (eds), *Women's Words: The Feminist Practice of Oral History* (New York and London: Routledge, Chapman and Hall, 1991), 77–92, p. 89.

28 Kate Fisher provides one such defence in the introduction to her DPhil thesis, which includes a comprehensive review and critical appraisal of the existing literature and debates. Fisher, 'Oral History of Birth Control Practice', pp. 31–80.

29 For example Penny Summerfield has demonstrated how the women she interviewed about their experiences of World War Two principally adopted two narrative models, the stoic and the heroic. Summerfield, *Reconstructing Women's Wartime Lives*.

30 Bronwen Davies, 'Women's subjectivity and feminist stories', in C. Ellis and M.G. Flaherty (eds), *Investigating Subjectivity: Researching on Lived Experience* (Newbury Park: Sage, 1992), 55–76, p. 55.

31 Joan Sangster, 'Telling our stories: feminist debates and the use of oral history', in Robert Perks and Alistair Thomson (eds), *The Oral History Reader* (London: Routledge, 1998), 87–100, p. 88.

32 Alessandro Portelli, *The Death of Luigi Trastulli and Other Stories: Form and Meaning in Oral History* (Albany: State University of New York Press, 1991), p. 50.

33 Philip Gardner, 'Oral history in education: teacher's memory and teachers' history', *History of Education*, 32 (2003), 175–88, p. 184.

34 Sally Alexander, 'Feminist history', in Elizabeth Wright (ed.), *Feminism and Psychoanalysis: A Critical Dictionary* (Oxford: Blackwell, 1992), 108–13, p. 108.

35 Alexander, *Becoming a Woman*, p. 109.

36 Alexander, 'Feminist history', p. 109.

37 Giles, 'Narratives of gender, class, and modernity', p. 24.

38 Graham Dawson, *Soldier Heroes: British Adventure, Empire, and the Imagining of Masculinities* (London: Routledge, 1994), pp. 48–52.

39 City of Oxford Annual Report of the Medical Officer of Health, 1935, p. 84 (hereafter Oxford MOH); Oxfordshire County Council Annual Reports of the County Medical Officer of Health and Principal School Medical Officer, 1967, p. 23 (hereafter Oxfordshire MOH).

40 Oxfordshire MOH, 1961, p. 9.

41 Oxford MOH, 1947, p. 23.

42 Oxford MOH, 1935, p. 84.

43 Oxfordshire MOH, 1967, p. 33.

44 Jessie Parfit, *The Health of a City: Oxford 1770–1974* (Oxford: The Amate Press, 1987), p. 95.

45 Agricultural Economics Research Institute Oxford, *Country Planning*, p. iii.

46 A.F.C. Bourdillon (ed.), *A Survey of the Social Services in the Oxford District, I, Economics and Government of a Changing Area* (Oxford: Oxford University Press, 1938), p. 139.

47 Richard C. Whiting, *The View from Cowley: The Impact of Industrialization upon Oxford 1918–1939* (Oxford: Clarendon Press, 1983), p. 39.

48 Bourdillon, *A Survey of the Social Services in the Oxford District, I*, pp. 25–46.

49 Donald Wood, 'A general survey', in A.G. Griffith, J. Henderson, M. Usborne and D. Wood, *Coloured Immigrants in Britain* (London: Oxford University Press, 1960), pp. 42–3.

50 Alison Shaw, *Kinship and Continuity: Pakistani Families in Britain* (London: Routledge, 2000), p. 53.

51 Alison Shaw, 'Pakistani Families in Oxford: Some Aspects of Migration' (DPhil dissertation, University of Oxford, 1984), pp. 13–14.

2

Family and community:
surveying women and the family

The lives of women and their families were subject to scrutiny throughout the second half of the twentieth century, with the issues of community, class and later ethnicity being of prime importance to social scientists. The particular focus of their concern, though, altered over the period, reflecting the changing nature of the society that they studied. For researchers writing in the 1950s and early 1960s there seemed many reasons for people to be content. After the war there was an array of new legislation that heralded the creation of the welfare state; the austerity of the immediate post-war years diminished and confidence grew that material conditions were on an upward trend. This mood of expectation conditioned the studies conducted during these years. Their authors believed that both the social and economic life of the country was improving, and that greater prosperity would positively affect patterns of community and family life. By the late 1960s and early 1970s this mood of optimism was tempered, as sociologists revealed the continuation of poverty, and feminists highlighted the problems that women in the family could face. The preoccupation of sociologists with the family then faded somewhat during the 1970s. Graham Allan believes that community and kinship studies were to some extent the victim of their own success, with later sociologists preferring to explore less well-researched areas.[1] Elements of the family experience did still attract attention though. Following the introduction of the 1969 Divorce Reform Act divorce rates rose significantly, encouraging the study of marriage breakdown. Growing numbers of ethnic minority families present in the country also formed a new focus for researchers. However, by the end of the century there was a move towards stressing continuities within people's experiences of family life despite the dramatic social changes that had occurred.

As well as family structure, sociologists were also interested in the vitality of the communities they were studying. In the years before and after World War Two, the consequences of the movement of families from traditional urban neighbourhoods in city centres to new suburban estates were a prime focus of concern. In her 1944 study of the problems of adjustment involved in the severance between the workplace and housing, Kate Liepmann commented upon the social disintegration she found in suburban estates due to 'the newness of the dormitories and the thinness of the urban fabric.'[2] Indeed Elizabeth Bott thought that by the 1940s it had become part of folklore that estates were responsible for marked losses of working-class sociability.[3] In the 1950s, Michael Young and Peter Willmott found that whereas in urban Bethnal Green residents had acquaintances in every direction, suburban 'Greenleigh' (Young and Willmott's fictitious name for Debden in Essex) was a far lonelier place. Comparing the two localities they asserted: 'In Bethnal Green, the kindred are at hand every day of the week. At Greenleigh the family has to wait for summer, for week-ends, for holidays, before they appear.'[4] Women in particular found the distances from their family prohibitive. Even when the distance moved was not great and transport was easily available, as was the case in Oxford, kin relations decayed. Of the households studied by John Mogey in city-centre St Ebbe's, 60 percent had regular kin contact whereas in Barton, only three miles away, half that number did.[5] Similarly, in her study of London house-wives first published in 1966, Hannah Gavron concluded that young working-class women living in new high-rise estates could feel isolated in a way that was unknown to previous generations, because the street-based life of old working-class communities had provided them with social contacts.[6]

Peter Willmott and Michael Young portrayed life in the suburb of Woodford (which they considered to be middle class[7]) in a far more positive light than that in 'Greenleigh'. Residents were deemed to be friendlier, more co-operative and supportive of one another. Willmott and Young thought the difference between the two areas was a result of class. They suggested that the middle-class residents of Woodford had a certain capacity or skill at 'making friends'. These friends were recruited amongst their neighbours and provided one another with a good deal of practical help. In contrast working-class Bethnal Greeners did not need this capacity to make friends because whether or not they made any effort they had plenty of friends around them, and were therefore 'lost when they were transported to the strange environment of the housing estate.'[8] Willmott and Young concluded therefore that the relative importance people attached towards friends and relatives was dependent on their class.

Such discourses of class dominated mid-twentieth-century Britain, and class was the prevailing mode of analysis for the authors of the post-war community studies. The period after the war was characterised as one of affluence and the question of whether or not there was embourgoisement of the working classes, and whether they were adopting middle-class patterns of life, encouraged great debate.[9] However, there were also those who noted the limitations of a simple class analysis. In their study of working-class attitudes to marriage in 1943, the social psychologists Elizabeth Slater and Moya Woodside proposed that the realisation of one's 'class' position emerged from routine activities of everyday life: it was the 'feeling of belonging' which was 'felt to be natural and was taken for granted'. They found their respondents were concerned as much with symbolic expressions of power in social relationships as with material realities.[10] Moreover, Peter Hiller and Herbert Moorhouse, who were both writing in the 1970s, found that within the space of one discussion people could change their definition of 'class' a number of times, without being aware of inconsistency.[11]

While class had been a traditional subject of concern for those investigating the family, as the post-war decades progressed sociologists also developed a new focus for their studies, 'race'. However, as Alison Shaw notes, there were few studies of migrant groups in the tradition of anthropological or community studies. Instead the main focus of many such studies was to address the question of whether or not immigrant groups could 'assimilate' into British lifestyles and values, and whether the experience of being second generation necessarily involved problems of 'cultural conflict' and of being 'between two cultures'.[12] The structure of immigrant families did receive attention though. It was considered different, and therefore inferior, by many commentators. Initially there was a particular stress on the deficiencies of West Indian families due to their low marriage rates, high illegitimacy, use of childminders and their practice of leaving their children behind with relatives when they migrated. In her study of Notting Hill, the sociologist Pearl Jephcott concluded, 'The migrants themselves plainly attach less importance than we do to the risk of separating children from their parents.'[13] Her allusion to post-war psychology's stress on the mother–child bond is noteworthy. Similarly, in Sheila Patterson's book *Dark Strangers*, published in 1963, about Jamaican immigrants in Brixton in the late 1950s and early 1960s, the sociologist described how 'London social workers are somewhat taken aback at the free and easy way in which many West Indian unmarried mothers discuss the disposal of their children.'[14] In actuality, migrant women who left their children with minders or in nurseries spoke of the difficulties they faced in reaching such decisions and the anxieties it caused them.[15] Indeed in her autobiography the teacher and novelist Beryl Gilroy, originally from British Guiana (now Guyana), reflected on the pressure she felt 'to be the perfect housewife and perfect mother. I must be above all possible white criticism.'[16] Initially, South Asian women did not come under the same scrutiny because of their smaller numbers and obviously strong family structure, with women occupying traditional roles. The writer Elspeth Huxley thought that, 'Of all immigrant groups, Indians and Pakistanis maintain the tightest family formations, the greatest social cohesion, the strictest moral code.'[17] However they still faced reproach for supposedly having too many children and consequently placing the health and welfare services under strain.

By the latter decades of the twentieth century new family forms within the wider population also became a subject of study.[18] There was a particular interest in how the dramatic rise in the divorce rate, the growth of couples cohabiting outside of marriage, and the formation of step-families due to remarriage, altered people's experience of family life. For instance in their study of step-families, conducted in the late 1970s, Jacqueline Burgoyne and David Clark reached two principal conclusions. Firstly, they found that apparently 'private' experiences of marriage breakup, divorce and remarriage were filled with public encounters, such as with solicitors, the courts, welfare and probation officers, doctors and social workers. Secondly, they discovered that the expectations and experiences surrounding second marriages were shaped and moulded to a considerable degree by the legacies of the past. These could include issues over the custody of children or maintenance payments, continuing ambivalent feelings about a previous partner, or anxieties about whether a 'better' choice had been made the second time around.[19] Moreover, while researchers found the experience of marriage for both the marriage partners and their children had changed, there were often continuities in attitudes towards marriage and family. In a study of family breakdown in Exeter, published in 1994, it was shown that, despite half of the children sampled living in families 're-ordered' by parental separation or divorce, people still held traditional ideas about family life, with lone parents and their children saying they did not feel themselves to be a part of a 'real' family.[20]

Similar patterns have emerged in terms of kinship structures as well. Although there were changes, continuities also exist. In the early 1990s Geoff Dench, Kate Gavron and Michael Young undertook a restudy of Young and Willmott's *Family and Kinship in East London*, research undertaken in the 1950s. They found that Bethnal Green 'had been transformed beyond recognition'. The most dramatic difference to emerge was in its ethnic composition. In 1953 there were few non-white people in Bethnal Green, and none recorded in the survey, but in 1992 only two-thirds of the respondents described themselves as white, while over one in five had been born in Bangladesh. Relatively large numbers of younger people born in the area had moved out – with more than half the children listed by older Bethnal Greeners now living outside London. However, despite these striking changes the family remained important to the study's informants. While the authors noted that many (middle-class) women now waited longer before becoming parents, they also found that, as in the first Bethnal Green study, women who did have children were pulled into extended family life. The authors concluded, therefore, that 'life for most people still seems to follow broadly the same path as it always has, that is from childhood, through a period of independence, on to parenthood and the interdependence between adults characteristic of married life … No one with children dependent on them can be independent of others. As they realise this, the mothers in our study rediscover that conventional families offer wide and durable networks, and are an effective basis for securing support.'[21] Nickie Charles, Charlotte Aul Davies and Chris Harris found a similar picture in their 2002 restudy of Colin Rosser and Chris Harris' 1960 survey of the family in Swansea.[22] They reported many differences between the social worlds of Swansea in 1960 and 2002, 'the most striking among them concern the late ages at which people form procreative households and the historically small proportions living in households comprising parents and immature children.' However, they also found that the character of family life and of the relationships formed by those people who did live in family based households in Swansea in 2002 was remarkably similar to that reported by Rosser and Harris for Swansea in 1960 and, indeed, by Young and Willmott for Bethnal Green in 1957. They therefore reached the conclusion that despite claims of radical change, 'The most striking finding of our study is that there is considerable continuity in family practices between 1960 and 2002. Thus, those who partner and parent in 2002 do so in very similar ways to those who partnered and parented in 1960; families are embedded in networks of kin and provide their members with substantial support over the life course; mothers and their adult daughters are at the heart of kinship networks and it is women who do the kin work.'[23]

Drawing on these themes of continuity and change, the remainder of this chapter will therefore investigate the role of the family and community in shaping women's experiences of motherhood over the second half of the century, with a particular focus on the questions of kinship, neighbourhood, women's organisations, class, ethnicity and locality.

Kinship

Rather than recalling an institution in decline, many women throughout the period 1945–2000 reported the centrality of the extended family to their lives. In both traditional urban and rural areas the extended family network offered women company and entertainment, with families coming together to celebrate rites of passage such as engagements, weddings, christenings and funerals.[24] In small villages individual families were firmly embedded in wider kinship networks. Maud was born in an Oxfordshire hamlet, Churchill Heath, in 1921 and moved to nearby Milton-under-Wychwood after her marriage in 1940. Her husband was a friend of the family whom she met through the Baptist church. She recalled her parents were approving of her choice because 'they knew him, they knew his people, they knew his father, well we called them uncle and aunty … but then of course they became my mother-in-law and father-in-law.'[25] Maud's extended family was central to her material and emotional life.[26] Bethany was born in her grandmother's home in Wallingford in 1944. Both her family and her husband's family lived in the area, and she moved to her husband's village of Preston Crowmarsh when she married in 1966. She described how important her extended family was to her parents when she was growing up: 'There were several cousins. We were very close really it was. My mother had five brothers and one sister. There were seven in the family and also there was a family farm. Life did revolve quite a lot around the family I think.' The extended family remained a centre of friendship and support for Bethany in her adult life too: 'I had quite a lot of cousins who had children at the same time … We used to go to the park and play tennis and the children would play as they grew bigger.'[27] These patterns of family sociability continued well into the second half of the twentieth century. Women who were born in the 1950s and 1960s recalled how important the extended family had been during their childhood. Moreover they also referred to the importance of family connections when they raised their own children in the 1970s, 1980s and 1990s. Jean's two children were born in 1987 and 1990. She lived in a small village in south Oxfordshire near her in-laws. The family's social life revolved around the family gatherings they held: 'They had a huge family because [my husband] has got three sisters and a brother, and we used to all go down there every Sunday, so there's be maybe up to about seventeen of us for Sunday lunches … [So] my kids were also brought up in a very big family sort of atmosphere.'[28]

As well as social and emotional support the extended family also provided women with more practical assistance. Madge was born in

Shipton-under-Wychwood in 1918 and grew up there before moving to the neighbouring village of Milton-under-Wychwood when she married in 1939. Her kinship network offered vital support during a period of illness when her children were young: 'I had a friend who not only had her own children, she used to foster them [too], and I was very friendly with her … and she was the one who looked after [my children], and then she went on holiday and my sister had [them], they had quite a different variety of mothers to look after them. And then I had others who I was friendly with. I had a great aunt who was living next to me and she used to take them out in a pram for a walk, oh yes I had quite a lot of help.'[29] It is also noteworthy that friends and relatives were interchangeable in Madge's account. She did not consider that a dichotomy existed between them as sociologists had thought existed in urban working-class communities. Another contrast to the findings of Michael Young and Peter Willmott was that the Oxfordshire women described living close to members of their extended family but rarely visiting them. Young and Willmott had found that women who had family living at close proximity saw them frequently (for example 55 percent of Bethnal Green women interviewed whose mother was alive had seen her in the previous twenty-four hours).[30] While close family relationships did exist among the Oxfordshire women, they also recalled them as being more nuanced. Doris and Tina were sisters-in-law who both lived in Benson when their children were young in the 1960s. While they felt they were a close family they said they did not see each other on a regular basis. Doris explained: 'I mean we know where one another is if we want one another … I mean I've got a brother living in the village but I don't live in his house. But there again I know where he is and he knows where I am.'[31]

The mother–daughter relationships recalled by the Oxfordshire interviewees were also somewhat different from those recalled by contemporary researchers. In her study of inner-city Liverpool in the 1950s Madeline Kerr found a common attitude was: 'I couldn't get on without my mother. I could get on without my husband. I don't notice him.'[32] Young and Willmott reported a similarly intimate mother–daughter relationship occurring in Bethnal Green.[33] However none of the Oxfordshire interviewees talked in this way. Regional differences may have been at work here. A number of the women interviewed by Elizabeth Roberts and Lucinda McCray Beier in Lancashire also recalled seeing their mothers almost every day; although there were also women who lived near their mothers but rarely saw them.[34] Nevertheless it seems likely that the close mother–daughter bond highlighted by the 1950s' researchers was over-sentimentalised. Young and Willmott were criticised by their contemporaries for over-emphasising the warmth of Bethnal Green life. Jennifer Platt contended that, 'A preference is implied for the social atmosphere of the working-class communities'. The weaknesses of working-class life were downplayed.[35] Indeed Michael Young later admitted that due to his desire to challenge 'superior people who looked down on people in places like Bethnal Green as being inferior', he painted Bethnal Green in 'too rosy colours'.[36] Reflecting on the early work of the Institute of Community Studies, Peter Townsend has also acknowledged that the Institute's enthusiastic portrayal of working-class life meant that there were 'certain oppressive factors about male domination, in terms of gender, which we were then less sensitive to'.[37]

Proximity did not necessarily equate to an intimate relationship. Not all working-class women had a close relationship with their mothers and some mothers did not want to be involved in helping their daughters with their children. They felt that they had already raised their own families and did not want to begin the process again. This experience contrasts with the findings of Young and Willmott in Bethnal Green who reported that when a woman 'wants to go out shopping' or 'wants to go out in the evening to the cinema with her husband, she does not have to look far for a "baby-sitter"'.[38] Ethel only lived a few minutes' walk away from her parents in Benson, but recalled with some resentment how her mother 'wouldn't baby-sit for me, occasionally if I wanted to go out somewhere for the day I could send [my daughter] up to her, but she wasn't very good about it, she'd had her six, and she said she'd had to look after them'.[39] Likewise the attitude of Madge's mother was: 'they're my children, I can get on with it'.[40] Such findings were not limited to Oxfordshire. Mrs Sykes, from Barrow in Lancashire, recalled that her mother 'didn't believe in looking after your children. She said, '"You have them, you look after them"'.[41] Women who had their children around the same time that their mothers were finishing raising their own families found their mothers often played a limited role, either by choice because they did not want to be involved in caring for small children again or necessity in that they were too busy to do so. While some women were close to their mothers, when reviewing these relationships from their current perspective in the 2000s (often as the mothers of adult daughters themselves) they remembered them as being more nuanced and somewhat less intimate than those depicted in contemporary writings on traditional working-class communities.

Women did express concern, though, that the extended family was declining due to the increasing mobility of its members. Zoe, a farmer's wife from north Oxfordshire, had four children between 1965 and 1976. She spoke fondly of the support her own maternal grandmother had provided when her children were young. Comparing her experiences with those of mothers in the 2000s, she said: 'a lot of young families miss out on that nowadays. They miss out on having the parents, let alone the grandparents.'[42] However not all women were so pessimistic. Several felt that grandparents in the 2000s, and particularly grandmothers, were as, if not more, important. Thelma had one child in 1972. She explained that she was far more involved with her grandchildren than her own mother had been. As was the case with Ethel, Madge and Mrs Sykes, Thelma's mother had told her that she was not there to baby-sit.[43] Their keenness to portray themselves in this way indicates not only that the interviewees thought grandmothers were still central to the family, but that at a time when family ties were deemed to be less strong they felt it necessary to defend their role. Moreover many thought that the increasing numbers of working mothers meant grandparents had to play a greater role in the provision of childcare. For example Ingrid told an anecdote about a conversation with her granddaughter to illustrate this point: 'certainly [my granddaughter] only the other day she said, "Granny we've never had an au pair", and then said, "Well I suppose really you're our au pair aren't you?".'[44] Increased mobility meant that some women were unable to take an active part in caring for their grandchildren, and there were always particular family circumstances which prevented such a relationship, but the majority of women did not present themselves as being any less involved with their grandchildren than their mother's generation had been.[45] Moreover at the end of the century new technologies made it easier for families to keep in touch. The widespread availability of telephones and the internet had come to the aid of families who lived at large geographical distances. Gina's daughter had emigrated from England to Australia. She said, 'Well thank goodness for the internet because we are able to, you know, not just talk to her, we use Skype and we have a webcam so we are able to sort of see her. We talk to her generally every week and we each sort of have the odd email in between.'[46]

One notable change over time that did emerge over the period 1945–2000 was that fewer women lived with members of their extended family in multi-generation households. This development coincided with the shift from privately rented housing to council housing and owner-occupation that accelerated in the decades after the war. In the 1940s and 1950s the housing shortage during and after World War Two meant that many women shared housing with their own or their husband's families. Geraldine was born in 1954 and recalled how her family lived with her grandparents. She said that it was 'a common thing to do at that time because there wasn't enough housing.'[47] Bobbie and her family were from

Milton-under-Wychwood. She met her husband, who was originally from Brighton, during the war when they were both in war-work at De Havilland's aircraft factory. Her husband chose to remain in Oxfordshire and joined Bobbie and her widowed mother in the family home after they married in 1948. Bobbie said, 'you couldn't get houses so we lived here with Mum, and we stayed here.'[48] The resigned manner in which Bobbie articulated this decision indicates that she had mixed feelings about the couple living with her mother. While she had a close relationship with her mother, and felt some degree of duty to remain with her, it seems the couple would have also liked to start married life in their own home. Eunice had four children in the 1950s. The first was born in Carlisle where her husband was from. Eunice, her husband and the baby lived in one room in a house that also contained her husband's mother, two sisters, a brother, the brother's wife and their little boy. Before they left Carlisle Eunice voluntarily moved into a home for unmarried mothers and other homeless women in the hope this would help get the family re-housed. When they were not, the family moved south where they squatted, lived in more homeless accommodation and then a Nissen hut before finally receiving council housing after Eunice became ill with tuberculosis.[49] Phyllis was originally from Burton-on-Trent, but joined the Land Army during the war and was sent to Shipton-under-Wychwood. She met her husband there and they married at the end of the war. Discussing the difficulty of finding housing Phyllis detailed the moves the couple made. To start with they lived 'with my sister-in-law, cos accommodation was very hard to get. And then we went into a farm cottage. And then we went from there to live with my mother-in-law. And then from that when my eldest daughter was about three we moved into a council house.'[50] Like many women in the country during these post-war years, Phyllis recalled her delight at moving into this council house – the first home of her own.

Families throughout the country faced similar difficulties in securing housing. Indeed the struggle that families could face in finding suitable housing was immortalised in the 1966 British Broadcasting Corporation (BBC) drama-documentary *Cathy Come Home*, written by Jeremy Sanford and directed by Ken Loach. The play tells the story of a young couple, Cathy and Reg, and their three young children. Reg loses his job as a lorry driver after an accident and they live with his unfriendly mother in Islington. They then move to a squalid council house from which they are evicted, before an arson attack drives them from a caravan site, leaving social services emergency accommodation, a rat-ridden hostel, as their only refuge. Reg is separated from his family, and Cathy eventually asks a friend to care for her eldest son after becoming concerned about his welfare. Finally, Cathy has her remaining two children taken away by social services. The play was inspired by a real-life experience. A neighbour of Sanford, the writer, had been evicted with her children from their home in Battersea and placed in Newington Lodge in Southwark, an accommodation centre for homeless families provided by the then London County Council.[51] The story would have resonated with women around the country. Mrs Boyle, from Preston, Lancashire, had ten lodgings in two years after the birth of her son in the mid-1950s. She said 'he squawked that much at night nobody would have him.'[52] Mrs Turnbull also lived in Lancashire when her first child was born in the early 1950s. She 'had a very job to get a house with a baby, because all our people wouldn't take people with children. It was the time when all the Polish people took over Regent Street, but they took us in with children, you know.'[53] It is noteworthy that Mrs Turnbull found that the only landlords who would rent to the family were Polish migrants. For migrant women, particularly those with children, the difficulties in obtaining housing were pronounced and they could find they were turned away from the limited housing that was available.[54] Beryl moved to England from Barbados in 1961. She told Mary Chamberlain that she experienced her 'first signs of prejudice' when looking for rooms after her son was born. People 'just slammed the door'. Her family eventually moved into a council house in 1980, but obtaining it was also a 'battle'.[55] Vi Chambers migrated from Jamaica in 1956. She lived in a series of rooms before finally receiving council housing in 1969. She explained: 'Actually it was amazing that they gave me this. I was so shocked when I came to see this place. It was so beautiful. There was no furniture in, so it looked massive, and I was so pleased because I didn't expect that they would have given me a new place. I was expecting a dump. That's what they always did to black people then.'[56]

However, the role of the extended family in providing housing was never completely eradicated. In moments of crisis, such as unemployment, death and increasingly divorce, women would seek the financial and emotional support that living with relatives provided. For example, Edna lived with her family after she separated from her husband in the early 1970s.[57] Such arrangements were also common nationwide. Mrs Burrell moved in with her mother when her son was born in the late 1950s as her husband was away at sea.[58] There were also variations in this general trend with women in some ethnic minority groups far more likely to live in multi-generation or extended family households. Common residence was the norm for many South Asian families who migrated to England in the late 1960s and early 1970s and has remained significant thereafter.[59] There were also differences in regards to locality and occupation. For example farmers' wives tended to move to live with their husband's families on the farms they ran. However it was often circumstance rather than choice that brought families together. Despite moving in with her mother when her first baby was born Mrs Burrell told Lucinda McCray Beier she was not really close to her mother and preferred her grandmother.[60]

Women who saw family members regularly might also do so out of duress. Elizabeth Roberts found that several of the Lancashire women she interviewed who married in the late 1950s and early 1960s felt trapped into entertaining or visiting their relatives regularly.[61] Doris and Tina, who were sisters-in-law from Benson, recalled the ambivalence they felt towards their mother-in-law. Doris had been born and brought up in the area and her family lived in Benson. Tina moved to nearby Wallingford as a child to live with foster parents after her own parents separated, and then moved to Benson when she married. They both remembered their mother-in-law as being an extremely influential, but difficult, figure in their lives:

> Doris: We used to have to go up there nearly every day didn't we?
> Tina: Yeah. If you didn't go up every day, if you were late it was, 'you should have been here half hour ago'. So if the kids needed feeding or something you didn't do it because of the routine.[62]

Tina felt this uneasy relationship with her mother-in-law was exacerbated by the fact that, unlike Doris, she did not have her own mother to turn to:

> I think actually she didn't mean it, it came across wrongly, I always thought that. But she'd say the most awful things. I was always in tears. I think I spent the first years just in tears because of something that she'd said. Like she'd come in without any notice, she'd just come up and walk in, and I can remember one day I was using the pressure cooker, which was the thing in the 1960s, and she said, '[My son's] never had food cooked in a pressure cooker. I don't know what you're doing to him.' And now I would just say well that's how I want to cook and that's it. But it was sort of really upsetting at the time, because I had no-one to really go and talk to about it. It really upset me.[63]

Peggy's mother had died when she was a child and like Tina she felt that this left her particularly vulnerable to the criticisms of her mother-in-law. After a number of years spent following her husband, a seaman, around the country, Peggy settled in his home village Middleton Cheney in the mid-1950s. Despite her mother-in-law living 'up the avenue' she was totally unsupportive of Peggy. Peggy remembered how she told her she was: '"Not good enough for my son", I don't know what she thought he was going to have … She said, "That's it, you've got no education". I thought, "We'll see about this", but oh she was hateful.'[64]

Indeed throughout the period the relationship between mother-in-law and daughter-in-law was frequently recalled as being a tense one. Often, this friction centred on competing ideas surrounding childcare and housewifery. Thelma struggled to meet the housekeeping standards of her mother-in-law whose house she felt was like something out of the magazine *Homes & Gardens*.[65] Carmel experienced her mother-in-law's disapproval in terms of her childcare practice: 'breastfeeding on demand she thought was absolutely appalling. Once every four hours and no more.'[66] The poor relationship that Kaye and her mother-in-law had meant that Kaye purposely tried to reject her mother-in-law's advice. She said that one reason she continued to breastfeed, despite the difficulties she faced in doing so, was that her mother-in-law said, 'Why don't you give him a bottle?'[67] These tensions seemed to be timeless and women recalled the difficulties that they faced with their own daughters-in-law. Again, differences in attitudes towards childcare were often at the heart of the problem. For example Shula said of her grandchildren: 'they don't really appreciate things and I think … I think it stems from our daughter-in-law really.'[68] However, not all the relationships were bad and indeed some women preferred the company and advice of their mother-in-law to that of their own mothers. For example Tasha wished that her mother-in-law rather than her mother had come to stay after her first baby was born in 1972: 'if I'd had my mother-in-law to stay, life would have been so different because she is a very calm, practical person … bags of common sense … you know, she was just such a calming influence … [in] comparison with my husband and my mother. Oh dear me.'[69] And Lorraine also recalled her mother-in-law as being her first port of call for advice when her three children (born between 1976 and 1983) were little, although interestingly she said this somewhat apologetically. 'I mean, my mum was really worried around little babies, she was all right when they got bigger, and I wouldn't have asked my mum … And my mother-in-law was a ward sister on the gynae ward for years and she was great and I would phone her rather than my own mum, I must admit.'[70]

Women in supposedly tight-knit communities who had kin nearby could therefore have ambivalent attitudes towards their family members. In addition, women who chose to leave their families and kinship networks may have provided less positive accounts of the communities in which they had lived. Nonetheless for many women the extended family provided help and assistance, friendship and support. While ties tended to be stronger in traditional urban and rural communities, and for working-class families, there was no strict rule in patterns of behaviour. And while by the second half of the century geographical mobility meant more women were living away from their families, new technologies and better access to transport meant that it was easier to keep in touch. Therefore it would be wrong to characterise the mid-century as a golden age for the extended family, which then fell into decline by the century's end. Furthermore, contemporary commentators, such as Michael Young and Peter Willmott, glossed over the tensions and ambiguities that could also occur within families. Indeed, musing on the importance of family support Donna concluded the extended family was surrounded by a fair amount of myth.[71] While families were always important to women they were not always benign.

Neighbourhood

In the late nineteenth and early twentieth centuries women were central in preserving the unity and coherence of traditional urban communities.[72] In relation to London at the beginning of the twentieth century Ellen Ross has demonstrated that 'Mum' was the centre of the 'survival networks' by which extended families looked out for each other. It was 'Mum' who negotiated mutual assistance with other matriarchs in those larger networks which tied together neighbouring extended families.[73] Elizabeth Roberts depicted a similar matriarchal community in Lancashire during the period 1890–1940. She revealed the mutual support and help women provided one another, but also the lengths to which they would go to in their determination to establish and preserve their concepts of decent moral behaviour.[74] Although in decline, such matriarchal figures did not disappear. For example they existed among immigrant communities later in the century, such as in those families who originated from the West Indies.[75] In her study of Jamaican immigrants to London in the early 1970s Nancy Foner commented upon the powerful bonds between mothers and daughters. She found that 'Jamaican women continue to have strong feelings for their mothers, even when separated by thousands of miles.'[76] There were also some parallels between the Oxford Pakistani community Alison Shaw depicted in the early 1980s and the pre-war Lancashire working-class communities described by Roberts, for example in women's management of the household finances and their policing of the communities' morals. Indeed echoing Ross' description of Edwardian London, Shaw noted that it was the Pakistani women who 'bind whole households into social networks.'[77]

It was also other women who featured most prominently in the

Oxfordshire women's accounts of their neighbourhood support systems. Reminiscing about Benson life during her childhood in the 1940s and 1950s, Gloria described an interdependency in the village based upon: 'Knowing families and knowing they're there if you need each other. I can see my mum now, we lived in the High Street and we were surrounded by elderly people, and no way would those people have been neglected. You didn't lock your doors or anything like that, you know if you were worried if they seemed ill or something, somebody would be in there to make sure they were okay.'[78] There was sadness in Gloria's account as she recalled what she felt was a vanishing world. This sense of loss was particularly upsetting as it highlighted the passing of a happy time in her life which may have caused her to exaggerate the villagers' closeness. Nonetheless, at several points during her interview Gloria demonstrated the importance of the village community to her. Theresa also spoke about the solidarity between women in the hamlet of Edgecote where she lived in the early 1950s stating: 'if anything was desperate I would just say to somebody … "Will you just keep an eye on the kids?" There was a woman opposite who had small children, and … she would come to me and say, "Oh will you watch mine, I'm off on [my bike]".'[79] What is interesting from the Oxfordshire evidence is that the patterns of neighbourhood and community that social scientists believed characterised traditional working-class urban areas could also be seen in rural localities. Moreover, it does not appear that such a community structure was limited to rural Oxfordshire. Shirley grew up in a Yorkshire village in the 1950s and recalled a very similar pattern. She said, 'Yes, I can probably still name all the immediate neighbours and yeah, we had little knitting schools and I played out and it was very much of the era where doors were open so you could just go in and visit and what have you.'[80]

Interviewees who lived in the city of Oxford also recalled tight-knit communities. Rebecca and her husband rented rooms in a house in Jericho when they had their first baby in the early 1950s. She explained: 'We had a very nice landlady … we were right up at the top of one of those houses backing onto the factory and we shared our tiny flat with seven undergraduates and there was one bathroom with the only loo in it. And the landlady was an absolute charmer, sweet, she loved the baby, she was very deaf. "Bring him downstairs I'll look after him when you go off to the cinema", and this was wonderful.'[81] In the absence of her own mother, Rebecca's landlady acted as a maternal figure to her and offered support and advice. Georgie recalled a similar picture of help from her landlady on the Cowley Road when her first baby was born in 1961.[82] As well as mother substitutes, women also recalled building up a quasi-extended family amongst their neighbours. Before moving to their own house in North Oxford, Emily and her husband had lived in a shared house in the city centre when their first baby was born. Emily found that there was a strong support system at work in the house and she missed this when the family moved. Having other mothers around had been beneficial to her. She stated: 'I didn't know what I would have done without that actually'. She had 'neighbours down below who had three children a little bit older, she was therefore an experienced mum. She really tutored me I would say ... And so if anything [happened] I always knew I could go and ask.'[83] Faith recalled how her neighbours in Jericho proved invaluable when she was left alone with her young baby after separating from her husband. In discussing how they had helped her she described a similar neighbour-hood-centred street life to that John Mogey had found in St Ebbe's:

> I was fortunate to have wonderful friends who helped me through it. Women who had children. They weren't university people, they were quite a different set. They were people who lived in Oxford and who had grown up here and who had lived in our neighbourhood and [we] became friends.
>   *So how had you come to meet them? Was it people you were living near?*
>   Yeah people I was living near. And I think people were very sociable. And we just got to know them and you know liked them enormously and they just kinda took us under their wing.[84]

While neighbours obviously proved a notable support network for women in traditional neighbourhoods, Young and Willmott had stressed that in Bethnal Greeners' conception of community neighbours were acquaintances rather than friends. They stated: 'Most people meet their acquaintances in the street, at the market, at the pub or at work. They do not usually invite them into their own houses.'[85] There was some evidence of this distinction in the Oxfordshire women's narratives. Olive was brought up in St Clement's but moved to Jericho after her first child was born in 1945. When asked whether she socialised much with the other mothers living around her she replied: 'I don't think I had many womenfolk in, I had children in and playing in the garden I think, but I don't think I would have had as many people in as I personally would have probably liked. I don't think we went to each other's houses either very much, we would meet mostly in the park or in the recreation ground or something of that nature.'[86] Maud lived in the village of Milton-under-Wychwood after her marriage in 1940. She stressed the strong sense of community that existed and the support villagers provided to one another. However she did not approve of what she considered to be the modern practice of neighbours forming friendships, arguing that, 'I think there'll be a lot of fighting before it's finished, cos people don't tend to get on with their neighbours, I don't think.'[87] Overall, though, interviewees did not stress a concern with respectability or the desire to keep themselves to themselves that some of Elizabeth Roberts' Lancashire respondents had done.[88] Indeed some of the women who had moved into these communities wished it had been possible to form closer bonds of friendship. For example, Lindsay moved to St Clement's to join her husband, and found it very difficult to integrate into the community because it was such a tight-knit neighbourhood.[89] As the period progressed, and increasing numbers of families were rehoused, the demographic make-up of the city-centre areas made it even harder for mothers who moved there. Young families tended to be the first to leave so women were left without their peer group. Mabel's husband was sent to Oxford during the war and she moved to join him, also living in St Clement's. When asked whether there were any other women with young children around, she answered that there were no other young mothers; her next-door neighbour did not have children and the other women around were older.[90]

Women who recalled growing up in urban areas in the 1950s and 1960s were also keen to dispel some of the myths surrounding traditional urban communities at this time. It is interesting that it was those women who grew up in the north of England who felt the strongest desire to challenge the popular image of these areas. Jemma was born and brought up in Liverpool. She told me: 'although people say northerners are very friendly and, you know, you're always in and out of each other's houses, that was never the case … and we addressed our friend's mums as "Mrs So-and-so" or aunty. You know, we never called them by their first name or anything. And we never went in each other's houses because we played in the street.'[91] Similarly Liz, who was from a small Lancashire cotton town, explained: 'everybody's got this idea, haven't they, from watching Coronation Street that northern people was [sic] in and out of each other's houses. Well we knew the neighbours' children to play with, cos they were a big Roman Catholic family. So we played lots with them. But our parents didn't go visiting usually. You know what I mean? It was purely family.'[92] April grew up in the north east, but described a very similar situation. She said, 'We weren't very kind of neighbourly really, against all the stereotypes, and obviously I'm from the north east but actually there wasn't that sense of neighbourliness I don't think. I remember once somebody's chip pan caught fire and everybody went round to kind of clean up the kitchen. But really there wasn't that sort of going in and out of peoples' houses and sharing life really in that way.'[93]

It was also notable from the interviews that women found estates to be places with a strong sense of neighbourhood. In contrast to the contemporary sociological orthodoxy – which negatively compared the feeling of community amongst residents in new estates with established housing stock – the women who were interviewed recalled enjoying the friendship and support of their neighbours. The feeling of community amongst women on estates was intensified by the fact that the estates tended to bring together people in like circumstances and at the same stage in the life cycle. Grace lived in a small, private estate in north Oxford when she had her first baby in the mid-1960s. She recalled her neighbour as being a hugely significant figure in her life and in doing so revealed the difficult time she faced after the birth of her first child:

> I had a very nice neighbour … she said, 'Why don't we have a tot lot? Why don't we take it', there were three of us with small babies, 'Why don't we on Monday, Wednesday and Friday one of us have all three children, let them play together all morning and give them lunch so mum can go off and do something.' And this was, you know as I was saying, I was pretty hopeless as a mother and I found it desperately lonely and desperately, you know, one worried and [my neighbour] was absolutely my salvation, it just transformed my life.[94]

Stories of the support women received from neighbours on these estates were common. Joanna lived in an estate of newly built houses in east Oxford when she had her children in the 1960s. She said: 'It was a little community. The children all went to the same school. And when [my daughter] was born, by chance, when she got to be sort of two or three, there were five families in the close, all with little girls strangely enough, about the same age … so it was like a small nursery, just five of us.'[95] In Polly's street, which was on a private estate built in Benson in the 1960s, each mother had all the children for one morning a week, allowing the other mothers some free time. Fiona lived on the same Benson estate as Polly. She said: 'I suppose really my closest friends were the people who lived near us. Lived on the same estate. It just so happened that there were people of like mind you know. And we used to have a lovely time.'[96] Fiona had enjoyed life on the Brighton estate she previously lived on so much that she had been determined to live on an estate again. For Agnes the neighbours on her newly built private estate in Ewelme also formed her social life. Indeed they enjoyed such sociability it was almost burdensome.[97]

In contrast to the findings of Michael Young and Peter Willmott in 'Greenleigh', working-class women in Oxfordshire remembered the same camaraderie existing on estates as their middle-class counterparts.

Doreen and Peggy were neighbours from a council estate built in the 1950s in the village of Middleton Cheney on the Oxfordshire–Northamptonshire border. They had enjoyed a close friendship since the time they had moved into their houses, and in the course of their interview (they chose to be interviewed together) both stressed how significant this had been throughout their lives. Peggy summed up what their friendship had meant to her: 'Yeah it's good to have a friend like that, no matter what happens.' She also stressed how happy she had been to move into the house, saying, 'I've never moved since, I wouldn't, the next place I go is over the back to the cemetery. I waited long enough for this, my god I did.'[98] Peggy's house and her relationship with her neighbours were a central theme of her narrative, demonstrating their importance to her. Rita was born and brought up in Adderbury. After they married, she and her husband lived there, initially with her parents before moving to a newly built council house on an estate in Kings Sutton in the mid-1950s. Although she recalled the distance from her family as being difficult – after her mother died she used to walk with the baby in the pram to Adderbury three miles away for the afternoon to visit her father – she still spoke of the happiness and improvement to their lives that the move brought. She remembered the friendship and support on the estate that she received from her neighbours, again sharing childcare together.[99] It is clear that in Oxfordshire women from a variety of class backgrounds and who lived in various types of estates, including those in suburban areas, villages, and which were both council and privately built, found that estates provided a strong sense of community. Neighbours were referred to as being extremely significant people in the women's lives. Moreover on moving from a traditional urban neighbourhood to a new housing estate some women actually discovered the patterns of neighbourliness that researchers had thought were confined to established areas. Glenda moved from London to Banbury and discussed the benefits of relocating: 'it was very boring in London, extremely boring. Because, well I suppose it was us in a way, because you were sat in this little house all day long from morning to night, it was a bit lonely, and you'd take the pram and do the shopping, come back and have a bit of lunch, take the pram out and then, yeah daytime was dull.' In contrast when the family moved to Banbury: 'we moved into a new house in a group of eight and everybody was very friendly, so for a start it was so much more friendly, this idea that London's all that pally is not true. It was very pleasant, we had three small children, we had quite a nice house, and it was a very pleasant little town.'[100]

It is important to note, though, that while in the minority some women did not recall living on new estates as a positive experience. For example, discussing living on an estate in Witney during the late 1970s when her daughter was little, Amy said:

> I was very lonely there and I didn't really fit in. I couldn't find it easy to find people, you know, like me really – whatever that may be. But I mean I just didn't find anybody, you know, [my daughter] would go to playschool. I didn't meet anybody there and I just don't think I was living the lifestyle that would have introduced me to people that I would have known and I wasn't, you see I wasn't working then. I wasn't meeting people at work … And so I was quite, quite isolated and we were in one of these ghastly huge estates which I always find so soulless and there I was stuck there and it really was a miserable time.[101]

Amy did have other difficulties at this time – a poor relationship with her then husband and financial troubles – which may have compounded the isolation that she felt and encouraged her to remember life on the estate in a particularly negative manner. However she also spoke of the great improvement she felt occurred when she moved away from Witney to a smaller village. Women may also have come to hold overly high expectations of the support networks amongst mothers that would exist on estates. For example Bev, who at the time lived on an estate in Sandhurst, said she was 'very lonely' when her first child was born in 1987. Her unhappiness was compounded by the fact that she 'had this picture book image you know, [of] walking down the street with the pram and meeting people.'[102] Furthermore, women felt that the neighbourhood's role as a place for women to meet was in decline. They felt the principal reason for this was the large number of mothers with small children who had entered the workforce at the end of the century. For example Patsy, who had her own children in the early 1970s said, 'I suppose there was much more of a community in those days because my daughter-in-law now, everybody's more or less working aren't they, but in our day they weren't, no mums were working so we were much more of a community and I suppose much more supportive of each other.'[103] Similarly Hilda, who had her two children in 1967 and 1970, thought, 'we all looked out for each other a lot more and I mean I don't know … but I should imagine they're a lot more insulated and also I think the fact is that they all go back to work very much earlier.'[104] While in part the women's views may have resulted from them romanticising their own past experiences, some of the younger women did also note this change. For example Cynthia, who had her only daughter in 1993, and returned to work shortly after her birth, said, 'In retrospect I am a bit sorry that I didn't have the whole mother and baby/toddlery [sic] thing. But anyway I didn't. I went back to work.'[105] There was also a change as neighbourhoods became less homogonous.

Pippa recalled living in east Oxford in the 1980s: 'We lived in Magdelen Road. And [on] the other side there was an Asian family, who we said hello to but I don't think they would have … or even we talked to the children and they were very friendly but there was no sort of real social interaction beyond that.'[106] Therefore while neighbourhoods remained important to women, the role of the neighbourhood in providing women with support networks was undergoing change and women increasingly sought friendship elsewhere.

Women's organisations

For women who did not find the support they needed amongst friends or neighbours, organised groups could be sought as a means of making social contacts. Caitriona Beaumont has demonstrated that despite losing members as a result of wartime disruption, these groups remained large successful national organisations for women in the post-war decades. For example two years after the end of hostilities, 876 Townswomen's Guilds had been established in England and Wales. Similarly the membership of the Women's Institute Movement had recovered by 1947 to reach a figure of 379,000. By 1950 the Mothers' Union had a worldwide membership of 5,000,000 although it never recovered its pre-war popularity in England and Wales. Moreover, despite the failure of older women's organisations to attract significant numbers of new and younger members in the early 1970s, and their continued association with middle-class values, the Mothers' Union, the Women's Institutes and the Townswomen's Guilds continued to represent hundreds of thousands of women.[107] The decline in numbers they did face may also be accounted for by the development of new groups, such as the National Childbirth Trust (NCT) and the Pre-school Playgroups Association (PPA) which joined the ranks of organisations that the women interviewed remembered as being particularly significant. In addition a group of women who had been part of Oxford Women's Liberation (OWL) were amongst those interviewed. The members of the group had continued to meet, although no longer under the auspices of Women's Liberation, and when they were interviewed in the 2000s were a reading group.

While the role of religion in society was generally in decline over the course of the second half of the twentieth century, formal social groups linked to the church were still recalled as an important way to make friends. Deborah had moved to Cowley as a teenager. She said, 'I didn't go to school here so I didn't have any school friends and we didn't [have friends] from work much either', but added that, 'Young Wives were good weren't they, we met a lot of people then.'[108] As well as national organisations such as the Mothers' Union and Young Wives, there were also groups specific to individual churches or denominations. Mother and toddler groups, parents' groups and playgroups were all referred to. For some women these groups were just one aspect of a wider social network formed through the church which acted as a focal point for the whole family. Of course this was true not only for Christian families. Both Rachel and Anna recalled the significance of their Jewish faith and the local Jewish community to their lives.[109] But in some areas the church was so much the centre of sociability that those women who did not attend church felt they missed out. Jackie had moved to Milton-under-Wychwood from London in the mid-1960s. She explained: 'Milton was, is, but was very much then a very non-conformist village, there were three Baptist chapels, two of them very strict and extreme, I think all but one's closed now. Neither [my husband] nor I attend church or chapel and so we didn't have an entrée into village life through church or chapel attendance and people found that odd I think and still do here, you know [being in] the church community you're in a network of people, we've never been in that network.'[110] However there was no guarantee that church attendance would lead to the making of friends. Winifred lived on a farm near Hereford when her first child was born in 1946. She recalled: 'I didn't have any very near neighbours on the farm so I wasn't able to make friends, I knew people at church, but I wasn't able to make friends with them.'[111] Neither was sociability always being sought. Viv, a Quaker, had her children in 1968 and 1971. She used to go to the meeting house in Wallingford for an escape from daily life: 'I used to go along and I used to find that, particularly after I'd had the kids I was so tired, I used to sit in [the] meeting … and it's quite a small meeting … It's very quiet. And when you've had a sleepless night it's perfect.'[112]

While women still attended the Mothers' Union, Women's Institute and Townswomen's Guild in the 1970s, 1980s and 1990s, by the latter decades of the century new groups, namely the NCT and PPA, became the organisations most frequently referred to by the interviewees. Indeed more women at this time said they used such formal organisations as a means of meeting other mothers. The division between formal and informal organisations was not strict however. For instance many women recalled that they continued to meet the people they had met at NCT antenatal classes on an informal basis after their children were born. Discussing how she coped with the depression she experienced after the birth of her first child in the late 1970s, Shirley said: 'But I do think that it was the friends that I made through antenatal class and the NCT classes.

I mean we had a good group and we would meet two or three times a week in each other's houses and we went for walks ... and that made a huge difference.[113] The opportunity to meet women in the same position was particularly welcome. Jean and Lorraine were still in touch with some of the mothers they had met at the classes over twenty years ago and Jemma said she had met some of her closest friends there.[114] By the end of the twentieth century attending NCT classes had become a standard way for women (although principally white, middle-class, town dwellers) to meet other mothers (particularly first-time mothers) of young children. Bertha's daughter had her children in the 1990s and Bertha said she had 'a group of friends that she'd met through that [NCT].'[115] Indeed Bertha wished that such a network had been available to her when she had her children in the early 1960s. However, not everyone spoke so positively. Harriet had her twins in 1986. She explained:

> I did go to a couple of the NCT meetings, afterwards, when everybody in the group had had their baby. But you know, I felt a complete stranger and totally and utterly inadequate because all their children were all beautifully dressed and ... sitting cooing on their laps. And I'd got two of them and I'm trying to ... I'm trying to deal with both babies. I'm trying to work out how I'm supposed to carry them both at the same time. It was just awful. I hated it. So, I really [pause] I completely discontinued that after about two visits. I really hated it.[116]

In contrast Geraldine had not wanted to attend NCT classes while she was pregnant because she thought they sounded too 'earnest', but after she had her children she did join the NCT and 'loved it'. She 'used to know so many people through that. We had talks and an amazingly sort of full social calendar. Going to different people's houses and doing different things. It was wonderful.'[117] However, as noted above, the NCT remained largely white and middle class and the interviewees commented upon this limitation. For example, April said, 'They were a little bit middle class, the NCT';[118] and Geraldine explained that 'the sort of people that took it up were again were fairly middle-class sort of people which upset me in a way cos ... it should have appealed to all sorts of people.'[119]

There was a shared membership across many groups, with women progressing from one group to another as their children grew older. For example, Linda set up a baby-sitting circle with some of the women she met at her antenatal class.[120] Sandra described how she took over the running of a playgroup: 'A few of us from the NCT decided, two of us actually decided to take it over, so we did.'[121] The national playgroup movement began in 1962, following a letter to the *Guardian* women's page in 1961, suggesting that because of the lack of nursery school places mothers might get together and provide their own substitutes. The PPA was formed later that year.[122] Although it initially saw playgroups as a temporary expedient to meet the unsatisfied demand for state-provided pre-schooling, the PPA came to promote playgroups as an alternative form of provision.[123] Several of the women interviewed reported they were involved in running playgroups. Lindsay described the 1960s as a revolutionary time when women were starting to form organisations and associations to enhance their lives. She said: 'this was the time also that the National Housewives Register was formed via the women's page of the *Guardian*, and of course a whole lot of other things were started there, the Pre-school Playgroups Association, that started with a letter in the *Guardian*.'[124] Jackie also remembered having first read about playgroups in the *Guardian* women's page. She co-founded the Wychwood's playgroup. When discussing why she got involved she explained it was largely to provide her with a break from her own children: 'having twins of course, I was rather keen that I should get them off my hands a bit [laughing], you see it was desperation, and reading the *Guardian* and hearing about this playgroup movement … I thought that this sounded like a good idea.'[125]

Janet Finch argues that playgroups operated on the model of paternal breadwinning and homely maternal care for children as they assumed the availability of the mother not only to provide the basic care for children when they were not at playgroup, but also to actually run the organisation.[126] While playgroups did not offer an alternative to full-time motherhood, they did provide women with the opportunity for social contacts, work outside the home and a break from their children, all of which were very welcome. A Mass Observation correspondent wrote how, 'in 1970 when my second son was three I became involved in the local playgroup and was its secretary. Being a rather elderly mum [forty] compared with others in my area, and finding small babies difficult to cope with, I emerged into the playgroup era delighted by all it had to offer.'[127] Playgroups have been categorised as a middle-class phenomenon. Not only did they begin on the *Guardian* women's page, but they flourished rapidly in suburban areas and small towns and villages. Finch suggests that setting up a voluntary organisation is fundamentally a middle-class activity and the tradition of voluntary work is rooted in the middle-class experience.[128] This picture is not altogether borne out by the Oxfordshire evidence. Diana was involved in starting the playgroup in Ewelme. She did find a divide in attitudes towards the playgroup in the village, but she defined this as being between old and new villagers rather than simply class based. Discussing reactions in the village when the playgroup was launched, she said, 'I suppose you'd call them the indigenous families, they resisted, they didn't believe in not bringing up the child themselves.'[129] In neighbouring Benson, Florence who was a 'native' of the village did express this view, refusing to send her children to the playgroup set up there.[130] Interestingly Florence was a 'working mother'. She was employed as a nurse and shared childcare with her husband by undertaking shift-work. Nonetheless she was critical of mothers who sent their children to the playgroup and was hostile to the idea because it seemed an unnecessary invention by incomers. This division between old and new villagers, and perhaps also between the generations, seems to be more significant than class. Marilyn felt she came from a working-class background. She left school at sixteen and worked as a typist before having her children in the early 1970s. After her marriage she moved to Benson with her husband for his work. Unlike Bridget she was happy to be involved in the Benson playgroup because it 'kept me out of the house and gave me something to do.'[131] Indeed many women who had their children between the 1970s and 1990s recalled the playgroup as being an important arena for making friends. While the aim of playgroups may have been to provide pre-school education for children, many mothers recalled that they used playgroups in order to make social contacts for themselves. Mary encapsulated this view, explaining how she enjoyed the group more than her children.[132]

Baby-sitting circles were a further way that women could offer one another friendship, support and of course help with childcare. Ellen and her neighbour set up a toddler group in Ewelme and she also belonged to baby-sitting circles in both Ewelme and Benson. She thought they were a 'good social contact, as well as being useful to have.'[133] Kaye lived in Wantage when her children were young in the 1980s. When asked if there were any mother and baby groups there, she replied: 'Yes there were and we had a baby-sitting circle. We were living on an estate and that was very good for getting to meet other mums and so forth.'[134] While not confined to estates, baby-sitting circles did seem to particularly flourish within them. Sonia explained what it was like when she moved into her house on a new estate in Sandhurst in the early 1980s: 'I suppose when we moved … [it was] to a new housing estate where everybody was pretty new to the area. There was a baby-sitting circle on the estate we lived on where, you know, all the mothers got together and you could baby-sit for each other with, you know, a token system. So that was a really good way of getting to know other families in the area.'[135] Gina was a friend of Sonia and lived on the same estate. She recalled how 'we had [a] thriving sort of baby-sitting circle and we had meetings of people as well as doing the baby-sitting and made lots of friends with lots of, you know, their children, that we still know now.'[136] However not all women were quite so positive in their accounts. Discussing the opportunities she had to meet people when her son was small Lynne responded more ambivalently about her baby-sitting group:

> There were these sort of quite intense North Oxfordy kind of baby-sitting circles and things, you know that was mainly how I met other mothers and things before he went to school. I suppose and I did always feel slightly different, I think, I don't know they seemed to be often much more accomplished, much more educated although they were not generally working themselves at that point but they seemed to be wives of academics or people who would go back into that sort of world themselves when their children were bigger and somehow also coping better than I at being a mum you know. It may just have been my take on it but that was how they made me feel rather. At the same time occasionally there was this nice feeling of a sort of solidarity … on odd occasions when we'd have a sort of baby-sitting circle tea or something or we would get together, it would just depend on the chemistry I suppose.[137]

Organised groups were certainly remembered as important to the interviewees in Oxfordshire. And for many women at the end of the century, who found it harder to meet other mothers through friends or family, organised groups formed an entrée into a network of new parents who then acted as their principal support system. However as Lynne's testimony indicates, not all women remembered such groups as being unproblematic.

Class, ethnicity and locality

One of the reasons for Lynne's discomfort may have been that she felt she was not quite of the same social standing as the other women in the baby-sitting circle. Class was important to women in defining their identities. The interviewees described how class distinctions had influenced their upbringing. Their mothers, especially, had stressed the appropriate behaviour for girls of their own social status. What was and what was not suitable employment seemed to have been an issue of particular importance. For example Deirdre came from a skilled working-class background in Banbury. Her father had worked as a gentleman's tailor, but her mother clearly had aspirations to improve the family's status and had a strong sense of what was 'respectable' behaviour. When discussing what she wanted to do when she left school during the war Deirdre recalled, 'I remember saying to my mum I would like to join the Wrens, "Oh for goodness sake" she said, "What do you want to go into the Wrens for?" she said, "You don't know who you're going to meet."'[138] Bet was from a similarly upwardly mobile family; her parents were shopkeepers. Bet's mother did not want her to go into nursing, telling her 'oh it's very dirty'.[139] Class was also important for the women in that they associated with people with similar class backgrounds. For Gloria the feeling of community in Benson was linked to class. She thought it was the working-class residents who shared a common way of life and were all 'in the same boat'.[140] The phrase 'in the same boat' seems to have been a popular way for members of the working class to describe themselves when referring to the 1950s and 1960s and was also used by Elizabeth Roberts' interviewees in Lancashire.[141] It was when women met people from outside their own class that distinctions became most apparent. Camilla came from a middle-class background in Sheffield and had been university educated, but she experienced an intense culture shock when confronted with upper-middle-class life after her husband got a job at Rugby School. In one anecdote she recalled how a senior wife had said, 'My dear you must remember that we never push out our own children and nobody [should do it] in the mornings'.[142] Kelly thought that class was a particularly important issue in Oxford as the city was rife with class divisions. She explained: 'there's a very strong class element round here'.[143] She was not alone in this view. Rebecca also said Oxford was polarised along class lines, arguing, 'Some [are] very poor and some pretty rich in Oxford as I'm sure you know'.[144]

But understandings of class did not remain static. For instance Tina thought that class distinctions had changed over time: 'I've heard [my husband] and I've heard [my brother-in-law] say it, "We're working class and proud of it", and I sort of say, "I'm not working class I'm working upwards mate", and it's sort of more that, and I don't think there is a class distinction as such. They don't say you're rich, you're poor, you're on a different level. It's moulded in a lot more. But there's always going to be obviously where you're born and who you're born to'.[145] As Tina's comments illustrate, definitions of class are both ambiguous and subject to change, with gender also influencing people's responses. Joanna Bourke suggests that this subjective perception of class position 'provides one way around the thorny problem of gender'. She stresses that employing categories such as occupation, income, or relationship to the means of production as indicators of 'class' is clearly problematical when focusing on women. Employed women may be categorised in terms of their own occupation, or that of the 'chief breadwinner' in the household, and women without paid employment are often allocated to the 'class' position of their husband or father.[146] Carolyn Steedman goes further, concluding women are 'without class, because the cut and fall of a skirt and good leather shoes can take you across the river on to the other side: the fairy-tales tell you that goose-girls may marry kings'.[147]

The difficulties in assigning women to a class were seen amongst the Oxfordshire interviewees. Marilyn came from a working-class family in Lewisham. She felt that she and her middle-class husband were from very different backgrounds and she was not happy to be viewed as middle class herself.[148] Indeed she found it uncomfortable to discuss the class difference between her own and her husband's families as there was some tension between them. Siobhan was married to a dentist and was herself university educated. She was, however, the daughter of a cooper from a family of Irish immigrants. She later worked as a receptionist at her husband's practice. If her class were to be determined by her father's occupation, her husband's occupation and her own occupation, each would have a different outcome. Siobhan herself did not think she was strongly attached to any class.[149] Indeed some women did not want to be assigned to a class. Mrs Critchley's father was a railway labourer and her mother a weaver in Lancaster. She herself was married to a policeman. She told Elizabeth Roberts: 'I think everybody who works is working class. I don't believe in all this class business, I think it's stupid.'[150] A woman's class position was not immobile, either. Some women married below their class. Lindsay's father was a civil engineer and her mother was a doctor, she was herself an Oxford graduate, but she married a local man who worked at the Atomic Energy Research Establishment at Harwell (she explained he was employed at the lowest grade), and they lived in St Clement's. While Lindsay did not explicitly say that she had fallen down the class hierarchy, at several points in her narrative she explained with some regret that she had not enjoyed the same standard of living as her parents had done.[151] It was not only individuals, but whole families that could move across the class spectrum. Carmel grew up in Lancashire in the 1950s and 1960s. She recalled that initially the family lived, 'In a pre-fab yes. We lived there until I was nine. Well it was pretty working class really. Yes it was. And I mean my family you would call them lower-middle class really, but I suppose aspiring, my parents moved and bought their own house which was a bit of a first you know.'[152]

Such mobility was not always easy for women, and women who moved between classes told of the difficulties they faced in doing so. For example Claudia, who came from a working-class background in Yorkshire, felt uncomfortable when she went to Oxford University because she felt like the 'poor relation'. She stated: 'Oh I was very intimidated by all the posh accents and the fact that most of the other girls came from private schools. I can certainly remember feeling that.'[153] Rose also had experienced difficulties in adjusting to life at university in Oxford when she too moved there from Yorkshire. Both her parents had worked in the local textile industry, although her mother stopped work upon marriage. She felt her education produced a degree of tension between them. 'I zoomed up the educational ladder [pause]. There had to be a certain amount of informal negotiating of the relationship but [pause] always it was a close relationship in which they clearly cared a lot for me and I felt a great deal of obligation to them.'[154] She found it difficult to talk about her relationship with her parents. At this point her narrative became disjointed, an indication of her ambiguous feelings. From their study of Woodford Peter Willmott and Michael Young had concluded that 'movement from one class to another creates a barrier inside the family only for men, not for women.'[155] While in part this view seems to be a simplification of the complex tensions that could exist for women, it is interesting that when Rose's father retired her parents came to live in Oxford and after her mother was widowed she moved in with Rose. Rose's experiences suggest that irrespective of women's social mobility family ties remained strong. Social mobility did not mean class was forgotten, though. Class (and linked to this the question of the north-south divide) was a constant theme in April's narrative. Indeed she joked that the interview would make her seem 'terribly obsessed' with class. She had grown up in the north east before moving to London to go to university. She explained:

> I did feel that ... it had a kind of class element ... I'd never been to the theatre before for instance except for a children's pantomime. Things like theatre, and there was no poetry in our house. My mum and dad read a lot but not in any kind of, it's a cultural thing I suppose. I found all that very, very scary. And of course having a northern accent, I mean you might think I've got a northern accent now but it was [nothing] compared to what it was like when I was seventeen. That was, everybody sounded [pause]. I think people don't always realise that if you've got a regional accent, people with a standard British accent sound aggressively posh. And people, I think, don't always realise that.[156]

Women's perceptions of their class identity were further complicated by ethnicity. A Jamaican woman who had migrated to London, interviewed by Nancy Foner, explained: 'It gives [sic] me at times to know that because of the colour of your skin they class you in that condition, beneath them in every way'. Another woman stated: 'I don't see a rich coloured in this country. They try to be independent. Just ordinary working-class people, just fighting it. It is a struggle for all of us, just trying to make [a] life.'[157] Irene was born in Barbados in 1939 and came to England to study nursing in 1960. Discussing her class position, Irene told Mary

Chamberlain that although some people argued 'if you're black, you're all working class', she disagreed. She felt she and her husband, who had also originally come from Barbados, had very different backgrounds and this caused difficulties for her and her family: 'I was being a working-class mum with working-class children and middle-class values and expectations which wasn't good.'[158] Moreover, just as class identities could be fluid and experienced at the individual level, so could ethnic identities. Tara was born in India, and described her background as Anglo-Indian and ethnically 'a bit confused.' However while her Anglo-Indian background was clearly influential upon her sense of identity she added that she could not 'remember anything at all about India.'[159] Women's sense of their own identities was also shaped by how others responded to them. Bet was white but her husband's background was Chinese. When their first son was born a Chinese friend said, '"He's gone to the English", it's like going to the dogs'. Bet then described what happened after the birth of her non-identical twins. She said her daughter 'looked really oriental, and [my son] was the Anglo-Saxon one', when visitors came to see the babies 'they all clustered around him because he looked English you see, and everybody that came in did the same thing, and I thought that was highly amusing, I didn't say anything but I thought this is good to sit here and observe this, they really like the baby that looks like what they are.'[160] Neither were experiences static. Discussing her Jewish background (her mother had come to England as a refugee), Anna recalled how differently she and her children had experienced their Jewish identity:

> my mother was Jewish, so I'm technically Jewish, but my mother knew very little about the religion except her identity. So the fact that I knew that I was Jewish was ... wouldn't have meant very much, but I had a Jewish friend at school who said you've got to go to Sunday school, so my mother agreed and so I did, so I knew a bit about it, but ... the fact that one was different was always a bit embarrassing for me. I think that was partly because my mother was not wholehearted about it, but I think it was partly the spirit of the age. And it interested me that my children weren't a bit embarrassed about it and if anything it was just rather interesting to their friends. And they sort of appreciated the ... you know the variety of the sort of culture. So I hope that it's one of these things where something has actually improved.[161]

Class, gender and ethnicity were all at work in determining women's identities. Locality could also be a significant factor. Rather than using a simple class analysis the sociologist Margaret Stacey offered an alternative dichotomy between the traditional and non-traditional in describing the residents of Banbury in her book *Tradition and Change*. The traditional residents were more likely to have been born in or near the place where they would spend their lives and so be physically close to their families. They were less occupationally mobile and often had a 'traditional' view of the social hierarchy. The non-traditional encompassed the large numbers of middle- and working-class newcomers who moved into the town in the 1930s after the construction of the aluminium factory. They were socially and geographically mobile, and were harder to place in the hierarchy.[162] This concept also seems applicable when talking about the rural communities in Oxfordshire. Agnes and Diana both moved into Ewelme in the 1950s and recalled the 'great deal of suspicion'[163] with which they were greeted by the native villagers. They felt this reaction was particularly strong because, as Stacey had also found in Banbury, they challenged the existing social hierarchy. Diana explained:

> It was the early 1960s and the only new houses that had been built since the war were council houses, so all the rest of the houses, as you know, had been there a long time, and they were either big houses or cottages. And then there were four bungalows built, and we bought one of those. So I was a bit different from people who lived in small cottagey places, cos they rented, so that made a difference. And it was when the children, well when my son started going to school and his best friend used to come and play but my son was never invited to go there ... But we were sort of kept separate, we were in a different category altogether. We weren't village people, we weren't big house people.[164]

Jackie faced a similar reception when she moved into Milton-under-Wychwood in the 1960s. The other villagers thought:

> we were very exotic as people, 'A' we came from London and 'B' we were in politics because [my husband] had been adopted as the [Liberal Party's parliamentary] candidate by then. So in a way we were a bit celebrities, people didn't know quite what to make of us. We were also very poor, and usually celebrities quote unquote are quite well off [laughing] and we weren't at all and we lived in this very small cottage. People didn't know what to make of us at all.[165]

Working-class women who moved into villages faced the same distrust and even hostility as their middle-class counterparts. Peggy had been born in Redditch, but spent much of her childhood in Banbury. When she moved into the nearby village of Middleton Cheney, which was where her husband was from, she found the villagers unfriendly.[166] Peggy's neighbour Doreen had been born and brought up in Lancashire and moved to the village to join her husband after the war. When asked what it was like to move there she replied: 'Well first of all I'd been in the forces, and when I got married, I mean there's always girls around you. Then when I got married … I didn't know a soul down there. The only people I knew was [sic] [my husband's] family up in the village here, so it was a big shock to me, shock to the system like.'[167] There was often particular hostility to incomers who had moved on to new estates built on a village's edge. Hilda moved to Dun's Tew, a village near Banbury where her husband had family, in the late 1960s. The couple lived initially on a new estate on the outskirts of the village before later moving to the older centre. She explained: 'Oh well, the far end of the village, the farmer sold his fields to a developer and … it was very much them and us, right. In fact we had lived on Dashwood Drive for seven years when we built this house. And one of the villagers, old time villager said "oh I'm glad you're now in the village". "No, we've been living here for seven years," you know. It was very much like that.'[168] Furthermore, while Shula felt that she had been helped to integrate into the village of Enstone through her children, she still was deemed a newcomer: 'But this village is a bit odd in there's a lot of older villagers, you know, original villagers and the new villagers and although we've been here over thirty years, we're still the newcomers.'[169] The native villagers did express ambivalent feelings about incomers to their villages. Alice, who lived in Middle Barton, thought people who moved into the village from towns were unsuited to village life, missed the amenities of towns and 'didn't last long, a couple of years and they were gone again.'[170] Commenting upon changes which had occurred in Benson, Florence said, 'There's a lot of people who only sleep here, yeah go to town to work, to London or to Oxford and they literally only come home at night, but also they don't all participate in things in the village, which I always think is a pity.'[171] Gloria, another Benson resident, thought that people who had been brought up and then continued to live in the same place, as she herself had done, enjoyed a better quality of life than those who were geographically mobile: 'I do feel sorry sometimes for people who sort of flit from one place to another and never really getting to know somebody properly, and really, really knowing them, and knowing their history.'[172]

However while it is therefore clear that class was only one factor among many, class differences did emerge in the women's experiences. Although most women seemed to form friendships amongst their neighbours, middle-class women were more likely to join organisations in order to find companionship – a trend that had been commented upon by social investigators at the time.[173] As noted above, from the 1940s until the 1960s the most popular groups amongst the Oxfordshire interviewees were those linked to churches, such as the Mothers' Union. There were also members of the Women's Institute, Townswomen's Guild and the

National Council of Women amongst the women interviewed. Then during the latter decades of the century the NCT and PPA became the most commonly referred to organisations. What these groups shared, however, were certain middle-class characteristics. But while middle-class women may have dominated such groups, they did not do so exclusively and several working-class women also attended them. Judy, who was a particularly active member of organisations and was involved in running the Florence Park community centre, came from a working-class background.[174] Other differences in patterns of sociability did emerge, though. For instance a number of highly educated women (although not necessarily middle-class) said they did not have a friendship network or even need this support. Rose came from a working-class background in Yorkshire, but won a scholarship to Oxford and went on to marry an Oxford don. When asked how much socialising she did with other mothers she regretfully replied, 'Virtually none, I think this is maybe the bugbear of a very academic background. What I valued most was time for myself and all the time the children were growing up I never, I can see that now I'm much older, went in for making friends.'[175] Hannah continued to work full-time as a university researcher after her children were born and felt that she had little in common with other mothers, and subsequently did not enjoy their company. She recalled how 'we used to go out to dinner too, and then after dinner people would separate and I used to be bored stiff listening to the conversation of [the other women], yes I felt quite isolated.'[176] It is significant that even amongst a group of women from a similar class and educational background Hannah felt separate from them due to her pursuit of a career. Similarly, when Kelly was asked how easy she found it to make friends when she moved from Oxford to Manchester, she replied: 'It wasn't. There were hardly any women in the university. I really had made no friends in Manchester. There were some people basically the parents of children who knew each other. I think everybody had their problems and no-one really understood mine or was interested in mine.'[177] This theme of having no close female friends ran throughout Kelly's narrative. Indeed the points in her story when she revealed her difficulties in adjusting to motherhood were also moments when she expressed sadness at having no female friends to support her.

Nonetheless, while perhaps more common amongst those interviewees who had been highly educated these feelings of isolation resulting from the absence of close female friends crossed class and generation. Women's personal circumstances and indeed their personalities were also influential in shaping their attitudes towards the communities they lived in. Donna, a teacher, whose mother was also a teacher, had her first child in 1969 and moved from Farringdon to Marlow in Buckingham-shire when her son was six months old. She said she was very lonely and isolated and spent an awful lot of time just sitting and crying over the baby.[178] Carol had grown up in a council estate in east Oxford with a large extended family around her. She moved to a small village outside the city when her first baby was born in her mid-teens in 1979 and was estranged from her family at that time.

> I was really sort of isolated. I didn't have, didn't keep in contact with any of my friends from school. You didn't have mobile phones in those days. We didn't have a phone where we lived. Again, it was a mobile home in Sanford. And so, you know, I didn't feel, I mean it was, I used to sort of look out the window and if a car [was] coming along that I thought might be somebody I knew, I'd be like 'gasp'. It was ever so, it was horrible. I was really lonely, and a bit scared.[179]

Bev had her first child in 1987 after moving to Owlsmoor, a new housing estate near Sandhurst. She said, she was, 'Very lonely with the first one. Immensely lonely … Because I couldn't drive and they didn't live close to me, I couldn't meet up with the few people that I had met. So I think that compounded the problems actually.'[180] Often it was simply being a stranger in a new area that was seen as the reason why women found it hard to integrate. Class was important in determining women's experi-ences, but it was only one factor among many. Class, ethnicity, and also locality could all work together to determine the type of community a woman lived in and how she experienced it.

Conclusions

The type of community a woman lived in had a great effect on her experi-ences of motherhood during the post-war decades. It influenced the patterns of marriage, kinship and friendship she enjoyed. Moreover these differences between neighbourhoods were intimately connected with variations that also occurred on the lines of locality, ethnicity and class. Social scientists who were investigating British social life at this time recorded similar findings. However, while the authors of these social surveys and community studies made some perceptive analyses of the variation that occurred in families during the period they also tended to operate on a class-based differentiation and assumed a value-laden division between urban, rural and suburban communities. Furthermore, there was a lack of appreciation of the ambivalent feelings women could hold towards their families. From the Oxfordshire interviews it is clear that women of all social strata shared mixed experiences of family. In addition there were similarities for women with regards to their experiences of being a mother that existed irrespective of their background. Whatever the type of neighbourhood women lived in having children seemed to provide them with an entrée into the community and other mothers of young children provided their principal support networks. Despite sociologists suggesting that in 'old' communities kin provided support and in 'new' communities friends did, this dichotomy does not seem to be reflected in the experiences of young mothers. Neighbours provided women in both sorts of area with social contacts. Women used their shared circumstance of being mothers of young children to develop social networks. While the ways in which they did so and their level of success depended upon factors such as their background and the locality they lived in, motherhood still served as a unifying experience for women in the post-war decades.

However changes were occurring over the period. While groups such as the Mothers' Union had always been a feature of some women's lives, new formal organisations, such as the NCT or PPA, became increasingly important as a means for women to meet other mothers. Neighbours were still recalled as significant figures in the lives of young mothers, but friendships were often formed through more structured associations, and the casual meeting of mothers of young children in the street seemed to be in decline. By the end of the century, with women returning to work outside the home when their children were at younger ages, this trend was even more pronounced. However, in many ways these new associations were following in the footsteps of earlier groups. Caitriona Beaumont has demonstrated that the contribution of groups such as the Mothers' Union, Women's Institute and Townswomen's Guild has been overlooked in the post-war decades. In reality they not only campaigned on women's issues, but gave women the opportunity to meet other women, share their experiences and interests, and engage in educational, domestic and recreational pursuits.[181] In addition to such formal organisations there were also more fluid groupings, such as neighbours coming together to share childcare, which the interviewees also recalled as being extremely significant. Therefore throughout the second half of the century women had sought to improve their lives as mothers through forming associations with their peers.

Notes

1 Graham Allan, *Kinship and Friendship in Modern Britain* (Oxford: Oxford University Press, 1996), p. 36.
2 Kate Liepmann, *The Journey to Work* (London: K. Paul, Trench, Trübner, 1944), p. 83.
3 Elizabeth Bott, *Family and Social Network: Roles, Norms and External Relationships in Ordinary Urban Families* (London: Tavistock, 1957), pp. 184–6.
4 Michael Young and Peter Willmott, *Family and Kinship in East London* (London: Routledge and Kegan Paul, 1957), p. 112.
5 John M. Mogey, *Family and Neighbourhood: Two Studies in Oxford* (Oxford: Oxford University Press, 1956), p. 81.
6 Hannah Gavron, *The Captive Wife* (Harmondsworth: Penguin, 1968), pp. 61– 2.
7 Although Willmott and Young classed it as middle class, Klein says Woodford offers a 'vivid picture of the upward-moving working-class family.' Josephine Klein, *Samples from English Cultures* (London: Routledge and Kegan Paul, 1965), p. 328.
8 Peter Willmott and Michael Young, *Family and Class in a London Suburb* (London: Routledge and Keegan Paul, 1960), p. 128.
9 Robert Millar's optimism was exemplary of the positive view. Robert Millar, *The New Classes* (London: Longmans and Green, 1966), p. 19; Goldthorpe *et al.*, thought this was not the case. John H. Goldthorpe, David Lockwood, Frank Bechofer and Jennifer Platt, *The Affluent Worker in the Class Structure* (Cambridge: Cambridge University Press, 1969), p. 26.
10 Elizabeth Slater and Moya Woodside, *Patterns of Marriage* (London: Cassell, 1951), p. 255.
11 Peter Hiller, 'Continuities and variations in everyday conceptual components of class', *Sociology*, 9 (1975), 255–87, p. 255; H.F. Moorhouse, 'Attitudes to class and class relationships in Britain', *Sociology*, 10 (1976), 469–96, p. 469.
12 Shaw, 'Pakistani Families in Oxford', p. 9.
13 Pearl Jephcott, *A Troubled Area: Notes on Notting Hill* (London: Faber and Faber, 1964), pp. 88–9.
14 Sheila Patterson, *Dark Strangers* (London: Tavistock Publications, 1963), p. 342.
15 Nancy Foner, *Jamaica Farewell: Jamaican Migrants in London* (London: Routledge and Kegan Paul, 1979), p. 161.
16 Beryl Gilroy, *Black Teacher* (London: Cassell, 1976), p. 109.
17 Elspeth Huxley, *Back Street New Worlds* (London: Chatto and Windus, 1964), p. 94.
18 Geoffrey Gorer, *Sex and Marriage in England Today* (St Albans: Panther, 1973); Lesley Rimmer, *Families in Focus: Marriage, Divorce and Family Patterns* (London: Study Commission on the Family, 1981); R.N. Rapoport, M.P. Fogarty and R. Rapoport (eds), *Families in Britain* (London: Routledge and Kegan Paul, 1982); Melanie Henwood, Lesley Rimmer and Malcolm Wicks, *Inside the Family: Changing Roles for Men and Women* (London: Family Policy Studies Centre, 1987); David Clark and Douglas Haldane, *Wedlocked? Intervention and Research in Marriage* (Cambridge: Polity Press, 1990); David Clark (ed.), *Marriage, Domestic Life and Social Change. Writings for Jacqueline Burgoyne (1944–88)* (London: Routledge, 1991).
19 Jacqueline Burgoyne and David Clark, *Making a Go of It: A Study of Step-families in Sheffield* (London: Routledge and Kegan Paul, 1984).
20 Monica Cockett and John Tripp, *The Exeter Family Study: Family Breakdown and its Impact on Children* (Exeter: University of Exeter Press, 1994), p. 10.

21 Geoff Dench, Kate Gavron and Michael Young, *The New East End: Kinship, Race and Conflict* (London: Profile Books, 2006), pp. 14, 114–16 and 236–9.

22 Colin Rosser and Christopher Harris, *The Family and Social Change* (London: Routledge and Kegan Paul, 1965).

23 Nickie Charles, Charlotte Aul Davies and Chris Harris, *Families in Transition: Social Change, Family Formation and Kin Relationships* (Bristol: Polity Press, 2008), pp. xii and 224–5.

24 Research on London has revealed a similar picture. Young and Willmott, *Family and Kinship*, p. 64; Michael Peplar, *Family Matters: A History of Ideas about the Family since 1945* (London: Longman, 2002), p. 115.

25 Maud, WY4, p. 5.

26 *Ibid.*, p. 1.

27 Bethany, EW4, p. 2.

28 Jean, EW14, pp. 8–9.

29 Madge, WY8, p. 14.

30 Young and Willmott, *Family and Kinship*, p. 30.

31 Doris, BE2, p. 23.

32 Madeline Kerr, *The People of Ship Street* (London: Routledge and Kegan Paul, 1958), p. 40.

33 Young and Willmott, *Family and Kinship*, pp. 28–43.

34 Elizabeth Roberts Archive, Centre for North-West Regional Studies (hereafter ERA), Mrs J. 1. B., p. 34; Mrs O. 1. B., p. 26; Mrs W. 5. L., p. 62; Mr and Mrs W. 6. L., p. 86; and Mrs H. 3. P., p. 38, saw their mothers most days. Mrs W. 6. B., p. 42, rarely saw her mother.

35 Jennifer Platt, *Social Research in Bethnal Green* (London: Macmillan, 1971), pp. 13–17.

36 Michael Young interviewed by Paul Thompson, 'Reflections on researching *Family and Kinship in East London*', *International Journal of Social Research Methodology*, 7 (2004), 35–44, p. 35.

37 Peter Townsend, 'Reflections on becoming a researcher', *International Journal of Social Research Methodology*, 7 (2004), 85–95, p. 90.

38 Young and Willmott, *Family and Kinship*, p. 38.

39 Ethel, BE6, p. 11.

40 Madge, WY8, pp. 17–18.

41 ERA, Mrs S. 3. B., p. 27.

42 Zoe, BA16, p. 14.

43 Thelma, CR6, p. 5.

44 Ingrid, SO11, p. 13.

45 Michael Peplar found his interviewees offered a similarly ambivalent response to whether the family had declined in importance. Peplar, *Family Matters*, p. 119.

46 Gina, SA8, p. 13.

47 Geraldine, CR9, p. 1.

48 Bobbie, WY7, p. 5.

49 Eunice, SA2, pp. 3–4.

50 Phyllis, WY3, p. 6.

51 Anthony Hayward, '*Cathy Come Home*. The true story behind Britain's most famous TV drama', *Independent* (3 November 2006).

52 ERA, Mrs. B. 11. P., p. 37.

53 ERA, Mrs T. 2. L., p. 17.

54 Wendy Webster, *Imagining Home: Gender, 'Race' and National Identity, 1945–64* (London: UCL Press, 1998), pp. 173–82.

55 'Beryl' as cited in Mary Chamberlain, *Narratives of Exile and Return* (London and Basingstoke: Macmillan, 1997), pp. 190, 192.

56 'Vi Chambers' as cited in Webster, *Imagining Home*, p. 18.

57 Edna, OX13, p. 4.

58 ERA, Mrs B. 2. B., p. 59.

59 Shaw, 'Pakistani Families in Oxford', pp. 89–91.

60 ERA, Mrs B. 2. B., p. 73.

61 Elizabeth Roberts, *Women and Families: An Oral History, 1940–1970* (Oxford: Blackwell, 1995), p. 187.

62 Doris, BE2, pp. 22–3; Tina, BE3, pp. 22–3.

63 Tina, BE2, p. 4.

64 Peggy, BA9, pp. 6–7.

65 Thelma, CR6, p. 22.

66 Carmel, NO16, p. 9.

67 Kaye, WY14, p. 4.

68 Shula, BA12, p. 11.

69 Tasha, SO14, p. 9.

70 Lorraine, SA6, p. 6.

71 Donna, TH1, p. 12.

72 Ross McKibbin, *Classes and Cultures: England 1918–1951* (Oxford: Oxford University Press, 1998), p. 170.

73 Ellen Ross, 'Survival networks: women's neighbourhood sharing in London before the First World War', *History Workshop Journal*, 15 (1983), 4–27.

74 Elizabeth Roberts, *A Woman's Place: An Oral History of Working-Class Women, 1890–1940* (Oxford: Blackwell, 1984), pp. 187–94.

75 Raymond T. Smith, *The Negro Family in British Guiana* (London: Routledge and Kegan Paul, 1956).

76 Foner, *Jamaica Farewell*, p. 61.

77 Shaw, 'Pakistani families in Oxford', pp. 206–7.

78 Gloria, BE14, pp. 21–2.

79 Theresa, BA10, p. 17.

80 Shirley, SA10, p. 1.

81 Rebecca, OX10, p. 11.

82 Georgie, OX2, p. 19.

83 Emily, NO8, p. 8.

84 Faith, SO12, p. 5.

85 Young and Willmott, *Family and Kinship*, p. 84.

86 Olive, OX6, p. 20.

87 Maud, WY4, p. 4.

88 Roberts, *Women and Families*, pp. 212–16.

89 Lindsay, OX12, p. 11.

90 Mabel, OX9, p. 4.

91 Jemma, SA13, p. 2.

92 Liz, SA5, p. 2.

93 April, SO16, p. 2.
94 Grace, NO7, p. 2.
95 Joanna, CO5, p. 5.
96 Fiona, BE10, p. 13.
97 Agnes, EW1, p. 19.
98 Peggy, BA9, p. 21.
99 Rita, BA6, pp. 8–9.
100 Glenda, BA2, p. 11.
101 Amy, WY13, p. 8.
102 Bev, CR10, p. 12.
103 Patsy, BA15, p. 6.
104 Hilda, BA11, p. 10.
105 Cynthia, WY12, p. 9.
106 Pippa, CO13, p. 6.
107 Caitriona Beaumont, 'Housewives, workers and citizens: voluntary women's organisations and the campaign for women's rights in England and Wales during the postwar period', in Nick Crowson, Matthew Hilton and James McKay (eds), *NGOs in Contemporary Britain: Non-State Actors in Society and Politics since 1945* (Houndmills: Palgrave Macmillan, 2009), 59–76, pp. 64 and 73.
108 Deborah,CO6, p. 27.
109 Rachel, OX7, p. 9; Anna NO13, p. 14.
110 Jackie, WY10, p. 4.
111 Winifred, CO4. p. 18.
112 Viv, EW12, p. 6.
113 Shirley, SA10, p. 6.
114 Jean, EW14, p. 6; Lorraine, SA6, p. 5; Jemma, SA13, p. 6.
115 Bertha, EW11, p. 13.
116 Harriet, CR8, p. 9.
117 Geraldine, CR9, p. 8.
118 April, SO16, p. 14.
119 Geraldine, CR9, p. 8.
120 Linda, TH2, pp. 21–2.
121 Sandra, EW13, p. 8.
122 The writer of the letter was Belle Tutaev who was concerned at the lack of nursery provision that was the result of a government embargo imposed in 1960. A trained teacher, she opened her own Nursery/Playgroup and encouraged other parents to do so. The National Association of Pre-school Playgroups was formally constituted on 10 July 1962 and in 1967 its name was changed to the Pre-school Playgroups Association. Joan Conway, 'The playgroup movement 1961–1987', in Judith Bray, Joan Conway, Marjorie Dykins, Leontia Slay, Ivy Webster and Wendy Hawkins (eds), *Memories of the Playgroup Movement in Wales 1961–1987* (Aberystwyth: Wales Pre-School Playgroups Association, 2008), 1–14, pp. 2–7.
123 Janet Finch, 'The deceit of self help: preschool playgroups and working class mothers', *Journal of Social Policy*, 13 (1984), 1–20, p. 3.
124 Lindsay, OX12, pp. 11–12. The 'Housebound Wives' Register' was also set up in 1961 through the women's page of the *Guardian*. From 1966 it was known as the 'National Housewives' Register'.

125 Jackie, WY10, p. 13.
126 Finch, 'The deceit of self help', p. 5.
127 Mass Observation Archive, University of Sussex (hereafter MOA), B1155, reply to 34: Spring Directive 1991, part 1 'Education'.
128 Finch, 'Self help', p. 4.
129 Diana, EW2, pp. 2–3.
130 Florence, BE8, p. 11.
131 Marilyn, BE13, p. 6.
132 Mary, TH5, pp. 23–4.
133 Ellen, EW3, p. 11.
134 Kaye, WY14, p. 6.
135 Sonia, SA11, p. 5.
136 Gina, SA8, p. 10.
137 Lynne, OX14, pp. 8–9.
138 Deirdre, BA1, p. 5.
139 Bet, CO1, p. 6.
140 Gloria, BE14, p. 25.
141 ERA, Mrs L. 2. L., p. 26.
142 Camilla, SO6, p. 5.
143 Kelly, SO10, p. 18.
144 Rebecca, OX10, p. 19.
145 Tina, BE3, p. 35.
146 Joanna Bourke, *Working-Class Cultures in Britain 1890–1960: Gender, Class and Ethnicity* (London: Routledge, 1994), p. 4.
147 Carolyn Steedman, *Landscape of a Good Woman: The Story of Two Lives* (London: Virago, 1986), pp. 15–16.
148 Marilyn, BE13, p. 5.
149 Siobhan, BE1, p. 1.
150 ERA, Mrs C. 7. L., p. 57.
151 Lindsay, OX12, pp. 6–8 and 10.
152 Carmel, NO16, p. 1.
153 Claudia, SO2, pp. 5–6.
154 Rose, NO12, pp. 1–2.
155 Willmott and Young, *Family and Class*, p. 86.
156 April, SO16, pp. 14 and 6.
157 Foner, *Jamaica Farewell*, pp. 41 and 134.
158 'Irene' as cited in Chamberlain, *Narratives of Exile and Return*, p. 146.
159 Tara, SO15, p. 1.
160 Bet, CO1, pp. 27–8.
161 Anna, NO13, p. 14.
162 Margaret Stacey, *Tradition and Change: A Study of Banbury* (Oxford: Oxford University Press, 1960), pp. 11–14.
163 Agnes, EW1, p. 18; Diana, EW2, p. 10.
164 Diana, EW2, p. 10.
165 Jackie, WY10, p. 4.
166 Peggy, BA9, p. 1.
167 Doreen, BA3, p. 1.

168 Hilda, BA11, p. 4.
169 Shula, BA12, p. 12.
170 Alice, WY2, pp. 11–12.
171 Florence, BE8, p. 13.
172 Gloria, BE14, pp. 21–2.
173 Willmott and Young, *Family and Class*, pp. 101–8.
174 Judy, CO10, p. 8.
175 Rose, NO12, pp. 14–15.
176 Hannah, SO7, pp. 4–5.
177 Kelly, SO10, pp. 13–14.
178 Donna, TH1, pp. 24–5.
179 Carol, TH14, p. 6.
180 Bev, CR10, p. 12.
181 Beaumont, 'Housewives, workers and citizens', pp. 60–3.

3

Educating mothers: family, school and antenatal education

During the second half of the twentieth century the question of how girls should be prepared for their future role as mothers provoked considerable debate. There was often disagreement about where the education of mothers should take place; and indeed if such education was necessary at all. Significant changes also took place over the period, as the assumption that all women would want to be mothers was challenged. Moreover, despite the rhetoric during these years about the need to educate girls to be mothers, it is questionable how successfully these aims were put into practice. Indeed personal testimony indicates how ignorant and ill-equipped many women felt with regards to pregnancy, childbirth and infant care. While the importance of motherhood for women, for their children and for society was widely accepted, the processes by which women came to see themselves as mothers were largely ignored or taken for granted. This chapter will explore how and to what extent women were being prepared for motherhood, where this preparation took place and whether patterns of experience crossed background and class.

Two principal schools of thought dominated understandings of how girls learnt to become adult women during the period 1945–2000. Firstly, psychoanalysis and the belief that girls unconsciously internalise maternal values and behaviours, and then relive their experiences of their relationship with their mothers when they in turn become mothers. Secondly, sociology and social learning theory, namely that girls learn to mother and to be like mothers by consistently and positively being reinforced when they imitate their mothers' behaviours.[1] With regard to psychoanalysis, Sigmund Freud's theories of the development of the individual, femininity and female sexuality were firmly established by the inter-war years. Freud had argued that the desire for motherhood was part of normal female psychic development.[2] In addition, psychoanalytic theory highlighted how the mother–daughter relationship was instilled with a renewed importance when a woman had a child of her own as she relived her experience of being mothered. The well-known post-war paediatrician and child psychoanalyst Donald Winnicott believed a woman could learn little from the medical profession, but argued that she 'may have learned a great deal from having been an infant and also from watching parents with babies and from taking part in the care of siblings, and most of all she has learned a great deal of vital importance when playing at mothers and fathers at a tender age.'[3] Writing in the early 1960s, the midwife and agony aunt Clare Raynor likewise believed, 'A little girl, playing with a doll, is more than a pretty sight. She is acting out her relationship with her mother, and, consequently, her future relationship with her own children.'[4] This concept of a maternal instinct was widely disseminated. As the medical sociologist Sally Macintyre noted in the mid-1970s, it was used within everyday society to imply that 'humans (and especially women) want to have babies, or have instinctual drives towards reproduction; that this drive has individual and species survival value; that pregnancy is normal; and that childbearing is woman's highest, yet most basic, function.'[5] Neither did such ideas go out of fashion later in the century. In the fourth edition of Hugh Jolly's *Book of Child Care*, published in 1985, the obstetrician told mothers that, 'Memories of the roles of father, mother and children during your own childhood remain to influence your new family.' Moreover, he explained that those mothers who had not experienced a good relationship with their own mothers were at a disadvantage. He stated: 'Fortunately, most of us bring to this task the in-built expertise given by our parents in the way they handled us as children. If we were "mothered" well by our parents we have at least a head start on those whose intellect is the same but whose childhood experiences were less happy.'[6]

Commentators also felt that girls learnt from their mothers in a more practical way. Mothering was a skill learnt by experience and passed down the generations. In *Family and Kinship* Michael Young and Peter Willmott argued that mothers and daughters could 'co-operate so effectively because the younger has not only the same work, but has learnt how to do it from the older woman.' Moreover they believed women continued to learn from their mothers after their children were born, with mothers providing their principal source of advice on childcare. They stated: 'When the wife gets contradictory advice from the welfare clinic and from her Mum, she usually listens to the person she trusts most.'[7] During the post-war decades this notion that girls should learn housewifery from watching and helping their mothers was commonly held. The educationalist Kathleen Ollerenshaw thought 'most girls do learn a great deal about homemaking from their mothers.'[8] Ruth Anderson Oakley, in her 1955 book on the role of mothers in educating their children, developed this theme, aiming to show that girls learnt not only within their own homes but also in those of others. She wrote, 'The natural training school for the nation's potential mothers were the homes of England, where thousands of women were employed as cooks, housemaids and nurses.'[9] She was therefore dismayed by the decline in domestic service, believing it was the logical arena for working-class girls to be educated about how to run a home. The class element here is notable and there was no mention of where middle-class girls were supposed to be similarly schooled.

Nonetheless, discussing the 1950s June Purvis argues that, 'For both middle class and working class girls, growing up and learning to be "feminine" meant socialization into a future ideal of wifehood and motherhood.'[10] Furthermore, as Stephanie Spencer has demonstrated, despite increases in employment opportunities during the post-war decades, the prevailing ideology of domesticity as the ultimate goal for girls remained embedded in a gendered curriculum in secondary modern and, to a lesser extent, grammar schools.[11] As Spencer intimates, however, the extent to which women received a domestic education was dependent upon the type of school they attended. The stress on domesticity was most pronounced for working-class girls who attended elementary and then secondary modern schools (or comprehensive schools after their introduction in the late 1960s[12]), where the teaching of domestic subjects was firmly entrenched. Grammar schools, where middle-class girls dominated, tended to provide a more academic education for their pupils. Purvis notes it was girls at secondary moderns who received the most limited education, being taught specifically domestic subjects, for instance caring for other people such as brothers and sisters, and domestic skills such as washing, cooking and darning. In short, they were socialised into a maternal role.[13] Significant developments were occurring by the 1970s, though. Encouraged by second-wave feminism, attention focused on this gendered education that girls were receiving. For example, writing in the late 1970s the sociologist Rosemary Deem argued that sexism in the curriculum was apparent in a number of ways: 'it is present in the characterization of some subjects as male and some subjects as female; it is found in the content of some disciplines, which emphasize male rather than female endeavour, or which take for granted the existing position of women in society; and it is found in the orientation of subjects towards boys or girls.'[14] Feminist campaigns to challenge the discrimination girls faced had some success. From the 1970s onwards girls did increasingly well in school, particularly in respect to their attainment of qualifications, and have continued to consistently outstrip their male counterparts. But despite these apparent improvements, schooling remained gendered. Even in the 1990s there were few subjects at GCSE examination level that girls and boys entered into in roughly equal numbers. For example in 1994 Physics, Design and Technology, and Economics, were male provinces. In contrast, Home Economics, Social Studies and Vocational Studies remained female preserves. Furthermore, gender biases were also reflected in young men's and women's choices of vocational courses, with young women still selecting business and commerce, hairdressing, and beauty and caring services, while young men chose engineering, construction and mainstream science subjects.[15]

Although schools provided girls with education in 'feminine' subjects, particularly those seen as related to running a home, they were less inclined to educate them about maternity itself. Schools were more comfortable providing domestic science lessons than sex education. While the instruction of children in general hygiene had been part of the school curriculum since the inception of state education in 1870 the idea of teaching children about sex was deemed more controversial.[16] A more active approach did develop by the 1940s with sex education seen as a vital means of counteracting the social upheavals perceived to exist at that time. Indeed by 1956 sex was considered to be the 'single most immediate problem' in the Ministry of Education's handbook on health education.[17] However, as AnnMarie Wolpe notes, sex education was still equated with teaching biological reproduction.[18] The 1949 film *Growing Girls*, which was about menstruation, and distributed free of charge to schools, youth clubs and Women's Institutes, began by showing farmyard scenes of chickens and cows to equate this to human development. Sexuality at this time was viewed as an 'impulse' or 'urge' that was properly channeled into marriage and parenthood.[19] While the 1963 report *Half our Future* (The Newsom Report) on secondary modern and comprehensive schools did recommend positive and realistic guidance on sexual behaviour, it asserted that religious instruction should play a part in providing young people with a firm basis for sexual morality. Furthermore it suggested that married teachers were best equipped to handle the teaching of sex education.[20]

During the 1970s sex education in schools was increasingly influenced by progressive educational pedagogies.[21] For instance Jane Pilcher has shown how advice contained within the 1977 edition of the handbook on the teaching of sex education was wholly transformed. For the first time the importance of educating both boys and girls about the experiences of the other sex during puberty was emphasised; masturbation, contraception, venereal diseases, 'sexual deviations' (an implicit discussion of paedophilia) and homosexuality were all explicitly identified as potential topics within sex education; and the fact that sex can and should be pleasurable was openly acknowledged.[22] However, changes at the policy level were not always translated into individual classrooms. The provision of sex education continued to vary greatly across the country, both in frequency and scope.[23] For example, in her survey of sex education in the early 1970s Christine Farrell found that most girls did recall they received sex education of some sort but they were also critical of their lessons because they had been told only about animal reproduction and nothing else.[24] Conservative attitudes remained. In the 1973 sex education film, *Don't be Like Brenda*, about the dangers of sexual encounters outside marriage, the audience is told that seventeen-year-old Brenda had her whole life ahead of her, until she got pregnant and gave her baby up for adoption. While no moral judgement is made against the father of her baby (who indeed goes on to marry someone else), the narrator of the film explains how 'in one unthinking moment, Brenda had ruined two lives, her own and her child's.' As if to make explicit Brenda's immorality, and that such actions warrant punishment, her baby is disabled. Moreover, the election of the Thatcher government in 1979 marked a retreat from the more liberal position of the earlier 1970s. For example, the 1986 Education Act allowed schools to provide no sex education whatsoever and also for parents to withdraw their children when it was offered. It also prescribed the content for sex education, requiring that any provision be given with due regard to moral considerations and the value of family life. Then in 1988 the infamous Section 28 of the Local Government Act banned local authorities from 'promoting' homosexuality. In 1993, a subsequent Education Act made sex education compulsory in secondary schools, but still gave parents the statutory right to withdraw their child from any or all parts of a school's sex education programme, and in May 1994 a Department of Education circular warned teachers against advising pupils about contraception and other aspects of sexual behaviour without parental knowledge and consent.[25]

Because of this reluctance to discuss sex or human reproduction in schools many members of the medical profession, including midwives, doctors and psychologists, thought the antenatal period was the best time to teach women about parenthood. The increasing medicalisation of maternity that took place in the years after 1945 also encouraged medical professionals to believe that they were particularly well-placed to provide women with this education. For example, midwife Jean Grime stated in the *Nursing Times* in 1965 that, 'The antenatal period has always been considered the period *par excellence* for health education of the mother';[26] and, writing in 1970, the psychiatrist P.S. Cook claimed: 'It is found that those who attend such courses come in a perceptive frame of mind, the majority being primiparae in the early stages of married life, with a common "crisis" ahead of them.'[27] There were also some doctors who argued that education for parenthood should begin before women became pregnant.[28] While there was no unified idea of what form preparation should take there was some agreement that women were not receiving this education at school. In Cook's words: 'At present many couples, who have spent years at school learning much that is not essential for healthy living, enter matrimony inadequately equipped to build a stable marriage, and much less well equipped to be good parents.'[29] Similarly in his 1960 educational book addressed to pregnant women, Dr Frederick Warren Goodrich wrote: 'There will be moments when you wonder why you feel the way you do, when you feel the way you do, when you wonder what is going on inside you, when you wonder why the doctor gave you such and such advice. At these times a knowledge of what is happening and what you can do about it is not one of the things you acquire at school.'[30] While by the later decades of the century the claims made for antenatal education were somewhat less effusive, its importance was still stressed. In a 1991 article summarising the standard antenatal care on offer to women, Geoffrey Chamberlain (then Chairman of the Department of Obstetrics and Gynaecology at St George's Hospital Medical School, London) stated: 'The visits to an antenatal clinic can act as a helpful time for the woman and her partner to learn about pregnancy. Formal antenatal education classes are held in most district hospitals, and couples are encouraged to attend a convenient course. Furthermore, informal discussions with midwives and doctors at the antenatal clinic are educational and much can be learnt from other mothers in the waiting time at the clinics.'[31]

The remainder of this chapter will examine the relationship between social constructions of motherhood and how women should be prepared for it, and women's own construction of their identities as mothers. It will examine how hypotheses surrounding the education of women for motherhood were interpreted in three different locales – the family, the classroom (during lessons on both domestic science and sex education), and the antenatal class.

The family

The idea that women learnt how to mother from their own mothers was a commonly expressed sentiment. Discussing girls growing up in the inter-war years, Sally Alexander argues: '[they] watched their mothers and fathers and learned what it meant to be a woman.'[32] The same was true for girls in the post-war years too. Tara was born in the mid-1950s and had her own children in 1988 and 1990. She said: 'I think my earliest impression of what it was to be a woman was to be a mother. That's what I remember, you know. Mum has the baby and it's literally holding the baby and dad's out there somewhere doing something called work.'[33] Using language informed by psychoanalytical thought, whether or not they were conscious they were doing so, interviewees explained how they thought the desire to care came naturally to mothers because they were reliving their own childhood experiences. For example, Sharon, whose two children were born in the early 1970s, believed that 'when you look after your children, you probably are recalling how your mother looked after you.'[34] Susan, who also had two children in the early 1970s, thought 'it does come you know sort of more naturally to you than you think.'[35] Other women talked of motherhood as being 'commonsense'.[36] Few interviewees believed the capacity to mother was entirely in-born, however. Many modified the idea of an instinct by combining it with elements from the discourse that motherhood was something to be learned. They took features from both these theories to create a model through which they could articulate how they believed women came to be mothers. For example Rachel, who had her first child in 1957, explained that she thought it was instinctive to want to care for her children, but knowing how to care needed to be taught.[37] During her narrative Rachel tried to reconcile how motherhood could feel both natural and alien to her at the same time. Rachel was not alone in this attempt at forming such a compromise. Siobhan reflected upon this same subject:

> I think it's something that you have to learn. I mean the instinct is that you want to care for your child, and you want to take good care of it. But knowing how, I don't think that comes instinctively at all. I mean if you hand [a baby to] someone who's never held a baby, they don't instinctively know to put a hand under its head to support its head and all that. I did know, but only because when I was a little girl there were babies in the house and you were taught how to hold them. But no I don't think any of it's instinctive.[38]

As Siobhan indicated, while some aspects of motherhood were viewed as instinctive, girls were also expected to learn the more practical elements of baby care in the home.

Indeed many of the Oxfordshire interviewees echoed the claims of social learning theory, namely that the skills deemed necessary to be a housewife, such as cookery or needlework, were passed down from mother to daughter. Resulting from such accepted beliefs, it was commonly argued in the post-war decades that if women felt unprepared for motherhood it was because this traditional way of learning within the family was being lost due to demographic changes and geographical mobility. However while women who did not live close to their families could feel that they missed out on traditional means of learning about motherhood, such as observing mothers, aunts and sisters, even those who were in close proximity to relations did not necessarily think they learnt from them. Lynne recalled that she had wanted to help her mother as a child, but her mother had not been encouraging:

> I can remember wanting to cook like mad as a small child and pretending, you know holding the frying pan on top of the cooker with nothing in it, you know ... but my mum was always sort of bustling and busy and didn't really seem to have much time to do cooking with me I don't think, and she herself didn't really like sewing and all those sort of things, she did it but you know, so that's slightly off putting I suppose. I do remember ... one of my aunts trying to teach me knitting and getting impatient very quickly which put me off.[39]

Nor did all women want to learn from their mothers. Ruby was born in 1939 and grew up in Benson. She did not get on with her mother and said '[I] spent most of my time with my dad'. As a result she learnt more about what her father did in his workshop than what her mother did in the kitchen.[40] Mrs Barlow, a Lancashire resident, remembered that when her own children were born (between 1955 and 1960) her mother told her she should do things in a certain way because 'that's what your grandma did'. She added that her mother 'used to be quite annoyed because I wouldn't.'[41]

Individual family circumstances meant that it was not always possible for girls to learn from their mothers in the home. Some women did not live with their mothers when they were growing up. For others, illness in the family meant traditional roles were challenged. Helen, from Greenwich in London, was interviewed by Michael Peplar. She told him how in her home in the 1940s and 1950s: 'things were a little different because my mother was ill quite a lot when we were children so therefore my father did a great deal of the shopping and the washing and the cleaning and that sort of thing.'[42] Sophie lived in Kent as a child in the 1940s and 1950s. Her father had multiple sclerosis and as a result she took on the 'men's work' in the home which he could not perform. She explained that while she was skilled in doing the gardening and decorating she had never cooked a meal until she had left home.[43] Interviewees' experiences of learning from their mothers also varied significantly according to class. Women from middle-class backgrounds thought they learnt far less from their mothers than their working-class counterparts. They contrasted their own experiences with that of the ideal of mothers and daughters sharing a common profession that characterised many sociological analyses. The mothers of middle-class girls born in the 1920s and 1930s often had domestic help, and servants were principally responsible for the more practical elements of the children's upbringing. For instance Louisa and Grace recalled how they were really brought up by their nannies.[44] Even after the war the situation had not entirely changed. Martha, who was born in 1945, said her mother, 'didn't take a tremendous amount of interest in me when I was a very small child, because she was too busy and preoccupied, but this nanny used to play with me.'[45] Recalling her mother's 'help', Kim, who was born in 1948, said, 'most of my bringing up, in a way, was to do with her'. She remembered: 'I used to go round and make the beds with her and learn how to do the ironing with her and hang out the washing with her.'[46] Middle-class women were also less likely to have their mothers at close proximity when raising their own families due to increased geographical mobility. It is interesting, though, that they sometimes thought they would have been of little use to them anyway.

In addition, despite the stress placed on the mother–daughter bond by sociologists and psychologists it is clear from the oral evidence that while women may have had close relationships with their mothers this did not mean that they would discuss topics such as sex and childbirth. These were 'taboo' subjects within many families. In this climate of secrecy it is questionable how much women really did pick up from family members. Some women's mothers were not only embarrassed by sex but thought of it as something shameful. Linda and Barbie were both born in 1947. Barbie explained that all her mother told her about sex was that it was dirty and horrible and she must not do it.[47] Linda's mother said it was dirty and filthy.[48] In her account of working-class attitudes towards sex in Lancashire, Lucinda McCray Beier concluded that attitudes and communication about sex had changed dramatically when comparing those interviewees born before 1930 and those born after 1930.[49] In contrast, the Oxfordshire interviewees indicated that for them this increasing openness towards sex occurred more gradually. Moreover while the overall trend may have been for the subject of sex to be more openly discussed in families as the period progressed there was still great variation within families. Olive was one of the oldest Oxfordshire interviewees, and was born in 1916. She recalled an intimate relationship with her mother and felt she could discuss anything with her. Her mother had particularly tried to be more open because of her own childhood experiences when her mother had not prepared her for her periods. Olive recalled that, 'we talked about anything that I wanted to know'.[50] In contrast, Mary who was one of the youngest women interviewed (she was born in 1959) recalled that her mother had not discussed sex or reproduction at all. She did not know anything about menstruation until the day her periods started. Mary recalled that she confronted her mother before she died over why she had been so reticent and her mother told her it was a result of her own upbringing. Nevertheless, Mary added that she was never able to forgive her mother for not speaking with her about it.[51]

While women were slowly receiving more information on menstruation, and even sex, ignorance surrounding childbirth remained common. Even Olive, who talked about her open relationship with her mother, said, 'I didn't realise, I don't think, that there were two stages ... So yes I mean I, it just amazes me that I could have been so ignorant, certainly much more than they are now, they certainly are much better prepared I think.'[52] Referring to childbirth Ivy, who had her first child in 1947, said, 'And you know it's terrible I didn't really know, you know, what happened, what to expect.'[53] Likewise Peggy explained, 'I hadn't got a clue, I thought perhaps me [sic] belly button opened or something, I just hadn't got a clue, now that's how ignorant I was, I was eighteen, I didn't know a lot.'[54] While the situation was improving as the post-war decades progressed, a considerable degree of ignorance about childbirth nevertheless remained. Fiona had her first child in 1966. When asked if she had been taught about childbirth at home or school Fiona replied, 'Oh no, no. First time I ever saw a picture of childbirth was when I was about to have one myself ... Yes it was rather a shock I must say.'[55] Mary had her children in the 1980s, but recalled being terrified by childbirth. She explained that she did not know what would happen and in consequence she had been too afraid to push. No-one had told her what it would feel like and she worried she was doing it wrong.[56] Therefore despite the ideal that women learnt to be mothers in the home, not all families fulfilled this role. The lack of communication that occurred within many families throughout the second half of the twentieth century also accounts for why some commentators believed it was so important for women to be educated for motherhood outside the home.

Domestic science

The classroom was one such place where this education could and did take place. All the women interviewed recalled receiving a gendered education designed to prepare them for their lives as adult women, but the form it took and the extent to which it was domestically orientated depended upon their class, presumed academic ability and the locality in which they lived. Girls who attended elementary schools in the 1930s and early 1940s, or secondary moderns after the 1944 reforms, reported that they received an inferior education and were denied the opportunities available to grammar school children; this sense of deprivation could be particularly strong for those who lived in rural areas.[57] Even for the most privileged girls educational opportunities were limited by gender – only 3,310 of 271,778 girls leaving school in 1959 went to university.[58] Mrs Barlow, who attended a grammar school in Lancashire in the 1940s, remembered her female head teacher saying 'girls were different from boys, and it … took more of their strength, physical strength to grow up so they shouldn't be pushed too hard mentally.'[59] Nicola attended a private school in Leicester which became a grammar school in the 1940s. She explained her contemporaries were not very academic: 'I mean 'A' levels were unheard of, well perhaps the odd one, we just about managed the odd 'O' levels.' She thought her school was preparing the girls to be 'young ladies' and this education consisted of poetry, art and drama.[60] Similarly discussing her education, a correspondent to the Mass Observation New Project who attended school in the late 1950s, wrote: 'I feel that the school was trying to prepare me for the kind of life that no longer exists – girls weren't suppose to have careers – just be able to find a rich husband.'[61]

However Yvonne's experience of Oxford High School, which she attended in the 1950s, was rather different. Discussing whether the school expected girls to get married she said: 'Not all that much, no the school ethos was definitely make the most of your education, become independent, marry later if you want, but it was historically the Girls' Public Day School Trust, we were made very aware that it was a great breakthrough for women to be able to choose whether or not to marry and that our school was part of what had made that possible.'[62] There is ambiguity in her narrative at this point. Yvonne intimated that girls had a choice either to marry or to have a career. While she aimed to show, with some pride, the opportunities which were presented to girls at her school, she also unwittingly described the limitations implicit in the school's philosophy. Girls were still expected to make choices that boys were not about pursuing either family life or a career. Furthermore, well into the

1970s women received a gendered education socialising them into the behaviour expected of adult women. Tara, Geraldine and Andrea all attended secondary school in the late 1960s and early 1970s and recalled their schools' similar expectations that girls would fulfil a feminine role. At Tara's school girls 'were set essays on things like, "What my children will be like" … And how to make a bed. And they had not looked at this, you know, the whole feminist thing had not started then … there was a large, great deal of pressure for the female role – [the] expectation that you would get married, quite likely, and that was the substantial part of your future.'[63] For Geraldine, 'there was the expectation that you'd get married and have children … well it was sort of set in stone, really, I mean even when I was at this grammar school, boys did woodwork and PE and girls did cookery and needlework.'[64] Andrea said, 'you basically had the choice, you could say do what was shorthand typing then or if you wanted to do the needlework and domestic science … And it was only the boys who were allowed to do woodwork or metalwork, anything like that. No way was a girl allowed to have that option.'[65]

The women who were interviewed held mixed opinions about this gendered education they received. Being successful at domestic skills could bring women a great deal of satisfaction. Even women who did not enjoy domestic science at school, and were keen to stop lessons as soon as possible, looked back on it as being of use. Indeed some regretted they had not been better at it, demonstrating the close association between domesticity and femininity. For example Lisa said, 'it was the only exam I ever failed, I burned my stewed apple, the only useful thing I learned at school and I, you know, failed it.'[66] Some women recalled how they still employed the lessons they had learnt. Shula, who attended school in the late 1950s, said: 'I remember so vividly the domestic science classes and sometimes the things, you thought it was ridiculous having to know that, but I still do things now that I learnt in my domestic science class.'[67] Similarly Nellie, at school in the 1960s, thought domestic science was 'very useful' and also said she still followed the lessons she had been taught.[68] Moreover some women enjoyed domestic science lessons because they thought it would help them reach their goal of marriage and mother-hood. Bet explained: 'I did home economics and I think I got a first class pass in that because I was interested. So I was well set up for domestic life and my dream was to be married, and the ultimate thing was to have a family and to have more than one [child].'[69] Her description of doing well in domestic science lessons because she was interested in the subject directly echoed the arguments of John Newsom, Chief Education Officer for Hertfordshire from 1940 to 1957, who thought that girls' education should be related to the home because this would evoke their intellectual interest and curiosity.[70] However this equation of domesticity with femininity repelled women from domestic science as well as attracting them. Margaret, who was at school in the 1950s, bemoaned the fact that 'they didn't teach us anything useful. They didn't even teach you how to rewire a plug. No, definitely not, no. We learnt how to cook revolting things and sew useless articles.'[71] Yvonne described domestic science lessons as:

> Awful. You were expected to make things you would never wear, maybe some of the others would've but not me, fancy aprons such as my mother didn't wear and peg bags which was something we didn't use, and my thread was always getting knotted and my needle was always coming unthreaded and it was very difficult for me to finish anything let alone to the standard they expected. And it was no better when we got onto machines either. I was no good at that either. I expect this was all a reaction against the domestic as well. It was books that I liked.[72]

Indeed Yvonne tried consciously to reject both domesticity and a conventional femininity by defining herself as someone who did not wear the 'fancy aprons' that the girls were expected to make. While domestic science (and later home economics) teaching was common in schools throughout much of the second half of the century, girls did not always feel they learnt much from these lessons and nor did they want to.

Sex education

Despite the focus in schools on training girls for their future careers as housewives there was little practical or emotional preparation for becoming a mother. A Mass Observation correspondent, born in 1930, explained: 'I wasn't even prepared for marriage and motherhood [at her Convent school] though it was accepted (by me and everyone else) that was my future.'[73] This limited preparation for motherhood was perhaps most clearly seen in the slow development of sex education in schools and was recalled in many of the Oxfordshire women's accounts.[74] When asked about sex education Rachel, who grew up in the 1930s and 1940s, emphatically replied that she learnt nothing.[75] In addition women recalled the sex education that did occur in school was really supplementary rather than an inherent part of the curriculum. For example June, who was at school in Oxford in the 1940s, explained her sex education only occurred incidentally in biology lessons.[76] When sex education was actually taught it focused more on the prevention of sexually transmitted diseases than the process of having children. Rebecca explained: 'Well we weren't taught about pregnancy and childbirth in school at all, but what we did have was, really they were very terrifying when I look back, slide shows about VD, I think this was an awful warning and they were very, very unpleasant, quite frightening.'[77]

In her oral history study of birth control practice in Oxford and south Wales between 1920 and 1950 Kate Fisher found that sex was not considered a suitable subject for women to discuss (irrespective of what their actual knowledge levels were).[78] This was also the attitude that many of the women interviewed for this book felt existed when they were young. The lack of sex education provided in schools seemed symptomatic of this belief that sex and reproduction, and indeed maternity itself, were not appropriate subjects to teach to girls. Josie explained that when she was in the sixth form of her girls' grammar school in the 1960s her class asked the head mistress for a talk on contraception. The head mistress replied that none of her girls should know about 'that' until they got married.[79] Religious beliefs could also be behind the reticence of schools to discuss sex. Alma attended a Catholic convent school in the 1960s and her sex education was provided by the nuns there. She said the nuns thought sex was appalling and therefore the girls' sex education was designed to be preventative rather than informative. For instance the girls were told it was a sin to sit on a man's knee without a phone book between them and that it was a sin to sit with a man in a car with the ignition off.[80] This association between moral teaching and sex education was not limited to Catholic schools. April was also at school in the late 1960s. Her school had changed from being a single sex grammar school to a mixed comprehensive during the course of her schooling. She recalled 'a talk from an anti-abortionist speaker who'd brought a foetus in a coffee jar … I mean the biggest one that you can get, and there was a foetus in it. And … that was a big shock to all these kind of fourteen-year-old girls. That's the only incursion of anything to do with babies that I can even slightly remember from school.'[81]

In her study of Lancashire Elizabeth Roberts found that there was a common belief that middle-class, grammar school girls were more informed about sex. Mrs Critchley attended Lancaster Girls' Grammar School from 1937 to 1942. She told Roberts that, 'My husband [who did not go to grammar school] always said that girls who were at the Grammar School were very fast because they learnt all about it at school. Well, I think that they did in the sixth form in biology, but we never did'.[82] However, as Mrs Critchely intimated, women who attended selective grammar schools did not think they received a greater level of information. Indeed some felt that girls at the non-selective secondary moderns were probably taught more. Donna's father was a teacher at the local secondary modern in Farringdon while she attended the grammar school. Her father brought home booklets about sex and reproduction that the all the girls at the secondary modern received and Donna did not. There was also a gender differential in what was acceptable knowledge about sex, and interviewees recalled their brothers were taught more than they were. Donna had been amazed to find out that her brother had been taught about girls' periods at his boys' grammar school while it had never been discussed at her school.[83] Alma also said her brother was her source of sex education. She explained how the day before she first went to university he took her to one side to talk to her about sex because he was concerned that no one else had.[84] Women from a variety of backgrounds could therefore find they had passed through their entire school careers having only learnt very little (and in some cases nothing at all) about reproduction.

The antenatal class

This lack of education in schools about pregnancy, childbirth and also childcare meant that antenatal classes were often women's main source of instruction. Until the mid-1960s antenatal education for women in Oxfordshire principally consisted of mothercraft classes. The first physiotherapy classes combined with parentcraft classes were introduced at Blackbird Leys Health Centre in November 1964. These were arranged jointly between the Oxford area supervisor of the NCT, the midwives and health visitors. The MOH for Oxford felt they 'proved most valuable and have been greatly appreciated by the women attending.'[85] The focus on preparation for labour in the classes (in the form of relaxation and exercises) quickly grew in the years that followed. By 1969 relaxation was considered to be an inherent part of the classes.[86] Indeed it is interesting that while mothercraft played such an important part in the early classes provided in Oxford, when asked what they learnt women generally said they were taught little about baby care. The time period was probably influential as by the 1960s the term mothercraft had gone out of vogue. Antenatal education thereafter became characterised as preparation for birth and so women prioritised this teaching in their accounts. Women seemed to think this was the format classes were expected to take. When asked what occurred during the classes they indicated that they felt this was a strange question – the answer was obvious. Ann Oakley has argued that antenatal classes were just about 'relaxation or breathing'[87] and many Oxfordshire interviewees echoed Oakley's contention.[88] Indeed some women did not even remember doing any exercises. Mary said that all she could remember about the antenatal classes she had attended was sitting with the other women and drinking tea.[89]

The proponents of antenatal education often held loftier ambitions.[90] While there was no universally accepted technique, most teaching was based on that of Grantly Dick-Read or psycho-prophylaxis or a mixture of both.[91] Mary Nolan argues that in practice Dick-Read and Fernand Lamaze advocated similar strategies for preparing women for childbirth, although the theory underpinning their approaches was different: Lamaze believed women should be taught to distract themselves from the pain of labour; Dick-Read thought labour was painful for women because they were afraid.[92] This emphasis on educating women about childbirth, on relieving pain through relaxation and breathing, and on demanding women be conscious throughout the entire birth process was revolutionary at the time.[93] However women held mixed opinions about this expert advice. Only one interviewee, Stephanie, recalled having a book by Lamaze, which she found very useful, but she may have been acquainted with him through her training as a physiotherapist.[94] Margaret said she was an enthusiastic follower of psycho-prophylaxis but had learned this from the Berkshire community midwives who ran her antenatal class.[95] Dick-Read proved to be more popular with the women and several had read his books. There was a class distinction in the women who were acquainted with Dick-Read, though. Educated and usually middle-class mothers were more familiar with him. Rose, who had her first baby in 1959, was the most enthusiastic of the women interviewed. She remembered his book as 'very sort of sober, explaining pregnancy and childbirth so you'd know all about it.'[96] A Dick-Read book was also Maxine's principal source of information about childbirth.[97] Marjorie thought the content of the book was extremely beneficial, explaining, 'I did believe in that. I was a great believer in relaxation and that sort of self-hypnosis.' However, she was less impressed by the manner in which Dick-Read wrote and recalled that 'it got awfully boring in parts and repetitive.'[98] Glenda religiously followed the exercises in the book she had, but when asked if they were useful she replied, 'No, not in the least, not in the least. It was all a big con, it does hurt!'[99] While in general the women who read one of Dick-Read's books did value them as a useful source of information about what occurred in childbirth, they were less certain that this knowledge made for an easier labour. In addition Dick-Read appeared to have gone out of fashion by the late 1960s. Karen was sent a copy of his book by a friend's mother, but while she did think it was useful she also felt it was a little dated by the time she had her first baby in 1967. She said, 'I suspect they were the thing at the time when she had her children.'[100]

By the end of the century Dick-Read was no longer recalled as an important figure. While his ideas remained very much present in the work of the NCT, women who had their children from the 1970s onwards did not refer to him personally.

Overall the interviewees who thought antenatal education was most useful to them were those who felt they had been unprepared for pregnancy and childbirth up to that point. It offered a last chance for those women who had missed out on any prior instruction. They recalled how the classes helped dispel their ignorance and taught them what to expect. For example Hope, who had her first baby in 1955, remembered being given 'details of what giving birth actually involved so you really felt clued up about the various stages.'[101] Bet recalled that her antenatal classes in the late 1960s were:

> led by an elderly lady, I should think she was about my age, you know just before retirement, and she'd obviously been a matron and all sorts of different things and she took us right through breathing exercises and exercises to prepare our muscles, our husbands were involved and we had to take them along to see the birth on a film and all the rest of it and so that was super, I was really well-prepared. I was in a way dreading it because it's like jumping off a cliff but I knew all there was to know, and so did [my husband].[102]

It is noteworthy that Bet stressed the matron's age and experience as much as her medical expertise in qualifying her to give advice. In Bet's account the matron assumed a motherly role passing on information to younger women. Indeed, women often stated it was the opportunity to talk to women who had already had children as being the most valuable part of the classes.[103]

However, while some interviewees found classes useful and said they put the ideas they learnt into practice, others felt the circumstances of their children's birth prevented them from doing so. The classes did give some welcome information on childbirth, but because they were principally concerned with techniques for labour they could not help women who had abnormal deliveries. Marilyn thought the classes 'teach you about childbirth, but I never had a normal delivery, I had two caesars [sic]. So you had quite a good idea of what went on in a normal birth. But they didn't really teach you until the last fortnight about what could happen, you know what could go wrong.'[104] Marilyn went on to describe the births of both her children in the early 1970s as being extremely traumatic and she found it upsetting to talk about them. Her lack of preparation was clearly something she regretted and felt was detrimental to her. She was not alone. Bonnie's first baby was born in 1978. She said women were not told in advance about caesarean section and she had not known it involved an operation. She was extremely traumatised on being given the news when she arrived at hospital that her baby would have to be cut out.[105] Tara had both her babies (born in 1988 and 1990) by caesarean section, the first being an emergency caesarean and the second elective. It is interesting that as she compared the births she recalled the emergency caesarean as the better experience. 'But the first time had been an emergency caesarean … When they just … put you out completely so that was in a way easy for me. What I didn't realise was the second time it was an elective caesarean and I had to be wide awake … at the time it was happening and it was far worse. And I sometimes think that if I'd known it was going to be like that I would have terminated the pregnancy. But you live and learn, don't you?'[106] Tara's lack of knowledge of the differences between an emergency and elective caesarean and the type of anaesthetic she would receive indicates how women could still feel uniformed about what could happen during their labours.[107] In addition, some younger women felt that their antenatal classes were too focused on breathing and relaxation and did not offer enough information on what would happen after their baby was born.[108] Cynthia had her only child in 1993. She said she was 'fairly ignorant about the whole process really' and therefore valued the antenatal classes she attended. However she added that, 'I would have liked some more classes sort of having given birth, but I don't think there were any at that point.'[109]

Oxfordshire was perhaps unusual and more advanced in relation to antenatal education than other areas of the country due to the fact Sheila Kitzinger, the social anthropologist and birth educator, was based there. Responding to an appeal from the NCT for women to show pregnant women how to breathe and relax for labour she ran the first couples' classes in the country from the late 1950s.[110] Several of the women interviewed had been aware of Kitzinger's work and commented upon it. A small number had also attended her classes. At the time there was a significant class bias in those she helped, which she herself acknowledged,[111] and it was only the middle-class mothers who remembered her. While generally thinking her work was a good thing, there was an element of ambivalence in their recollections of the classes. Monika was dismissive: 'Sheila Kitzinger was carrying on about this, and natural childbirth was a great cry. I wasn't at all sold on natural childbirth, I thought the easier the better thank you very much.'[112] Claire attended a class but felt unsure about it. When asked what it was like she replied, 'Oh we saw photographs of Sheila giving birth, surrounded by dogs and with Sheila in the middle … But I only went to one class.'[113] There were women who had more positive experiences. Emily remembered Kitzinger as being a highly significant figure. 'She was the guru and we went to her classes and [my husband] must have been one of the first men to have gone to classes as well.' Emily held Kitzinger in high regard and thought 'she was a very, very inspirational writer, and she interviewed us all and followed us all up and all the rest of it so that was important, a very important feature of the time.'[114] Perhaps the most interesting recollection came from Grace, who attended Kitzinger's classes; she found them 'very supportive' and appreciated the opportunity to meet 'other mums in the same position'. However she also recalled that 'when I had a caesarean I terribly felt I'd let her down which was perhaps silly but that's how it was, it was a great shock.'[115] Her guilt at having a caesarean reveals the pressure she felt to have a natural birth. Echoing the belief that motherhood was innate to women Grace felt that successful childbirth meant receiving as little medical intervention as possible. She thought her capability as a mother was threatened by not doing so.

As noted in the previous chapter, the NCT grew substantially during the 1970s and 1980s and this was reflected in the growing number of women who reported attending NCT classes. While these classes were positively remembered as a means of making friends with other mothers the educational content of the classes was recalled somewhat more ambivalently. Some interviewees spoke positively about the classes. For example Carmel thought the NCT classes were 'good because, you know, the people running the NCT classes were young mothers themselves on the whole.'[116] April, said she 'was a great believer in the principle of the NCT … that part of pain is fear, and that if you know that it's meant to be doing this then it's not so frightening.'[117] In contrast, Geraldine said she knew about the NCT, but 'thought they sounded rather earnest. And I didn't want to get involved with them at that time.'[118] Geraldine's scepticism is particularly interesting as she later became very active within the NCT. Her turnaround was not a reaction to a bad birth experience, but because she came to value the social side of the NCT. There were also women who felt they had been misled by the natural childbirth movement into expecting a 'natural' birth which they did not then enjoy. For example Sheilagh, who had her children in the early 1970s, felt that the NCT encouraged women to have unattainably high expectations of birth which meant they could feel like failures when these were not realised.[119] Commenting on the lack of preparation she had received for a caesarean in the early 1980s Tara thought the NCT was to some extent at fault. She explained: 'Before I had the baby we went to the NCT classes. I suppose lots of people tell you they went to NCT classes. We had to pay for those … But it wasn't very expensive. And they're really in favour of natural childbirth. And I think that they should've realised that me being very small and thirty-three already it was not going to be a natural childbirth situation.'[120] Harriet had decided to deliver her twins vaginally but now believed she should have had a caesarean section. She believed she had been swept up by the feeling in the mid-1980s that natural childbirth should be promoted. 'I think I thought … I ought to give it a try … You know, I'm not just going to go along with what the doctors say … if the NCT and everyone else I'm talking to seems to say, well you know, just try and see what happens. And I was fairly determined that that was what I was going to do.' However Harriet now felt that 'if I knew [then] what I know now and [what] I went through afterwards, I think I probably shouldn't have tried to deliver them normally.'[121]

The availability of NCT classes, and indeed antenatal classes more generally, was also highly dependent on where women lived. Many of the women interviewed had not attended any classes, well into the 1960s. Mildred's first child was born in 1965 when she was living just over the Oxfordshire border in Haddenham, Buckinghamshire. She said she received no antenatal education at all and was not even shown around the hospital where she was to have her baby. Interestingly when she had her second child in Thame there were antenatal classes available but Mildred chose not to attend them.[122] Fiona, who had her first child in 1966 in Brighton, recalled that there were no classes there because the consultant at the hospital did not agree with them. Strikingly this consultant was a woman, dispelling the myth that female medical professionals would necessarily be more progressive in respect to maternal care than their male counterparts. Fiona had to go to private classes for her second child after having none for her first. She explained that classes: 'didn't happen in Brighton, not on the National Health it didn't, because the number one consultant at the Sussex Maternity, who happened to be a mother of four, didn't believe in it. I don't know quite what she was on about, but you know, you just had to grin and bear it apparently.'[123] In contrast she found the classes on offer when she had her third baby in Benson to be very good. This local variation reflected a wider uncertainty within the health services about their role in preparing women for motherhood. Local health departments accepted different levels of responsibility for providing antenatal education. Women living in Oxford benefited from a forward thinking authority which offered a range of services, but it is clear that this was not the case nationwide.

Furthermore, as was the case with Mildred, women were not always willing recipients of the antenatal care that was offered to them. The 'old hard-core' of non- or late attenders were older women who had multiple pregnancies, classified as class V according to the Registrar General's classification.[124] Young mothers, working mothers and those mothers from ethnic minority backgrounds were also less likely to attend. Some of the common problems for these women were the long journeys needed to keep hospital appointments, transportation costs, responsibility for other children and long waiting times at clinics. Working mothers also found it difficult to find the time to attend. Valerie had three children in the 1970s. Discussing antenatal classes she said: 'I stayed working, and I worked up until a month before baby was born, I think I only went to a couple. Because … you see, when you were pregnant you were meant to give up work in those days, I think the antenatal classes didn't really take into account people like me who were still working.'[125] Young mothers could be subject to judgemental staff. Yvonne had her first child in 1959 when she was nineteen and unmarried. She said, 'I do remember that I had to start going to the antenatal department at the Radcliffe, and had to put a ring on and pretend to be married and absurdities like that.'[126] Ethnic minority women could also be prevented from accessing antenatal care due to language and communication problems, intrusive examinations, the lack of explanations, negative stereotyping and the racist attitudes of health professionals.[127] They could also face the ignorance of other mothers.[128]

Many women felt ambivalent about the information they received however. Despite describing how she actively sought out private antenatal classes, Fiona felt that her lack of knowledge about medical matters was actually a good thing because if she did not know there was a problem she could not worry about it. Indeed this somewhat contradictory view was one she expressed on several occasions. For example when her first baby was born he had the umbilical cord around his neck and did not cry, but she 'was so ignorant that I didn't realise this was actually something to worry about'. Her second son had to have a blood transfusion and again she said, 'ignorance is bliss. I mean it never occurred to me that he might not be alright, and he was alright.'[129] Further developing this line of thought Polly felt that the antenatal care women currently receive can cause them unnecessary stress: 'I must say I don't think I would want to go through what people go through today. Scans and things like that, because I think that gives you more worry … I never even thought that I would have a deformed baby. I don't think you worried about, at least I didn't worry about things like that. So I'm not sure whether these, all these tests and what not are good now.'[130] Siobhan believed that access to information was the principal difference between what it was like when she was a mother of young children in the 1970s and for mothers in the 2000s, and similarly thought that this information could increase concern: 'I mean there were ways of finding out about bringing up your children, or about nutrition, or diseases or whatever, but it wasn't always straight-forward or easy, whereas now most people have computers and you can call things up on the internet and you get a worrying amount of informa-tion and sometimes sorting it all out, that can be another difficult thing now. Whereas when I was young you just went and asked your mother.'[131] Indeed Siobhan was not alone in thinking that the internet could be as much a source of worry as that of comfort. For example Harriet thought that the internet made information 'readily accessible and available', which was empowering for women, but she also felt that it could mean women were left confused by unreliable information.[132] Similarly Kaye concluded that the internet meant people could 'worry themselves sick with all the things that could happen or could go wrong.'[133] The women were uncer-tain whether increased access to information was beneficial or harmful to women and expressed contradictory opinions. Several of the women stated that not knowing what was going on led to stress, particularly in the area of childbirth. However, they also felt that knowledge equated to worry. The women seemed to find this dilemma irresolvable, perhaps reflecting the contemporary debate in the post-war years over whether it was necessary or desirable to educate women for motherhood.

Conclusions

When addressing women's experiences of becoming a mother in the period 1945–2000 it is important to consider how the preparation of girls for motherhood was a source of competing discourses during these years. Women embraced elements of these discourses and used their language within their own narratives. They did so in complex ways, however, and borrowed different strands from the varying ways of thinking in order to construct an identity of motherhood that was acceptable to them. Indeed Bronwen Davies believes this practice of 'taking up as one's own those discourses through which one is constituted as female' is an inherent part of the experience of 'being "a woman".'[134] The process of incorporating these discourses into their own accounts was not unproblematic, however. The difficulties women experienced were revealed in the contradictory statements interviewees made about how they believed they developed as mothers. For example many said they thought the ability to mother was innate to them, but then also explained that it was something they had to learn. They tried to reconcile the fantasy of motherhood being instinctive and effortless with the real need for instruction that many had also felt.

These fantasies are significant, however, because as Sally Alexander has demonstrated, 'fantasy draws on the immediate and historical for aspects of its content, form and context.'[135] Interviewees' fantasies of being 'natural' mothers demonstrate the pressure women could feel in the second half of the century to fulfil the ideal of the 'perfect' mother.

There was also a gulf between women's own experiences and the portrayals of how girls were supposed to develop into mothers. It was often assumed that women would learn about maternity in the home, but it seems clear that the reluctance of families to talk about sex and childbirth meant that for many women this was not the case. Despite the ideal of motherhood being a shared tradition passed down generations of women, a significant number of women reported they had very little experience of babies and childcare. This situation could be particularly problematic for women because schools often abdicated from the responsibility of providing sex education for their pupils on the premise that parents wanted to perform this role. The reluctance of national government to require schools to play an active role in educating children about sex meant that numerous interviewees reported that animal reproduction was the extent of what they were taught. For many women, therefore, as late as the 1960s (and for some even later), the antenatal period was the first time they were educated about pregnancy and childbirth. Despite the instruction they then received interviewees often recalled how they still entered into motherhood feeling decidedly ill-equipped. In addition women themselves held equivocal attitudes towards education for motherhood. The women interviewed were uncertain about whether increased access to information was beneficial or harmful to women and expressed contradictory opinions. Several of the Oxfordshire respondents stated that not knowing what was going on led to stress, particularly in the area of childbirth. However they also indicated that they felt women in the 2000s could be burdened by knowledge and spoke of their reticence about advising their own daughters, fearing it would not be welcomed. Women were ambivalent about the question of preparation for motherhood and seemed to find the dilemma between knowing too little, or indeed knowing too much, irresolvable. This uncertainty in their accounts was linked to the ambiguity over whether motherhood came naturally to women or needed to be taught. To the women themselves, however, their accounts were not inconsistent. They were endeavouring to reconcile the conflicting ideals surrounding preparation for motherhood with which they were confronted.

Notes

1   Carol Boyd, 'Mothers and daughters: a discussion of theory and research', *Journal of Marriage and the Family*, 51 (1989), 291–301, p. 291.

2   Sigmund Freud, 'Femininity' [orig. 1933], in *Standard Edition*, Vol. 22, 112–35, p. 128.

3   D.W. Winnicott, *Babies and Their Mothers* (London: Free Association Press, 1988), p. 61.

4   Clare Raynor, *Mothers and Midwives* (London: George Allen and Unwin, Ltd, 1962), p. 14.

5   Sally Macintyre, '"Who wants babies?" The social construction of instincts', in Sheila Allen and Diana Leonard Barker (eds), *Sexual Divisions and Society: Process and Change* (London: Tavistock Publications, 1976), 150–73, p. 151.

6   Hugh Jolly, *Book of Child Care* (London: George Allen & Unwin, 1985), pp. 1 and 240.

7   Young and Willmott, *Family and Kinship*, pp. 159 and 164.

8   Kathleen Ollerenshaw, *Education for Girls* (London: Faber and Faber, 1961), p. xiv.

9   Ruth Anderson Oakley, *Challenge to Heritage* (London: The Saint Catherine Press Ltd, 1955), p. 97.

10 June Purvis, 'Domestic subjects since 1870', in Ivor Goodson (ed.), *Social Histories of the Secondary Curriculum: Subjects for Study* (Lewes: Falmer Press, 1985), 145–76, p. 147.

11 Stephanie Spencer, 'Reflections on the site of struggle: girls' experience of secondary education in the late 1950s', *History of Education*, 33 (2004), 437–49, p. 446.

12 In the ten years between 1965 and 1975 the vast majority of state secondary schools in England went comprehensive.

13 Purvis, 'Domestic subjects since 1870', p. 164.

14 Rosemary Deem, *Women and Schooling* (London: Routledge and Kegan Paul, 1978), p. 46.

15 Madeline Arnot, John Gray, Mary James and Jean Ruddick with Gerard Duveen, *Recent Research on Gender and Education Performance* (London: The Stationery Office, 1998), pp. 12 and 68.

16 See Jane Pilcher, 'School sex education in England 1870–2000', *Sex Education*, 5 (2005), 153–70; Angela Davis, '"Oh no, nothing, we didn't learn anything" Sex education and the preparation of girls for motherhood, c. 1930–1970', *History of Education*, 37 (2008), 551–678; Lesley A. Hall, 'In ignorance and in knowledge: reflections on the history of sex education in Britain', in Lutz Sauerteig and Roger Davidson (eds), *Shaping Sexual Knowledge: A Cultural History of Sex Education in Twentieth Century Europe* (London and New York: Routledge, 2009), 19–36.

17 Ministry of Education, *Health Education* (London: HMSO, 1956), p. 44.

18 AnnMarie Wolpe, 'Sex in schools: back to the future', *Feminist Review*, 27 (1987), 37–47, p. 40.

19 Ministry of Education, *Health Education*, pp. 44 and 51–3.

20 Ministry of Education, *Half our Future* (London: HMSO, 1963), pp. 54, 61 and 70–1.

21 Rachel Thomson, 'Moral rhetoric and public health pragmatism: the recent politics of sex education', *Feminist Review*, 48 (1994), 40–60.

22 Pilcher, 'School sex education in England 1870–2000', p. 164.

23 Marie-Ann Doggett, 'The development of sex education in British schools: a review of the literature', in Isobel Allen (ed.), *Education in Sex and Personal Relationships* (London: Policy Studies Institute, 1987), 212–38, pp. 213 and 217.

24 Christine Farrell, *My Mother Said... The Way Young People Learn About Sex and Birth Control* (London: Routledge & Kegan Paul, 1978), p. 124.

25 Pilcher, 'School sex education in England 1870–2000', pp. 165–6.

26 Jean Grime, 'The maternity patient in hospital: an experiment in health education', *Nursing Times*, 61 (1965), 249–50, p. 249.

27 P.S. Cook, 'Antenatal education for parenthood, as an aspect of preventive psychiatry: some suggestions for programme content and objective', *Medical Journal of Australia* 13 (1970), 676–81, p. 677.

28 Ben M. Peckham, 'Optimal maternal care', *Obstetrics and Gynaecology*, 33 (1969), 862–8, p. 864.

29 Cook, 'Antenatal education', p. 676.

30 Frederick Warren Goodrich, *Maternity: A Guide to Prospective Motherhood* (London: Staples Press, 1960), pp. 17–18.

31 Geoffrey Chamberlain, 'ABC of antenatal care. Normal antenatal management', *BMJ* (30 March 1991), 774–9, p. 779.

32 Alexander, *Becoming a Woman*, p. 220.

33 Tara, SO15, p. 2.

34 Sharon, EW9, p. 14.

35 Susan, WY11, p. 6.

36 Monika, SO1, p. 7; Mabel, OX9, p. 4.

37 Rachel, OX7, p. 8.

38 Siobhan, BE1, pp. 15–16.

39 Lynne, OX14, p. 3.

40 Ruby, BE5, pp. 3 and 20.

41 ERA, Mrs B. 3. B., p. 11.

42 Peplar, *Family Matters*, pp. 108–9.

43 Sophie, TH12, p. 1.

44 Louisa, SO5, p. 3; Grace, NO7, p. 1.

45 Martha, NO14, p. 3

46 Kim, OX15, pp. 1–2.

47 Barbie, TH4, p. 19.

48 Linda, TH2, p. 19.

49 Lucinda McCray Beier, '"We were green as grass": learning about sex and reproduction in three working-class Lancashire communities, 1900–1970', *Social History of Medicine*, 16 (2003), 461–80, p. 475.

50 Olive, OX6, p. 15.

51 Mary, TH5, pp. 15–16.

52 Olive, OX6, p. 15.

53 Ivy, BE4, p. 8.

54 Peggy, BA9, p. 15.

55 Fiona, BE10, pp. 21–2.

56 Mary, TH5, p. 9.

57 Discussed further in Angela Davis, '"So it wasn't a brilliant education, not really I don't think": class, gender and locality: women's accounts of school in rural Oxfordshire, c. 1930–1960', *History of Education Researcher*, 78 (2006), 72–83.

58 Ministry of Education, *Education in 1959. Report of the Ministry of Education and Statistics for England and Wales* (London: HMSO, 1960), p. 142.

59 ERA, Mrs B. 3. B., p. 22.
60 Nicola, BA5, p. 3.
61 MOA, R1227, reply to 34: Spring Directive 1991, part 1 'Education'.
62 Yvonne, NO3, p. 7.
63 Tara, SO15, p. 4.
64 Geraldine, CR9, p. 5.
65 Andrea, SA9, p. 2.
66 Lisa, CO12, p. 3.
67 Shula, BA12, p. 4.
68 Nellie, BA14, pp. 2–3.
69 Bet, CO1, p. 7.
70 John Newsom, *The Education of Girls* (London: Faber and Faber, 1948), p. 109.
71 Margaret, EW15, p. 7.
72 Yvonne, NO3, pp. 3–4.
73 MOA, A2168, reply to 34: Spring Directive 1991, part 1 'Education'.
74 The Oral History of Contraception confirms this was a widespread experience. British Library, C644 Oral History of Birth Control.
75 Rachel, OX7, p. 3.
76 June, CO2, pp. 2–3.
77 Rebecca, OX10, p. 4.
78 Kate Fisher, "'She was quite satisfied with the arrangements I made': gender and birth control in Britain 1920–1950', *Past and Present*, 169 (2000), 161–93, p. 189.
79 Josie, TH6, pp. 13–14.
80 Alma, TH7, p. 14.
81 April, SO16, pp. 3–4.
82 ERA, Mrs C. 7. L., p. 31.
83 Donna, TH1, p. 14.
84 Alma, TH7, p. 15.
85 Oxford MOH, 1961, pp. 63 and 98.
86 *Ibid.*, p. 122.
87 Ann Oakley, *Women Confined: Towards a Sociology of Childbirth* (Oxford: Martin Robertson, 1980), p. 37.
88 Stella, CR5, pp. 13–14; Amelia, CO15, p. 35–6; Katherine, SA12, p. 5; Tasha, SO14, p. 7; Alma, TH7, pp. 21–2; Natalie, SA14, p. 6; Jemma, SA13, p. 6; April, NO16, pp. 14–15; Bethany, EW4, p. 10; Sharon, EW9, p. 9; Nicola, BA5, p. 5.
89 Mary, TH5, pp. 21–2.
90 C.W.F. Burnett, 'The value of antenatal exercises', *Journal of Obstetrics and Gynaecology of the British Empire*, 63 (1956), 40–57; F.M. Hardy, 'Antenatal care', *Nursing Times*, 58 (1962), 571–3; W.C.W. Nixon, 'Refresher course for general practitioners: antenatal care – 1. Advice for the expectant mother', *British Medical Journal*, 4804 (1953), 268.
91 D.A. Mandelstam, 'The value of antenatal preparation – a statistical survey', *Midwife and Health Visitor*, 7 (1971), 217–24, p. 217.
92 Mary Nolan, *Antenatal Education: A Dynamic Approach* (London: Baillierè Tindall, 1998), p. 4.
93 Mary Thomas, *Post-War Mothers: Childbirth Letters to Grantly Dick-Read, 1946–1956* (Rochester: University of Rochester Press, 1997), p. ix; Grantly Dick-Read, *Natural Childbirth* (London: Heineman, 1933).

94 Stephanie, EW7, p. 5.

95 Margaret, EW15, pp. 4–5.

96 Rose, NO12, p. 6.

97 Maxine, WY6, p. 5.

98 Marjorie, NO10, p. 15.

99 Glenda, BA2, p. 7.

100 Karen, SO4, pp. 9–10.

101 Hope, CO11, pp. 7–8.

102 Bet, CO1, p. 12.

103 See Audrey Wood, 'Education for parenthood through the maternity services', *The International Journal of Nursing Studies*, 314 (1966), 199–205.

104 Marilyn, BE13, p. 7.

105 Bonnie, CR14, p. 24.

106 Tara, SO15, pp. 14–16.

107 An elective caesarean is performed before labour has begun and an emergency caesarean is carried out as a result of some complication arising during labour. By the 1980s epidural anaesthesia was preferred over general anaesthesia in elective caesareans because it was deemed safer for the mother and allowed the mother to be awake and to immediately interact with her baby. General anaesthetic was still used in emergency caesareans because it could be given very quickly when there was an immediate threat to life.

108 Beatrice, CR4, pp. 13–14; Nina, TH3, pp. 21–2; Pippa, CO13, p. 10; Gina, SA8, p. 7; Liz, SA5, pp. 12–13.

109 Cynthia, WY12, pp. 6–7.

110 Sheila Kitzinger, *The Politics of Birth* (London: Elsevier, 2005), p. 46.

111 Sheila Kitzinger in conversation with the author. See also Kitzinger, *Politics of Birth*, pp. 48–9.

112 Monika, SO1, p. 11.

113 Claire, NO1, p. 4.

114 Emily, NO8, p. 9.

115 Grace, NO7, p. 1.

116 Carmel, NO16, p. 14.

117 April, NO16, pp. 14–15.

118 Geraldine, CR9, p. 6.

119 Sheilagh, CO17, p. 37.

120 Tara, SO15, pp. 14–16.

121 Harriet, CR8, p. 5.

122 Mildra, TH9, pp. 3–4.

123 Fiona, BE10, p. 20.

124 John B. McKinlay, 'The new late comers for antenatal care', *British Journal of Preventative and Social Medicine*, 24 (1970), 52–7.

125 Valerie, SA4, p. 5.

126 Yvonne, NO3, p. 8.

127 Savita Katbamna, *'Race' and Childbirth* (Buckingham: University Press, 2000), p. 11.

128 Gilroy, *Black Teacher*, p. 112.

129 Fiona, BE10, pp. 8 and 23.

130 Polly, BE7, p. 7.

131 Siobhan, BE1, pp. 26–7.
132 Harriet, CR8, p. 13.
133 Kaye, WY14, p. 11.
134 Davies, 'Women's subjectivity and feminist stories', p. 54.
135 Alexander, *Becoming a Woman*, p. 206.

4

Pregnancy and childbirth: antenatal care, birth and postnatal care

The introduction of the NHS in 1948 gave rise to a renewed interest in maternal and, to an even greater extent, child health. Women and children were perhaps the NHS's greatest beneficiaries as they had gained least from the pre-war insurance schemes. However there was never any clear and universally agreed upon idea of what form maternity care should take. Policies were continually being modified in response to changing medical opinions and technological developments. Initially the creation of the NHS dramatically increased the role of general practitioners (GPs) and it seemed they would be the principal providers of maternal care. This situation was already being altered by the 1950s, however, with a shift to the hospital as the locus for both childbirth and antenatal care. The Cranbrook report of 1959 called for 70 percent of births to take place in hospital.[1] The resulting move to hospital as being the primary location for childbirth was a dramatic change. Nationally the proportion of deliveries in hospital was 63.7 percent in 1954 and only slightly more, 64.7 percent, in 1960, but between 1963 and 1972 the rate rose from 68.2 percent to 91.4 percent, and from 1975 onwards it never fell below 95 percent.[2] It is not true to say that all women wanted to have their children at home but were forced to have their children in hospitals. Indeed feminist campaigners of the first half of the twentieth century had argued for an increase in hospital provision. Early in the post-war period there were still more women wanting hospital births than there were beds to accommodate them. Prior to the introduction of the NHS, and in the years immediately following, private maternity homes helped satisfy this demand for beds amongst those who could afford to pay for them. However homebirths were clearly popular with women. *Maternity in Great Britain*, the report of the 1948 Joint Committee of the Royal College of Obstetricians and Gynaecologists and the Population Investigation Committee, found that most women wanted to have their babies at home.[3] Consequently the developing argument that hospital was the only safe place to give birth (in 1970 the Peel Committee recommended provision for 100 percent of confinements to take place in hospital[4]) meant that in the latter decades of the century women's right to choose was severely curtailed; when women were being told that hospital was the only safe place to give birth it was hard to dissent.

Other changes taking place during the 1970s resulted from the introduction of new technologies. With respect to antenatal care, new antenatal testing and monitoring were available, most notably in the introduction of ultrasound. By the 1980s ultrasound became the accepted way of viewing the foetus and it became routinely used to screen for gestational age. Originally used as a diagnostic aid in high risk pregnancies, the ultrasound scan became widely accepted as a crucial rite of passage in pregnancy, the point at which the embryo became a 'real baby'.[5] During the 1970s intervention also became a feature of birth itself. In a national study of all deliveries which took place during one week in 1970 entitled *British Births*, the National Birthday Trust Fund revealed an increased use of oxytocics, episiotomy and caesarean sections. Gas (nitrous oxide) and pure oxygen had almost entirely replaced gas and air for pain relief, and there had been a considerable decline in the use of the anaesthetic Trilene (trichloroethylene).[6] Until the 1960s British clinicians had viewed episiotomy as an emergency procedure, but by the 1970s it was routine in many consultant units.[7] The incidence of induction, through artificial rupture of the membranes and/or the use of oxytocin administered by an intravenous drip, was also at its peak during the 1970s. In 1965 only an estimated 15 percent of labours were induced; in 1974 it was around 41 percent.[8] Proponents of induction argued it reduced perinatal deaths by preventing babies going beyond term,[9] but others argued it was being overused.[10] The rise in the induction rate was an issue that provoked much debate. Indeed it inspired a wider feminist, anti-doctor critique of obstetric care to develop. Sally Macintyre has described how the mid-1970s witnessed a vigorous public debate about obstetric practices: 'it seemed as though a dam of hitherto latent antagonism to the obstetric profession had burst, flooding medical, nursing and midwifery journals, the quality and popular press, television and, ultimately, parliament, with debate and controversy about obstetric practices.'[11] By the time *Reducing the Risk*, a report by the Department of Health and Social Security, was published in 1977 its authors could reflect on how, 'The value and increased use of induction has been a source of discussion and controversy for some time among doctors and midwives and the general public.'[12]

As intimated here, running alongside the medicalisation of childbirth, was a growing criticism of such intervention. The complaints of the 1970s were not without precedent. Grantly Dick-Read had argued as early as the 1930s that most women did not need medical intervention. Opposition to the medicalisation of childbirth continued to gather in the years after the introduction of the NHS. Prunella Briance, whose baby had died after conventional obstetric care, launched the Natural Childbirth Association of Great Britain in 1957 to promote Dick-Read's teaching. After a period of internal conflict it became a charitable trust, changing its name to the National Childbirth Trust or NCT in 1961. The NCT aimed to teach pregnant women skills in relaxation and breathing but also tried to persuade medical authorities to facilitate homebirths, or at least to provide a more homely environment for institutional births, which included allowing the presence of husbands or other companions. Initially the organisation tried to work with the medical profession, but increasingly it found itself in opposition to the medical establishment as the period progressed. The NCT has therefore fulfilled a number of different functions for women. It is an educational organisation (providing instruction and information through both its classes and literature); it has acted as a pressure group campaigning for women's rights in respect to medical care; but, as discussed in chapter 2, it also offered new parents an entrée into a social network. Other organisations which campaigned for a new approach to maternity care were also formed at this time. In 1958, after a distressing stay in hospital for the birth of her child, Sally Wilmington tried repeatedly to find a newspaper willing to print her letter asking if other women had shared her unhappy experience. Childbirth was still considered such a taboo subject in the 1950s that it took her a year to get the letter published. The response to her letter once it did appear, however, gave rise to a voluntary organisation, originally called the Society for the Prevention of Cruelty to Pregnant Women, but from 1960 the Association for Improvements in the Maternity Services or AIMS.[13] Unlike the NCT, AIMS was not, at least initially, arguing for less medical intervention, but rather wanted to see more (although also improved) provision for hospital delivery. The work of bodies such as the NCT and AIMS did have some effect on women's experience of maternity care as the period progressed. While deference to medical staff was common at least until the 1970s, hospitals became less regimented and more attuned to the needs of their patients.

In many ways the pressure groups of the 1970s built upon these pre-existing campaigns, but they also became more vocal and overtly political in their tone. In the late 1950s and early 1960s it had been hard for groups such as the NCT to bring their campaigns to public attention. By the 1970s the social climate had changed, with discussions of childbirth and critiques of maternal care beginning to enter the mainstream. For example, in her article in *The Times* published in 1973 Margaret Allen challenged the move from home to hospital as the place of birth.[14] The NCT reacted to the increasingly interventionist practices seen in obstetrics in the 1970s by pursuing a less accommodating approach to medical professionals. During the 1980s the NCT explicitly espoused the 'right to choose' in a way it had never done in the 1960s.[15] Similarly AIMS also adapted to the changing circumstances of the 1970s and 1980s. Its formation in 1960, when home confinements were common, was largely inspired by a body of women demanding the right to hospital births. By the 1980s, with homebirths being less than 1 percent of all deliveries, AIMS also focused its campaigns on choice in the place of birth, including the right to home confinements.[16] Moreover new groups began to emerge. The 1970s and 1980s saw the creation of the Foundation for the Study of Infant Deaths, the Stillbirth and Neonatal Death Society (SANDS), Baby Life Support Systems (BLISS), and the Pre-eclamptic Toxaemia Society, which all sought to represent the interests of specific groups of parents and babies. By the end of the century the internet had also become a new arena for women to share views and to campaign for mothers' interests. Perhaps the most famous of such groups is Mumsnet set up in 2000 as a forum for parenting support and the discussion of issues connected with parenting. The creation of these groups reflected both changes in medical technology, particularly neonatal care, and a growing belief in specialised pressure groups as a means for achieving change.

Responses at the policy level to these campaigns were often slow, however, as can be seen in the advice relating to homebirth. Arguing why women should not have homebirths the 1977 report *Reducing the Risk* asserted: 'Even if a woman is "low risk" and likely to have a normal birth, one cannot be sure it is normal until it is over. Hospitals are better able to cope with emergencies and to provide the special care some babies need at birth. It is not possible to provide such facilities at home and the travel and delay in getting a baby from home to hospital in an emergency may be harmful.'[17] This was still the official view in the 1980s. The 1984 second report of the Maternity Services Advisory Committee stated: 'No labour or birth can be completely free of the risk of complications. Most mothers will know this and understand that special measures may need to be taken.'[18] The report argued that, 'As unforeseen complications can occur in any birth, every mother should be encouraged to have her baby in a maternity unit where emergency facilities are readily available.'[19]

These attitudes were reflected in practice and the years between 1985 and 1988 saw the lowest ever recorded rate of homebirth, 0.9 percent.[20] By the early 1990s there had been a significant change in the rhetoric surrounding choice, even if in reality a woman's ability to decide where and how to give birth often remained restricted. The work of the pressure groups, campaigners, and patient advocate groups were important here. So too was Marjorie Tew's work, which challenged the assumptions that hospital birth was safer than homebirth, and that falling maternal and neonatal mortality rates were directly attributable to increased intervention.[21] National policy, although not always local practice, was altered in response to these campaigns. By the early 1990s, a women's right to choose where to give birth was on the agenda. For example the 1993 Report of the Expert Maternity Group, *Changing Childbirth*, which was taken up by the Department of Health, explicitly criticised unsympathetic doctors and midwives who used 'safety' as a reason to try and impose arrangements or interventions which the mothers found unhelpful and disturbing.[22]

Perhaps the most public and dramatic moment came in 1985 when the obstetrician Wendy Savage was suspended from her post as Honorary Consultant in Obstetrics and Gynaecology to the Tower Hamlets Health Authority for allegedly being a danger to her patients.[23] Savage qualified as a doctor in 1960, and in 1977 became Senior Lecturer in Obstetrics and Gynaecology and Honorary Consultant at the London Hospital and Medical College, the first woman to hold the post. Savage believed in minimum surgical intervention during labour and birth, asserting that pregnancy is normal unless there are clear indications that something is wrong. She argued women should not be labelled 'high-risk' on the basis of statistical rather than individual information, as this led to far too many women attending hospital clinics rather than having the more personal care of a doctor or midwife closer to home. She was therefore a controversial figure because of her anti-interventionist views and practice. On 24 April 1985 Savage was suspended for alleged incompetence in five obstetric cases. However in February 1986 she was exonerated by a public inquiry and five months later reinstated. The three-man inquiry panel – Mr Christopher Beaumont, a barrister, and two obstetricians, Mr Leonard Harvey of Rugby and Professor Peter Howie of Dundee – found that while Savage failed in some instances to attain the highest possible standards of care, her treatment and clinical management of the five cases fell within the broad limits of acceptable medical practice. The panel disagreed with, or found invalid, most of the criticisms in the particulars of the case against her.[24] Helen Jones posits that the court case helped to bring an important aspect of women's reproductive rights to the fore.[25]

Histories of the maternity care provided to women during pregnancy and childbirth, both from a medical history approach such as Philip Rhodes' history of clinical midwifery and feminist interpretations such as those of Ann Oakley and Marjorie Tew, have detailed these developments and debates surrounding maternity provision in the second half of the twentieth century.[26] The inter-professional rivalries between midwives and doctors were also identified.[27] However research has often focused on clinical and professional developments rather than the thoughts and feelings of the women who were at the receiving end of maternity care. This chapter will therefore look at how debates surrounding maternity provision in the decades after World War Two determined the services on offer to women and how they experienced this care.

Antenatal care

In the 1940s antenatal care for mothers in Oxfordshire consisted of three examinations, one made early in pregnancy, the second in the seventh or eighth month, and the third six weeks after the date of confinement.[28] The women interviewed who gave birth to their children during this time described how they received very little care during pregnancy. They reported how either they made one or two visits to their GP or district nurse, or the doctor or nurse visited them. Women in urban areas could also attend antenatal clinics provided by the local health authority, although these were in decline by the 1940s. Madge, a resident of Milton-under-Wychwood, represented the typical experience. She recalled that her doctor turned up without warning just once or twice to check her over.[29] In the late 1940s and early 1950s in Benson, before the village got a resident GP, antenatal care for villagers was usually performed by the district nurse, and the women could not remember ever seeing a doctor. However, the provision of antenatal care was expanding. The obstetrician and champion of antenatal care Francis J. Browne wrote in 1935, 'It is probable that 80 percent of all parturient women in England and Wales receive antenatal care of some kind of degree.'[30] By 1955 he thought that, 'nearly all expectant mothers now come under supervision.'[31] Nonetheless, even in the 1960s there were women who recalled that they did not seek antenatal care until relatively late in pregnancy during the third or fourth month. Rather than going to their GP to see whether they were pregnant, they waited until they were sure they were before they went. In the context of the period this was a rational course of action to take. Until the 1970s pregnancy testing was neither reliable nor widespread. Consequently a woman's doctor could rarely tell her more than she knew herself. As the century progressed pregnant women came under increased supervision. In the mid-1970s the feminist sociologist Ann Oakley conducted a study of women's views of first-time motherhood during their pregnancies, labour and deliveries, and their experiences at five and twenty weeks postpartum, based on interviews with fifty-five first-time mothers. The degree of medical involvement she found was striking: 100 percent of the mothers in the sample had taken medication of some kind in pregnancy; 100 percent had blood and urine tests; 68 percent were given ultrasound; 19 percent had X-rays; and 30 percent had other tests. The average number of antenatal visits was thirteen.[32] However, despite this increased monitoring women did still slip through the net. Older multiparous women, teenage mothers, working mothers, and women from ethnic minority backgrounds were among those who were non- or late attenders. The tripartite nature of the NHS in the years before 1974 could also cause problems.[33] Fiona missed out on antenatal care with her third child born in 1970 because her local GP in Benson thought that she was having her antenatal care provided by the hospital in Oxford and vice versa.[34]

Women who were booked for hospital confinements attended the antenatal clinics that the hospital ran. Interviewees who went for their antenatal check-ups at hospitals were not very complementary about the care they received. Yvonne, for instance, who had her first baby in the Radcliffe Infirmary in 1959, listed her complaints: 'Big waiting room, waited a long time, not knowing the people, no regular relationship with doctors or anybody … I don't even remember if I was seen by a midwife or a doctor.'[35] The women did not go as far as arguing that the care they received was neglectful, but they did say that it was rather inattentive. A constant refrain was that they never got to see the same person twice, whether this was a doctor, midwife or nurse. The long waiting times that women experienced were another common complaint. Often there was either no appointment system or appointments were disregarded. Ingrid had two children in the early 1960s at Oxford's Churchill Hospital. She said, 'what you learnt was that no matter what time people got their appointment given to them, they all went at the earliest time, and they didn't stick to appointment times, they took them in the order they booked them in, so if you innocently think that you're queuing you weren't at all.'[36] It was assumed that women's time was less valuable than that of the medical professionals so it would not matter if women had to wait; this was a particular inconvenience for the women who were still working during their pregnancies. Georgie, a teacher, had her first baby in 1961 and described having to rush to the clinic at the Radcliffe

Infirmary in her lunch hour, 'so of course I then tore down to Walton Street for my prenatal check-up and my blood pressure had shot up, well there's a surprise, you know, there I was, what eight months pregnant and tearing around like a thing possessed and [they] wondered why my blood pressure had shot up.'[37] The negative experiences women had at the clinic reflected the wider culture of the health service at this time, namely that patients should fit in with the hospital's needs and requirements rather than the other way around.

A further complaint women made about their antenatal care was that medical professionals discounted women's knowledge of their own bodies. Bet had twins with her last pregnancy in 1975, but this was not diagnosed until late on because both her doctor and her midwife had not believed her protestations that she was carrying them. She said her midwife told her, '"I'm getting fed up with you asking", and she wrote in red pen, "One big baby".'[38] Rather than alleviate such conflicts the introduction of routine ultrasound scans during the 1980s could in fact exacerbate the problem. Indeed not all women who were offered an ultrasound scan wanted to have one at all. Pippa said she had to 'fight' not to have one when she was pregnant with her daughter in the late 1980s and that medical staff were 'cross' with her for refusing.[39] Andrea had three children in 1978, 1981 and 1984. She had an ultrasound scan with her third child and was sceptical whether it really was beneficial: 'And in fact that was the only one they actually queried the dates on. But I knew my dates were right.'[40] Andrea felt her own knowledge and experience had been challenged by the use of a technology which was itself ultimately discredited as the predicted due date was incorrect. Tara also had a story of a scan which was proved wrong. She had her first child in 1988 by emergency caesarean and had hoped to deliver her second baby, born in 1990, vaginally. However, 'they did one of those scans … And they told me the baby was actually quite large.' As a result of the scan Tara opted for an elective caesarean but found the experience 'nerve wracking and immediately the baby was delivered I got really, shockingly depressed.' In actuality Tara's daughter was 'tiny'. She was 'five and a half pounds', and Tara concluded: 'I would probably have been wiser to try and deliver her normally but what do you know?'[41] Nonetheless despite these interviewees' doubts about the medical benefits of ultrasound, by the end of the century it had become an established part of antenatal care, and having an ultrasound scan made some women feel for the first time that they were 'really pregnant'. For example Cynthia, who had her only child in 1993, said, 'certainly until I had my first scan I really had this sort of notion that it wasn't real.'[42] However, women's reasons for undergoing the scans were rather different than those intended by the maternity services. Women welcomed the opportunity to see their unborn child, but they seemed rather less enthusiastic about ultrasound's medical uses. Indeed the tensions which characterised the interviewees' accounts of ultrasound, and the sometimes conflicting desires of women and the medical staff who attended them, reflected their wider uncertainties about the benefits and limitations of their antenatal care.

Birth

The most striking development that occurred in relation to maternity care during the second half of the twentieth century was the growth in the number of hospital deliveries. This was not a gradual trend, rather there was a dramatic shift over the course of ten years from the mid-1960s until the mid-1970s. Roughly two-thirds of births took place in hospital and one-third at home between the late 1940s and mid-1960s, but in the decade that followed, the number of homebirths fell to under 5 percent and remained at this low level throughout the remainder of the century. This move to hospital deliveries was significant because hospital deliveries were often recalled unfavourably by the women interviewed. The main consultant-run maternity unit in Oxfordshire was Oxford's Radcliffe Infirmary, and after 1973 the John Radcliffe Hospital. Jackie, who had twin girls in the early 1960s at the Radcliffe Infirmary, remembered how women waited in rows in trolleys along the corridors until it was considered time to take them to the delivery room; she was, 'just one in a sort of sausage machine'.[43] This trolley system seems to have been the norm at the hospital and it was recalled by most of the women who were there. Siobhan had her first baby in the Radcliffe Infirmary in 1970 and found 'the hanging round on a trolley in a corridor in the hospital a bit tedious. It happened to be a very busy day, the day that [my son] was born.'[44] Women who had their first child at the Radcliffe Infirmary and then a later one at home or in a maternity or community hospital found significant improvements. For example Ruby had her first child in the Radcliffe Infirmary because she was over thirty and therefore considered at risk, but because all went well she was allowed to have her second baby in the maternity hospital in Wallingford. She found the staff at the Radcliffe Infirmary were unfriendly and patronising and she therefore discharged herself early. In contrast she recalled the birth of her second son at Wallingford as a much improved experience.[45] Gloria described the same contrast with regards to being moved from the Radcliffe Infirmary to Wallingford to convalesce after the birth of her first child. At the Radcliffe Infirmary the staff were 'off handed'. Gloria had not been out of bed for over a week because no one helped her up. Conversely she remembers arriving at Wallingford and 'the first words they said, "Is there anything you want?", [I said] "Can I have a bath?" "Course you can", immediately, you know, "Haven't you had a bath?" "No, and I'd love to wash my hair". And I got there and that was all sorted out, all done. Marvellous.'[46]

Indeed many women remembered hospital staff as being dismissive of their female patients. Penny, who was pregnant with her third child in the early 1960s, recalled what happened when she visited her consultant to undergo a procedure designed to prevent the risk of miscarriage:

> There was a Professor of Gynaecology … and I went to him. And he explained about this new technique and what a success this was going to be. [Pause]. And I think it was eighteen weeks that they put these sutures in, well I had been going to him regularly for antenatal check-ups and I went one day, and he was in a hurry and just fitting me in, and he examined me and he estimated the length of the pregnancy. And he did this, and then he said, 'Oh it's all going very nicely, you know in a couple of weeks time when you're eighteen weeks pregnant we'll do this.' And I was saying to him, 'But I'm eighteen weeks now!' [Bangs her fist on table]. He didn't take any notice. [Pause]. Within a week I had lost the baby. I was furious, I could have sued him, but what's the point.

Penny's distress was still evident as she told this story. The breaks and pauses in her narrative demonstrate the difficulty with which she did so. Penny went on to have another successful pregnancy, but she recalled how this experience of losing her baby had been a revelation. She said, 'in those days of course people paid such reverence to somebody with a medical coat, it really was an education.'[47] 'Rebecca worked at the maternity department at the John Radcliffe Hospital in Oxford when it opened in the early 1970s. She was shocked by the disparaging attitudes some of the male consultants held towards their female patients and that there were no female gynaecologists or obstetricians. As a result she felt that all the important decisions in the department 'were taken by men' despite the fact that 'all the patients were women'. She said it was, 'One of the things that made me into a feminist.'[48] Such experiences seemed to occur nationwide. Responding to a Mass Observation New Project Directive about the NHS, a correspondent wrote about her first baby being born in the early 1950s in Bristol: 'The consultant used to appear with his entourage, formally dressed and never speaking to anybody. The poor sister had to remember everything he said to her and come back and tell the mother after he had gone. We were not allowed, whilst he was in the room, to get out of bed for any reason at all. Going to the loo or asking for a bedpan was forbidden.'[49] However, it was not only consultants, but also midwives who received criticism. Another Mass Observation correspondent, whose children were born in 1958 and 1961, stated: 'When I had my confinements many years ago, the midwives, who were usually of sister status, seemed very hard and even callous ... [they] were very concerned with their own power and needed psychological guidance on how to treat women in pain.'[50] Another correspondent, who had her first child in 1949, wrote: 'I had our baby in a small prison (for that's what it seemed like) with a black-gowned matron who ruled us with a rod of iron.'[51] Women's criticisms of their hospital care were therefore focused mainly upon members of the hospital staff. Women could feel that while they received good medical care, the emotional care was lacking.

Whether in home or hospital women who felt they had established a relationship with their attendants in labour recalled having a better birth experience. Polly experienced continuity in her care because her GP delivered her baby. He was her family doctor and someone she felt she could trust implicitly. She explained how he told her, 'he would have put me into the Battle [Hospital], and I'm quite happy I wasn't there, because I'd gone through six or seven months with his care, so no way would I have been happy going into the Battle.'[52] It was also easier for women who had homebirths to establish a relationship with their midwife because she provided both antenatal and postnatal care. A woman's prior contact with her midwife or GP meant that she usually felt comfortable and relaxed with them. Emily had her baby at home in Oxford in 1963. She remembered her midwife as being 'very attentive all the time, the whole way, from whatever time they started beforehand ... and they were like limpets the week before and during labour they just sat there or they had a trainee you know one of their youngsters in, and I still remember the cross stitch she was doing.' Moreover, she thought the midwifery service was excellent because of the consistency of the care it provided, 'I'm not sure when health visitors turned up on the scene in the history, but certainly ... it was a kind of pretty seamless thing because the midwives stayed for two weeks after you gave birth and then handed you over to the health visitor and you'd be expected then to go to the clinics but they would come and call on you, they kept a sort of diary on you.'[53] Interviewees valued this continuity of personnel.[54] The alienation from their attendants which women often felt in large hospitals was one reason why they preferred to have babies at home, in maternity homes or later, when they were introduced, GP units. Moreover, it was not simply a result of subsequent labours being easier. Women who went to hospital for later births also commented that they had preferred giving birth at home. A Mass Observation correspondent writing on the subject of birth in 1993 explained: 'I had my first baby in 1947, a home delivery with a wonderful midwife in Selly Oak Birmingham …[In] 1949 I had twin boys. This time in Sorrento Nursing Home, Moseley, due to the fact I had toxaemia. This was my first experience of hospital and I didn't like it at all.[55]

However, while the overwhelming response from women who had homebirths was that it was a fulfilling experience for them, problems did occur and could be frightening. Tina's second two children were born at home in 1968 and 1971 and she remembers that giving birth at home had both positive and negative aspects:

> It had some advantages because … it doesn't seem so frightening because you've got your own, everything of yours around you so you sort of felt that life's going on as normal … Then I had [my daughter], but I had problems when I had [my daughter] and I was seriously ill then, because I don't actually know the name for what it's called, but she was born face forward, and she was a very big baby, and I was very tiny then, and so I was rushed into hospital, and [my husband] told me later that they had given me twenty minutes to live, because I'd lost, I just haemorrhaged really, so I didn't have any more then, that did end it, so that was a bit scary.[56]

Amanda also recalled how stressful it was when she had her second child at home in 1966 and had difficulties getting hold of the midwife.[57] Having children at home could be a satisfying experience for women if things went well. Problems during a homebirth however, such as Tina haemorrhaging or Amanda not being able to get in contact with her midwife, meant that it could be just as traumatic as at hospital, if not more so. This fear of something going wrong at home is one reason why women may have wanted to give birth in hospital. Moreover while statistical evidence, at least for Oxfordshire, does not indicate homebirths were more risky (this is complicated by the fact that difficult deliveries were done in hospital), women were also being told that hospital was safer. In addition, by the 1970s technological advances meant that hospitals had equipment that was not available at home, particularly in respect to neonatal care. Before then the rationale for going to hospital was less certain.

These changes resulted in a dramatic shift in attitudes towards homebirths. In 1958, the year before the Cranbrook report, the MOH for Oxfordshire, P.W. Bothwell, indicated that he thought the question of where a woman should give birth was open to debate. He wrote:

> While many mothers prefer hospitalisation for their confinements there are many people who consider that home is the proper place in which to be born. Contact with the family and children and the personal general practitioner is not then lost. On the other hand, specialised assistance is

not so readily available, even with a Flying Squad Maternity Emergency Unit, and many general practitioners would feel happier to be able to conduct their own cases at home antenatally and in a G.P. hospital bed if hospital care is necessary.[58]

After the Cranbrook report in 1959 called for 70 percent of births to take place in hospital the debate in Oxfordshire was over. In 1966 the policy of discharging early those patients who delivered in consultant units was introduced to provide for as many hospital births as possible.[59] In other areas the trend towards hospital delivery may have been occurring earlier, reflecting how women's care was highly dependent on the individual practitioners involved.[60] In Preston in Lancashire only 19 percent of babies were born at home in 1957.[61] Mrs Barlow's first baby was born in 1958. She said her doctor 'definitely pushed me towards hospital' and she thought this was because he 'didn't want to be bothered with it.'[62]

By the 1970s homebirths were virtually nonexistent throughout the whole of the country. The Peel Report of 1970, which advocated 100 percent hospitalisation of births, had proved a turning point. Margaret's children were born at home, in 1969 and 1970, and she explained that she faced a lot of pressure to go into hospital from her GP and was only able to have her babies at home due to the sympathetic community midwives in Berkshire where she was then living.[63] Not all midwives were of the same opinion, though. Kaye was a midwife in Oxfordshire. She talked at length about how she felt birth had become too interventionist in large consultant hospitals during the 1970s and that she favoured the midwife-run smaller units which enabled a more 'natural birth'. She said, 'I was never that happy with homebirths because you just never know what might happen and I only did seven in my three years in Oxford and I'd done none before that whatsoever. So although there weren't any problems with them, I still felt it was a pointless risk.'[64] For the interviewees who had their children after 1970 being delivered at home by a midwife was no longer considered mainstream. It had become seen as old-fashioned – something their mothers had done – or the preserve of eccentrics. For example when asked whether she had considered a homebirth, Jean replied: 'No, I'm not that adventurous. No.'[65] Similarly, April 'didn't want to have children at home, I just thought that was something hippyish.'[66] Very few women recalled being prevented from having a homebirth by doctors, or by the fear of medical complications. Only Amelia said she had asked to have a homebirth but was refused because at over thirty she was told she was too old.[67] Rather, the interviewees presented homebirth as something that was never even an option. For example, Bev said, 'homebirths was another thing that sort of didn't occur to me.'[68] The pace of change is astonishing.

In the ten years from the mid-1960s to the mid-1970s homebirth had gone from being viewed as normal to extraordinary. Women's experience of hospital delivery also changed during the 1970s. Induction and acceleration of labour became routine procedures in many hospitals. However there was great variation between individual hospitals. In consequence whether or not a woman was induced was highly dependent on the policy of the hospital in which she was delivered. Kaye discussed the different policies towards induction at the various hospitals where she worked as a midwife. 'At St Thomas' [London] where I did my obstetrics, you know, the consultants would routinely induce people when it suited them sort of thing, not at weekends, and I thought that was all wrong. So yes I thought it was, you know, much more natural the way they did things at the smaller hospitals and the midwives were, you know, skilled in normal deliveries without using episiotomies routinely and that sort of thing.' She continued: 'At the Royal Bucks [Buckinghamshire] it wasn't very good. The doctors sort of interfered unnecessarily and if a labour wasn't going as fast as they'd like they'd stick a drip [in] ... to speed things along.' Kaye also explained that she turned down a job at Oxford's John Radcliffe Hospital because, 'their induction rate was so high at the time which I thought was terrible. It was something like 37 percent. This was in the mid-1970s.'[69] Women therefore found their care was determined by hospital policies and practices rather than medical need.

Reflecting the contemporary uncertainty surrounding induction, many interviewees' accounts indicate their doubts about whether induction or acceleration of labour were beneficial, detrimental or of no consequence. Patsy had two children in 1970 and 1972. Comparing the births she spoke of the great improvement with her second child. He was 'induced early because of the problems I'd had with [my first son], so he was induced and, of course, I had no problems whatsoever and I think I probably only stayed twenty-four hours before I came home.'[70] In contrast Liz was unsure about the procedure. Her third baby was induced in 1980 because she had not been putting on weight. She was told:

'You'd better come in tomorrow and we'll put you on a drip.' And I'd never had a drip before. And I thought no, I just want to do it the way I know ... So, the doctor came round and said, 'Oh we'll have to put you on that drip anyway.' And I [thought] 'Ooo you nasty man.' Oh and he wasn't gentle at all when he, cos I went red, the midwife was so sympathetic. She was lovely. So I think he ... I think he broke the waters, that's what he did. He put me on the drip and then that.[71]

Liz's account touches on a number of different issues that were present in maternity care at this time – the change in practice over time, the division between doctors and midwives and the power relations between them and their patients. However while some women were unhappy that their labours had been accelerated or induced, the strongest impression that emerges from the interviews is that women were accepting of the judgements made by medical professionals. At the time they had believed decisions were taken in the best interests of their babies, and they still felt this way from their current perspective in the 2000s. For example Viv was induced with her second child at Reading's Royal Berkshire Hospital in 1971. While she could have presented the birth as a traumatic event – she had high blood pressure; a trolley system was in operation at the hospital; and her labour was long – instead Viv used humour in her account. She said the hospital was 'fantastic' and told the story in a light-hearted manner, joking that she was not allowed to eat or drink as she was nil by mouth and remembering how she spent her time 'getting up and wandering and chatting to everybody else.'[72]

The interviews with Oxfordshire women revealed a similarly complex picture surrounding women's experiences of epidural anaesthesia and caesarean section. The consequences of having an epidural were often not separated from women's memories of the birth process more generally. Epidurals were rarely presented as turning points in women's stories of birth, leading either to an 'easy' or 'difficult' birth, but rather were just another procedure to be undergone. For example, describing the birth of her first son in 1983 Pippa associated epidural anaesthesia with the processes of being induced and foetal scalp monitoring. One followed on from the other: 'It hadn't started naturally the night before, and I spent most of the day there and nothing much happening … and then they wired me up and [I was in] a lot of pain but not much happening [pause] got really, really tired [pause] and eventually I had an epidural, which sort of did speed things up … and that had worn off and I did, sort of, push him out.'[73] The various procedures women underwent were therefore often not differentiated in their recollections. Katherine's first child was born by caesarean in 1983 at Frimley Park Hospital in Camberley, Surrey. When asked how the birth went she replied, 'Oh, very traumatic. Yes, they decided, he was a big baby … And they decided that they would induce me … Sort of nothing happened for all day … And then suddenly the distress [call] went out and they, you know, did all sorts of things and it was an emergency caesarean by the evening.' However while recalling her experience of giving birth to her son as traumatic she then added that she did not regret having a caesarean: 'I was glad because he was a big baby.'[74] Bev had both her children at St Peter's Hospital in Chertsey, Surrey, rather than at her local hospital, Frimley Park, as she was considered high risk.

She felt that she was well-prepared for a caesarean but was critical of what happened after the birth:

> I felt up to that point, I was given everything I wanted and listened to. But after he was born, when things went a little bit squiff, I felt like I wasn't in control at all. Now whether that was my mental state or whether that was how things really were, I don't know, I wouldn't like to say. I felt I was like, in a German concentration camp. The nurse was 'Get up. Do this. Do this. Do this.' You know. The baby was, you know, I was manhandled to feed him. And [pause] I wasn't well.[75]

Therefore while interviewees could report unhappiness with some of the procedures they underwent, as with the women who had their children in the 1940s, 1950s and 1960s it was poor interpersonal relationships and their consequences that featured most prominently in their accounts.

Nevertheless some changes were occurring in maternity wards over the second half of the century. Visiting hours greatly increased and husbands were allowed to remain present throughout labour. The husbands of women who had their children in the 1940s and 1950s had definitely not been welcome at the birth. Childbirth was considered to be a female preserve. Describing visiting hours when she was in the Radlciffe Infirmary with her first child in 1951 Rebecca recalled: 'only fathers could visit and only something like four evenings in this week you stayed in hospital then, and because of the [time of day] when my son was born, our son was born, it was over two days before [my husband] saw him and he was desperate and he rang his parents in Austria and said, "What's wrong with him, what's wrong".[76] Even during homebirths, many husbands chose to remain out of the room, or indeed midwives kept them out. When her first baby was born at home in Benson in 1943 Enid's midwife sent her husband on an erroneous errand to Wallingford because she did not want him in the house. This attitude had softened by the 1960s with fathers increasingly being present, although it was still not the norm. Mrs Rowlandson had her first child in 1969 in Preston. She recalled how her husband 'dropped me off and said, "Goodbye, have a nice time," and went back home again. Among our group none of the husbands did [attend the birth] because it wasn't done. It was the woman's personal thing wasn't it?'[77] Women were also fairly ambivalent in their attitudes towards husbands being present. Some said they were glad their husbands were not there, and that they would not have wanted them to be present; however others who had hospital births and experienced long periods left on their own would have enjoyed the support of their husbands or another companion. Furthermore those women whose husbands were at the birth said it was a good experience. For example Fiona felt her husband developed a closer relationship with their second child than with their first because he was present. She explained how, 'it was very happy and it was lovely [my husband] was that more involved I think with [our second child]. Because I think he'd been there and it wasn't this sort of women's mystery. And I was much happier having him there. Because he didn't see [our first child] until, he didn't even know he had a son until nine o'clock that morning when he rang up.'[78] From the 1970s onwards attitudes further changed. Fathers found they were now expected to be present at their children's births. During the 1980s and 1990s the majority of the Oxfordshire interviewees had their husbands present. Moreover this was a national trend. In her study of fathers in labour wards, published in 1990, Rosaline Barbour found that midwives had come to welcome paternal attendance, as they felt it had made their own jobs easier.[79]

Whatever the reasons for the change, women spoke positively about its effects. Carol's first baby was born in 1979 and her last in 1996, both in the John Radcliffe Hospital in Oxford. With her first baby she experienced many of the features of 1970s' maternity care that were so criticised. She was induced, had to give birth in the lithotomy position and was given a routine episiotomy. She explained:

> Well, the first baby, I went into hospital and they said they wanted to keep me in. Cos I was getting late … I was about a week late … So they started me off. And that was horrendous. [The contractions] sort of started every two minutes. You know the gradual build up. And I wanted to have a natural birth. I didn't want any drugs or anything. And I said, 'Oo, how much longer?' And this had been going on about an hour. And she said, 'Oh, it's your first one. You'll have about another 18 hours of this.' And I said, 'Oh my God, I can't cope with that.' And I said, 'Oh can I have something?' And they gave me some Pethidine. By the time they'd given me the Pethidine [pause]. Oh sorry, I had to have a gown, lay on the bed, have my socks on and legs in stirrups and you weren't to move and just lay there. But anyway, they gave me this Pethidine. And my son was born about twenty minutes later. And I think it was routine as well, to give you an episiotomy on your first. And so, because he was being born so quick I had no injection, to numb the pain. And they said, 'just a little snip'. And, nobody told me they did that routine. They just did it. And it was just, felt like a pair of shears, just cutting into you. It was the only time out of all five children that I let out a scream. Cos that was just really painful. And shocking as well, cos they didn't tell you. And, of course, he was born and they took him straight out of the room.

Dramatic improvements had occurred by the time Carol's fifth baby was born:

the most relaxed birth was [my last] because my Mum came in ... I wanted my Mum to video it. Because I've never seen one of my children being born. I've missed out on that. So, my Mum came but my brother, from America, gave my Mum a lift. And he come in to say hello and that. And I don't know how, but he ended up staying there. Cos his wife was pregnant in America and he'd come over to visit. And he was sort of quite interested. And he said, 'you don' t mind if I stay, love, do you?' He said 'I'm going to stay at this end.' He stayed at the head end. Didn't go down that way. And, he was sort of like mopping my brow. My Mum was there with the video camera and [my partner] was sort of back holding my hand and talking to me. But again, there, you know, I could walk around. I chose what music I wanted to play. I chose that I wanted soft lighting. I chose that I wanted [my partner] to tell me the sex of the baby and to cut the cord. You know, there was all these things that you felt much more empowered and in control at the birth. And it was just so much nicer.

Carol concluded: 'You know when I think back to how my first one was. Well, I think, you know, I'm surprised I ever had any more after that. Yeah. So big changes from 1979 to 1996. All for the better.'[80]

Postnatal care

As with their antenatal care, and indeed the birth, there were also significant variations in the postnatal care women were offered. Moreover the place where they gave birth, namely at home or in hospital, greatly affected the care they received after their babies were born. Lisa was living in Cowley when her baby was born at home in 1960. Her postnatal care followed on seamlessly after the birth and she described how this process worked: 'I had the baby at home, the midwife came and delivered it ... And then the midwife came in every day for the first week and then every other day for the next couple of weeks.'[81] This continuity did not exist for women coming home after giving birth in hospital, who often experienced a marked break when they left the hospital's care. For these women the maternity services available offered piecemeal provision rather than a unified service. For example after her first child was born in 1953 Florence had to travel to Oxford with her new baby on the bus in order to have an abscess on her breast treated because her GP said as she had been under the hospital for the birth, he could not see her. Although she now thought this was ludicrous, at the time she accepted it unquestioningly.[82] Katherine's first baby was born in 1983. She recalled what happened when she returned to the maternity unit at Frimley Park Hospital in Camberley for her six week check: 'when I got in the doctor took one look at me and said, "I don't see postnatal." Sort of, you know, I just felt awful. And the nurse actually was very kind ... And in the end he had to and he was a bit brutal. So, it was just a horrible experience ... I think the nurse realised how horrible he was and she was terribly nice to me. But, you know, it wasn't her fault.'[83] Moreover for women who felt they had been supported while in hospital, and given help with breastfeeding, bathing and caring for their babies, leaving hospital could be traumatic. Siobhan explained: 'You suddenly realise that you're responsible for this little person which when you're in the hospital, because there are nursery nurses caring for the babies, you didn't feel particularly responsible for them. You did feel that bond with your baby, I think it's just something that happens instantaneously, but you didn't feel that you were responsible for them at all, that was quite a shock when you got home.'[84]

After the 1950s, when women stayed in hospital for fourteen days after giving birth, the length of time women spent in hospital started to decrease, a trend hastened in the 1960s as the policy of discharging women early from hospital into the care of community midwives was introduced. While this policy was originally a response to the shortage of hospital beds, many women preferred leaving hospital early and then being cared for in their own homes. It also meant that community midwives began to perform an important role in women's postnatal care. For example Sharon, who had her first baby in 1972, remembered 'the midwives coming to visit, they were important. Cos the midwife would come to visit for I think they would come for the first ten days, but I can't remember them now but I did, if they didn't come I was very disappointed. Cos, I definitely found them supportive.'[85] Women's desire for integrated postnatal care provision was an area of need that was recognised by both policy makers and practitioners. As a result some improvements were being made by the latter decades of the century. April had her first baby in Oxford in 1978 under the Domino (Domiciliary In and Out) system at the GP Unit at the John Radcliffe Hospital. Under this system women received their antenatal and postnatal care from the same team of community midwives who would then also deliver them within the GP Unit. April said:

> It was just great. You know you went to your GP and your GP had midwives, I don't know how many actually. They had some midwives attached to the surgery and you bonded with [them], or saw [them] regularly, you went for these antenatal appointments and met the midwives and got friendly with the midwives. And then with any luck they were the midwives, there'd be a kind of senior one and a junior one I think I remember. And they were the people who were there at the birth and you were in the sort of special bit [GP Unit], it wasn't quite the hospital.[86]

When the midwife's visits concluded, the care of women and their babies was supposed to pass into the hands of the health visitor. However the women interviewed had mixed feelings about their health visitors' efficacy and this was true throughout the period. Some reported them as being useful figures who would be the first person they turned to if they had any questions or problems. Carol, whose first baby was born in 1979, recalled her health visitor as being her 'surrogate Mum'.[87] Jane, herself a doctor, had her first child in 1974. She had also hoped for a 'homely, maternal health visitor who's had three or four children to arrive on my doorstep'. In actuality, 'this tall, bearded, long-haired young man arrived and said, "I'm Mr Such and Such, your health visitor"'. However, while he may not have been what she expected Jane also spoke positively about the support he offered: 'He came in, talked to me and he was absolutely super.'[88] Women could also show deference to their health visitors and indicated that they felt they ought to follow their health visitors' expert advice. Mrs Burrell had three children in Lancashire in the 1950s and 1960s. She explained that she would rather ask for advice from her health visitor than her mother. She thought 'the health visitor was the one to ask'.[89] However other women resented the health visitor coming, thinking that she (or he) was interfering and passing judgement on their ability to care for their children. Eve's first baby was born in 1957. She described her health visitor as being 'very strict and you know, "Are you doing this, are you doing that, are you doing this?"'.[90] Andrea had her first child over twenty years later in 1978, but recalled similar feelings towards her health visitor. She also felt her health visitor was too strict, and she disagreed with the health visitor's advice to give her baby water at night, preferring to follow her own mother's advice to give 'a spoonful of custard'.[91] These ideas that health visitors were interfering, and that it was necessary to take their advice with a healthy scepticism, were common in the first half of the century and it is noteworthy that similar attitudes existed throughout the post-war decades too.[92] It is also interesting how this opinion crossed class, challenging the traditional stereotype that it was working-class women who resented the middle-class health visitor entering their homes. Grace was university educated and was married to a university lecturer. However, she was very uncomfortable when the health visitor came after her second child was born, and presumed she was passing judgment upon her: 'I was pretty chaotic. We were living up the road in a little house which had one big room downstairs and these tiny babies and the health visitor used to come and visit invariably when the [eldest] baby was sort of crawling round the floor in a filthy nappy.'[93]

A significant group of women held an indifferent attitude towards their health visitor. She either made little impact during her visits or her visits were rare. Such an attitude was not unusual and a Mass Observation report from 1949, based on interviews with 150 women from Hammersmith and Camden, found that few of the women interviewed expressed any definite attitude towards their health visitor.[94] Such views may have resulted from the fact that while women could feel their health visitors dealt with practical problems they did not provide much emotional support. Michelle was not critical of the practical advice her health visitor gave her, indeed she thought 'they were invaluable cos they took over when the nurses left and they followed you up'. However she also said that 'you didn't get the emotional sort of support, really I don't think, it was quite practical.'[95] Similarly Lindsay did not think her health visitor was 'that wonderful. I remember her coming in and telling me kindly that, "Was I aware that if it was windy I could pull the pram hood up", but yes there I was stuck with this screaming entity, and of course again postnatal depression wasn't terribly recognised. Well it hit me actually really badly after [my daughter] was born.'[96] It was middle-class women that were most critical, reflecting how they felt neglected by their health visitors.[97] Emily explained: 'I remember one time, the baby would be crying and crying and crying and I can remember this health visitor coming in and asking me was I alright, she could see the baby was you know crying a lot, and of course being a good, stiff-upper-lip, middle-class girl I said, "Oh yes I'm fine", but I wasn't, I could have battered that child.'[98] Indeed there was little provision for women who did suffer from mental health problems after the birth of their children. Penny suffered from postnatal depression after her baby was born in 1955. When asked if she received any help for her condition, she answered, 'Oh no, pull yourself together … But you know it, was absolutely … awful, absolutely dreadful.'[99] Moreover, the situation was slow to improve. Shirley became depressed after the birth of her first child in 1978, but described a similar experience. She recalled that it was her neighbour who had detected she had a problem and encouraged her to seek help, although with limited success. 'Well I did go along [to] my GP, this is the surgery in Sandhurst and I saw [pause] it happened to be the elderly doctor in the practice who really was no help, he just prescribed valium and said, "Oh just go home and it'll all pass".'[100] The lack of support women received therefore compounded the difficulties they faced.

The other prominent feature of women's accounts of postnatal care was their visits to the baby clinic. Women valued the baby clinic because they felt they could ask things of the health visitor or doctor at the clinic with which they did not want to trouble their own GP. Hope explained that she liked to go to the clinic because, 'you felt that you could go to the health visitor sometimes with a problem that wasn't big enough to take to the doctor.'[101] Yvonne described the clinic as 'reassuring and a place you could get advice.'[102] The clinics also provided the opportunity for women to buy baby foods and products at reduced rates. Mabel said that the only reason she went to the clinic when her children were little in the 1940s was to get the cod liver oil and orange juice.[103] The clinics dispensed these products in large quantities. In 1954, for example, 78,103 tins of National Dried Milk, 109, 858 bottles of orange juice, 21,807 packets of cod liver oil and 6,216 packets of vitamins were distributed in Oxfordshire during the year.[104] Moreover, the clinics also provided an occasion for women to meet other mothers over a cup of tea and this was something they valued as highly as any medical care or advice. When asked about the clinic Cherie said, 'I used to quite enjoy going to the baby clinic cos you got the chance of sort of being with other mums and finding out how much weight had gone on and, and it was just generally a nice little occasion I used to quite look forward to it … yes I enjoyed going there and meeting the other mums.'[105] Going to the clinic was an important feature of women's accounts of their care and was an experience that stayed with them. Indeed Hayley, who had three children in the late 1950s, said, 'I don't remember any antenatal or postnatal care at all except the clinics.'[106]

However, despite the women's endorsement of the clinics their role in Oxfordshire, as in the country at large, was under some debate. In 1958, P.W. Bothwell, the MOH for the county, wrote in his annual report that, 'The persistence of the Infant Welfare Clinics on such a wide scale will, however, need careful scrutiny. The regular weighing of entirely healthy infants is probably more persistent than useful and it is possible that the Health Visitors' time could more profitably be spent on selective home visiting of mothers who never bring their children to a clinic.'[107] However two years later, in 1960, the then MOH M.J. Pleydell advocated a very different policy:

> The Committee have adopted the policy of providing child welfare clinics for comparatively small communities in rural areas … In a rural county like Oxfordshire, the clinics serve a very useful purpose from a social point of view, as mothers' clubs. Mothers, living under isolated conditions, welcome the regular opportunities of discussing with each other their different parental problems. In addition, the health education given by the health visitors, the doctors' advice and reassurance, and the provision of the necessary welfare foods help to make the clinics a fundamental part of our health services and social life.[108]

Eight years later there had been a complete reversal of this policy in response to the Sheldon Report of 1967 which had argued that GPs should take over the services provided by local authority child health clinics.[109] The function of selling infant foods was removed; immunisations were now to be done by appointment at the GP's surgery; and the clinics were to have a purely medical, rather than social, function.[110] Women did still recall going to the clinic in the decades after 1970. Jean had her two children in Wallingford in 1987 and 1990. She described how the clinic continued to be a place to meet other mothers: 'We used to meet and chat in the clinics because you, you know, waited to have your baby weighed and measured, so you used to sort of see people and chat a bit then.'[111] However, as Jean also intimated, the clinic had been stripped of its other functions and was now, for many mothers, simply remembered as the place where they got their babies weighed. The example of baby clinics demonstrates how quickly attitudes changed towards services at the national and local level, but also, as a result, the gulf in expectations which could exist between women and policy makers.

Conclusions

During the second half of the twentieth century important developments occurred in relation to maternity provision. Both midwife-supervised homebirths and GP-supervised births in home or hospital were in decline and instead delivery at consultant-led hospital units became the norm. While the initial result of the increased number of hospital beds meant a hospital delivery became available to some women for the first time, by the 1970s women lost the opportunity to decide where they wanted to give birth as hospital became the only option. In the latter decades of the century hospitals were making some efforts to improve the quality of care they could offer. Women spoke positively about these developments: husbands were allowed to be present at the birth; less deference was expected by the hospital staff; women were kept more informed about and included in the decisions being made. However, this process was by no means complete and in many areas it took a long time to take effect.

Writing in the 1970s, feminist writers such as Ann Oakley portrayed the medicalisation of childbirth, which reached its pinnacle in the second half of the century, as resulting from the desire of doctors to exert control over women's bodies. Oakley argued, 'It is only by an ideological transformation of the 'natural' to the 'cultural' that doctors can legitimate reproduction as a medical speciality.'[112] However in recent years historians of women's health have shown how the process of medicalisation and the relationships between women and medicine are considerably more nuanced than such earlier analyses allowed for.[113] While it cannot be denied that medical intervention in pregnancy and childbirth increased over the second half of the century, the reasons for this were complex. They included women's desire for doctor-attended labours, the state's concern with infant and maternal mortality as a social problem, and technological advances. Moreover, analysing women's own accounts of these changes indicates that they had a rather ambivalent response to them. While women often reported their unhappiness with obstetric interventions, this seemed as much a criticism of the lack of information they received, the lack of choice they felt that they had in their care, and their dissatisfaction with their medical attendants (doctors, midwives and nurses), as their dislike of the procedures themselves. Indeed women could feel they received excellent medical care, but criticised their treatment by hospital staff. Furthermore, despite the changes that were taking place women's complaints remained remarkably similar throughout the whole of the period. They were unhappy at their treatment by self-important medical professionals who believed that they rather than their patients knew best. The women felt they were left uninformed about the procedures being carried out and that their emotional needs were not being met. Interviewees who objectively had similar birth experiences, for example the same length of labour, technical interventions, or pain relief, could recall them very differently. Those women who said they knew and trusted their attendants, and believed they acted in their best interests, remembered their care far more positively. When reflecting back upon their experiences from their current perspective in the 2000s, it was poor interpersonal relationships and their consequences that featured most prominently in the interviewees' accounts.

Notes

1 Ministry of Health, *Report of the Maternity Services Committee* (London: HMSO, 1959). The Cranbrook Committee set a target for hospital deliveries of 70 percent of all births. Given correct selection for hospital or home confinement the committee felt that the remaining 30 percent of mothers could safely and appropriately be delivered in their own homes.

2 Ann Oakley, *The Captured Womb: A History of the Medical Care of Pregnant Women* (Oxford: Basil Blackwell, 1984), p. 215; D. Christie and E. Tansey (eds), *Maternal care: Wellcome Witnesses to Twentieth Century Medicine* (12) (London: Wellcome Trust Centre for the History of Medicine at UCL, 2001), p. 74.

3 Joint Committee of the Royal College of Obstetricians and Gynaecologists and the Population Investigation Committee, *Maternity in Great Britain* (London: Oxford University Press, 1948).

4 Department of Health and Social Security, *Report of the Sub-Committee on Domiciliary and Maternity Bed Needs* (London: HMSO, 1970). The Domiciliary Midwifery and Maternity Bed Needs (Peel Report), published in 1970, was the report of a Sub-committee of the Standing Maternity and Midwifery Advisory Committee chaired by Sir John Peel. It recommended 100 percent hospital deliveries, and that medical and midwifery care should be provided by consultants, GPs and midwifes working as teams, with GP units in district general hospitals sharing the same staff and facilities.

5 Clare Hanson, *A Cultural History of Pregnancy: Pregnancy, Medicine and Culture, 1750-2000* (Houndmills: Palgrave Macmillan, 2004), p. 158.

6 Roma Chamberlain, Geoffrey Chamberlain, Brian Howlett and Aalbert Claireaux, *British Births 1970* (London: William Heinemann Medical Books, 1975), p. vii.

7 James L. Reynolds and P.L. Yudkin, 'Changes in the management of labour: 2. Perineal management', *CMAJ*, 136 (1987), 1041–9, p. 1048.

8 Ann Cartwright, *The Dignity of Labour: A Study of Childbearing and Induction* (London: Tavistock Publications, 1979), p. 1.

9 M.B. McNay ,G.M. McIlwaine, P.W. Howie and M.C. MacNaughton, 'Perinatal deaths: analysis by clinical cause to assess value of induction of labour', *BMJ* (5 February 1977), 347–50.

10 I. Chalmers, J.G. Lawson, and A.C. Turnbull, 'Evaluation of different approaches to obstetric care: part II', *British Journal of Obstetrics and Gynaecology* (83) 1976, 930–3.

11 Sally Macintyre, 'The sociology of reproduction', *Sociology of Health and Illness*, 2 (1980), 215–22, p. 217.

12 Department of Health and Social Security, *Reducing the Risk: Safer Pregnancy and Childbirth* (London: HMSO, 1977), p. 39.

13 Marjorie Tew, *Safer Childbirth? A Critical History of Maternity Care* (London: Chapman and Hall, 1995), pp. 235–6.

14 Margaret Allen, 'Viewpoint', in *The Times* (13 August 1973), p. 8.

15 Jenny Kitzinger, 'Strategies of the early childbirth movement: a case-study of the National Childbirth Trust', in Jo Garcia, Robert Kilpatrick and Martin Richards (eds), *The Politics of Maternity Care* (Oxford: Clarendon Press, 1990), 92–115, pp. 109–11.

16 Lyn Durand and Ruth Evans, 'Pressure groups and maternity care', in Garcia, Kilpatrick and Richards (eds), *The Politics of Maternity Care*, 256–74, p. 260.

17 Department of Health and Social Security, *Reducing the Risk*, p. 35.

18 Maternity Services Advisory Committee, *Second Report. Maternity Care in Action: Part II – Care During Childbirth (Intrapartum Care)* (London: HMSO, 1984), p. 17.

19 *Ibid.*, p. 23.

20 'Home birth rate in UK falls', www.nursingtimes.net (10 November 2010).

21 Tew, *Safer Childbirth?*

22 Department of Health, *Changing Childbirth. Part 1: Report of the Expert Maternity Group* (London: HMSO, 1993), p. 10.

23 For a full discussion of the case see Wendy Savage, *A Savage Enquiry: Who Controls Childbirth?* (London: Virago, 1986).

24 Clare Dyer, 'Mrs Savage reinstated: "all over in five minutes"', *BMJ* (2 August 1986), 340, p. 340.

25 Helen Jones, *Health and Society in Twentieth-Century Britain* (London: Longman, 1994), pp. 159–60.

26 Philip Rhodes, *A Short History of Clinical Midwifery* (Hale: Books for Midwives Press,

1995); Oakley, *Captured Womb*; Tew, *Safer Childbirth?*

27 Jean Donnison, *Midwives and Medical Men: A History of the Struggle for the Control of Childbirth* (New Barnett: Historical Publications, 1988).

28 Oxfordshire MOH, 1938, p. 44.

29 Madge, WY8, p. 6.

30 Francis J. Browne, *Antenatal and Postnatal Care* (London: Churchill, 1935), p. 15.

31 F.J. Browne and J.C. McClure Browne, *Antenatal and Postnatal Care* (London: Churchill, 1955), p. 12.

32 Oakley, *Women Confined*, p. 20.

33 Between 1948 and 1974 the NHS had a tripartite structure, with three branches – hospitals, primary care and local authority health services. In 1974, a 'unified' structure was introduced, with management at the regional level.

34 Fiona, BE10, p. 20.

35 Yvonne, NO3, p. 9.

36 Ingrid, SO11, p. 6.

37 Georgie, OX2, p. 10.

38 Bet, CO1, pp. 21–2.

39 Pippa, CO13, p. 13.

40 Andrea, SA9, p. 3.

41 Tara, SO15, pp. 14–16.

42 Cynthia, WY12, p. 7.

43 Jackie, WY10, p. 12.

44 Siobhan, BE1, p. 13.

45 Ruby, BE5, pp. 16–18.

46 Gloria, BE14, p. 11.

47 Penny, CO7, p. 11.

48 Rebecca, OX10, p. 17.

49 MOA, C2570, reply to 50: Spring Directive 1997, part 1 'You and the NHS'.

50 MOA, B89, reply to 50: Spring Directive 1997, part 1 'You and the NHS'.

51 MOA, F1560, reply to 41: Autumn/Winter Directive 1993, part 2 'Birth'.

52 Polly, BE7, pp. 7–8.

53 Emily, NO8, p. 11.

54 Lisa, CO12, p. 10; Tania, EW8, p. 9; Molly, NO4, p. 11.

55 MOA, A1733, reply to 41: Autumn/Winter Directive 1993, part 2 'Birth'.

56 Tina, BE3, pp. 8–9.

57 Amanda, BE9, 11.

58 Oxfordshire MOH, 1958, p. 5.

59 Oxfordshire MOH, 1966, p. 19.

60 For a more in-depth discussion of the role of locality in determining the provision of care see Angela Davis, 'A revolution in maternity care? Women and the maternity services, Oxfordshire c. 1948–1974', *Social History of Medicine* (2011, doi: 10.1093/shm/hkq092).

61 Lucinda McCray Beier, 'Expertise and control: childbearing in three twentieth-century working-class Lancashire communities', *Bulletin of the History of Medicine*, 78 (2004), 379–409, p. 405. See also Lucinda McCray Beier, *For Their Own Good: The Transformation of English Working-Class Health Culture, 1880–1970* (Columbus: The Ohio State University Press, 2008).

62 ERA, Mrs B. 3. B., p. 63.
63 Margaret, EW15, p. 4.
64 Kaye, WY14, p. 4.
65 Jean, EW14, p. 4.
66 April, SO16, p. 11.
67 Amelia, CO15, p. 37.
68 Bev, CR10, p. 10.
69 Kaye, WY14, pp. 2 and 7.
70 Patsy, BA15, pp. 11–12.
71 Liz, SA5, pp. 13–14.
72 Viv, EW12, pp. 8–9.
73 Pippa, CO13, p. 9.
74 Katherine, SA12, pp. 5–6.
75 Bev, CR10, pp. 10–11.
76 Rebecca, OX10, p. 10.
77 ERA, Mrs. R. 1. P., p. 66.
78 Fiona, BE10, p. 24.
79 Rosaline S. Barbour, 'Fathers: the emergence of a new consumer group', in Garcia, Kilpatrick and Richards (eds), *The Politics of Maternity Care*, 202–16, p. 212. Judith Leavitt has charted men's increasing participation in American birth during the second half of the twentieth century, although no equivalent work currently exists for the English context. J.W. Leavitt, *Make Room for Daddy: The Journey from Waiting Room to Birthing Room* (Chapel Hill: University of North Carolina Press, 2009).
80 Carol, TH14, pp. 10–11.
81 Lisa, CO12, p. 10.
82 Florence, BE8, pp. 7–8.
83 Katherine, SA12, p. 7.
84 Siobhan, BE1, p. 14.
85 Sharon, EW9, pp. 12–13.
86 April, SO16, p. 11.
87 Carol, TH14, p. 7.
88 Jane, NO17, p. 8.
89 ERA, Mrs B. 2. B, p. 50.
90 Eve, CO8, p. 13.
91 Andrea, SA9, p. 5.
92 Graham Smith, 'Protest is better for infants: motherhood, health and welfare in a woman's town, c. 1911–1931', *Oral History*, 23 (1995), 63–70, p. 66.
93 Grace, NO7, pp. 1–2.
94 MOA, FR 3097 'A Report on Baby Foods', March 1949, p. 9.
95 Michelle, OX8, p. 9.
96 Lindsay, OX12, p. 8.
97 Juliet, NO9, p. 5; Fiona, BE10, p. 27; Amanda, BE9, pp. 9–10.
98 Emily, NO8, pp. 11–12.
99 Penny, CO7, p. 3.
100 Shirley, SA10, p. 5.
101 Hope, CO11, p. 10.
102 Yvonne, NO3, p. 12.

103 Mabel, OX9, p. 7.
104 Oxfordshire MOH, 1955, p. 23.
105 Cherie, CO9, p. 11.
106 Hayley, NO5, p. 5.
107 Oxfordshire MOH, 1958, p. 5.
108 Oxfordshire MOH, 1960, p. 12.
109 Report of a Sub-Committee of the Standing Medical Advisory Committee on Child Welfare, *Sheldon Report* (London: HMSO, 1967).
110 Oxfordshire MOH, 1968, p. 27.
111 Jean, EW14, p. 6.
112 Oakley, *Women Confined*, p. 18.
113 See, for example, Judith A. Houck, *Hot and Bothered: Women, Medicine, and Menopause in Modern America* (Cambridge, MA: Harvard University Press, 2006); and Linda Bryder, *Women's Bodies and Medical Science: An Inquiry into Cervical Cancer* (Houndmills: Palgrave Macmillan, 2010).

5

Experts and childcare 'bibles': mothers and advice literature

Childcare manuals were abundant throughout the twentieth century and many self-proclaimed experts were writing on the subject. Their advice was by no means consistent though, and mothers were under pressure to conform to conflicting models of care. The writings of the experts were influenced by contemporary theories of child development. Thinking on child development in the years after 1945 was greatly influenced by the experiences of World War Two, with children experiencing family breakdown, separation and evacuation. Anna Freud advanced her hypothesis of maternal separation on the basis of her work in war nurseries; John Bowlby reported on the mental health of homeless children in post-war Europe for the World Health Organization (WHO). The war years also gave Donald Winnicott the opportunity to work with seriously disturbed children who had been evacuated from London and other big cities, and separated from their families.[1] Perhaps the most significant and contentious idea which arose was Bowlby's concept of maternal deprivation. Denise Riley argues that:

> Feminist writings, looking back, have often assumed that the return of women to their homes after the last war was intimately linked with, if not positively engineered by, Bowlby's psychology, whose anti-nursery tenets were in harmony with the government's desire to get shot of its wartime labour force, and reassert its 'normal' male one. Not unreasonably, given all the orchestrated appearances, feminism tends to hold to a vision of post-war collusion between the government and psychology to get working women back to their kitchens, and pin them there under the weight of Bowlby's theory of maternal deprivation in an endless dream of maternity throughout the 1950s.[2]

The moral panic over latchkey children and juvenile delinquency during and after the war did promote concern about the role of mothers.

Mothers were blamed for their children's problems while fathers' role in childrearing was neglected and masculine failings attributed to inadequate mothering. In their 1947 book, *Modern Woman: The Lost Sex*, the American economist Ferdinand Lundberg and psychiatrist Marynia Farnham stated in reference to perceived psychological problems among young people, that, 'The bases for most of this unhappiness, as we have shown, are laid in the childhood home. The principal instruments of their creation are women.'[3] Such views were also common in England. Writing in 1955 the social commentator Ruth Anderson Oakley asserted, 'It is within the province and the power of good mothers to eradicate most of the prisons and the asylums.'[4]

However John Bowlby's writings were often misinterpreted and taken to extremes he did not intend.[5] Furthermore, at no point did Bowlby's theories hold sway over every psychologist and sociologist in post-war Britain, and by the late 1960s and 1970s his views were increasingly being challenged. Writing in 1972, the psychologist Michael Rutter argued that the concept of 'maternal deprivation' was erroneous. He thought the evidence strongly suggested that most of the long-term consequences of a child being separated from its mother were due to privation rather than loss which meant the 'deprivation' half of the concept was somewhat misleading. He added that the 'maternal' half of the concept was also inaccurate in that the deleterious influences concerned the care of the child or relationships with people rather than any specific defect of the mother.[6] Lawrence Casler's criticism was even stronger: 'the human organism does not need maternal love in order to function normally.'[7] Other psychologists also supported the view that the infants Bowlby had studied suffered not from maternal deprivation but from perceptual deprivation. While it was important that infants received suitable care this did not have to be from the mother.[8] The view that juvenile delinquency resulted from maternal deprivation was also tempered in later studies. By 1965 Bowlby's colleague Mary Salter Ainsworth considered that 'delinquency has not been found to be a *common* outcome of maternal deprivation or early mother–child separation.'[9] Robert Andry looked at the link between paternal deprivation and delinquency, finding that 'faulty *paternal* relationships rather than faulty *maternal* relationships primarily occur for the type of delinquent boy studied.'[10] Therefore while the concept of maternal deprivation was extremely influential in the post-war period it did not have universal acceptance. Many psychologists were aware that the impact and consequences of maternal deprivation could be overstated at the expense of other factors. In addition, feminists from the late 1960s onwards increasingly highlighted the loneliness and isolation that mothers who spent their days entirely in the company of young children could feel.[11] Riley concludes that the development of psychological beliefs in the post-war years was far more fragile than the feminist vision of collusion between Bowlby and the government allows. There was, in fact, no concerted attack to keep women in the home.[12] Nonetheless Bowlby's ideas did hold great sway in society at large and were extremely popular. For instance in her survey of teachers in the 1960s, Elizabeth Jane Goodacre found that they commonly viewed working mothers as a detrimental factor in a child's success at school.[13] Bowlby's theories were also influential on parents who thought that even short mother–infant separations could psychologically harm their children.

This chapter will investigate the effects upon mothers themselves of these debates surrounding the care of children. In order to do so, six principal authorities on child development who were popular from the 1940s to the 2000s will be considered. While by no means the only experts writing books on childcare at this time, they have been chosen because they or their theories featured most prominently in the accounts of the Oxfordshire women interviewed. They are Frederick Truby King, John Bowlby, Donald Winnicott, Benjamin Spock, Penelope Leach and Gina Ford. The chapter will examine both the content and tone of the literature and the authors' influence in reinforcing certain stereotypes of mother-hood, but its main focus will be on the relationship between the experts' pronouncements and the thoughts and feelings of the women inter-viewed. Undertaking such an analysis is not a straightforward exercise. As Jay Mechling has demonstrated, the relationship between women and experts is complex. Mothers could ignore advice or act in the opposite way to experts' recommendations.[14] Just because mothers had 'the book' it didn't mean they used it. Gina remembered how, 'We did have, we had Penelope somebody or other … We had her on the shelf. Then in reality I didn't really look at it at all.'[15] Nonetheless childcare experts and the advice they extolled were recalled as significant in the lives of many women. Moreover the competing theories of child development which were inherent within the literature were also influential within society more generally. The tensions, ambiguities, and indeed the contradictions that are present in the women's accounts reveal wider concerns about how best to care for small children in the light of the tremendous changes, particularly in women's lives, that took place during the second half of the twentieth century.

Frederick Truby King

Frederick Truby King was a New Zealand doctor famous for his work on child welfare. His first book about the care of babies was published in 1913.[16] Although he died in 1938 his influence continued in the following decades with his books remaining in print and his daughter Mary also publishing on the subject. The principal thread running through the advice of Truby King is that babies need strict routines. He told mothers: 'Regular habits of the baby are of first importance. A baby cannot be expected to thrive if his mother is not regular and punctual in the matter of all details in his daily routine.'[17] Indeed he went as far as to argue that mothers themselves should follow a routine, urging, 'Come what may, the taking of a regular daily walk, regardless of weather, should be an absolute rule of life.'[18] Truby King aimed his books principally at middle-class mothers. For instance he often refers to nurses and nannies. He also assumed his readership would be educated, telling them, 'the exercise of intelligence cannot be dispensed with. Indeed, reason becomes continually more necessary for women as they depart further and further from the simple ways of Nature.'[19] In Oxfordshire, however, women with a range of backgrounds recalled following strict routines with their babies. Although they did not necessarily specify they were followers of Truby King many women who had their children in the late 1940s recalled being influenced by his beliefs. When asked what she thought were the principal changes in childcare between the 1940s, when she had her children, and the 2000s, Maud, a farmer's wife, replied, 'Well we had a proper routine. That's what we had.'[20] Similarly Mavis, who lived in Ewelme and was married to a beekeeper at the honey farm there, thought a lack of routine caused difficulties for mothers in the 2000s: 'I used to work to a routine, I found it better. They get in the habit of doing it then and it helps a lot. If you don't, a lot of women today don't, and they get in such a state, you know they can't cope.'[21] Winifred was a nurse who had two children in 1946 and 1951. Like Mavis she spoke with regret about the lack of routine she felt characterised current childrearing practice in the 2000s. Directly echoing Frederick Truby King's pronouncements she stated, 'I think if you allow children to just wander as they will, they grow up with no sense of order at all.'[22] Sarah had four children in the 1940s and 1950s and lived in North Oxford. She was a self-confessed follower of Truby King and had attended a clinic run by Oxford's Truby King Society in Summertown in the 1940s. She thought his books were supportive of mothers because following a routine made life easier for them. 'I think there's something to be said for it, babies do settle down and they do get used to a routine and it does mean the mother's less worn out.'[23]

An important part of a baby's routine was supposed to be their daily dose of fresh air. Truby King told mothers to, 'Keep baby in open air and sunlight as much as possible'.[24] The belief that babies needed regular fresh air for their health and wellbeing was popular with the Oxfordshire women and was supported by mothers who had their children from the 1940s to the 1980s and across all social classes.[25] Phyllis, who had her first baby in Shipton-under-Wychwood in 1946, explained: 'I used to take my baby out every day. If I didn't manage to get out I always put her outside to sleep you know, and she never came to any harm.'[26] Similarly Celia, who had her first baby in the early 1950s, recalled: 'Well we were told that you put them outside every day in all weather other than fog, it didn't matter if it rained, it didn't matter if it was cold, they were supposed to be outside.'[27] It is interesting that Celia remembered being 'told' to put her baby outside. Although she did not say who had instructed her to do so she clearly associated the recommendation with authority and remembered it as being the official viewpoint. Unlike some of the other elements of his advice, Truby King's ideas about the beneficial nature of time spent outside for small babies held currency into the 1970s and 1980s. Ellen was a university graduate who brought up six children in Ewelme born between 1975 and 1985. She still believed a routine, including time spent outside, was vital for small children, explaining, 'I've always been a great believer in fresh air and exercise … you've got to have your daily ration of fresh air and exercise.'[28]

However, the routine Truby King believed was most crucial was a feeding routine. He asserted that four-hourly feeding was necessary for babies, and threatened women with dire consequences if they disregarded his advice, stating, 'Never give a baby food merely to pacify him or to stop his crying; it will damage him in the long run.' For Truby King feeding meant breastfeeding. He argued that practically every mother could breastfeed if she wanted to and was encouraged to, and that women should not abandon attempts at breastfeeding for some weeks after childbirth. Again he told mothers the consequences of not breastfeeding would be severe. 'Babies don't make themselves delicate and sickly; they become so through faulty treatment – mainly though bottle-feeding.' Babies would then need to be weighed before and after feeding as this was the only means of ascertaining whether a breastfed baby was getting the right quantity of food. Furthermore he told mothers, 'This rule is absolute.'[29] The belief that babies needed a feeding routine was a highly influential element of Truby King's philosophy. For example, on their own initiative Janice, Cherie and Jackie kept diaries documenting when their babies were fed and how much they weighed.[30] When asked what were the contemporary ideas about childcare when she had her children in the 1940s Olive answered, 'I think that most people [thought] you had a certain time [to feed] and if they cry you leave them.' Despite saying this was the orthodox method of feeding babies, Olive also added that she 'wasn't very keen.'[31] Olive was ambivalent about routines. Her doubts may have been the result of looking back with hindsight, which led her to change her attitudes. Esther had her children in 1959 and 1963 and expressed a similar position. When asked if she followed feeding routines she replied: 'Yes [emphasis]. I was very strict. I didn't believe in demand feeding, it was every four hours. I've changed my mind though since then ... I don't think it's good to be that strict.'[32] It is interesting that as Truby King's ideas had become discredited in the years after Esther had her children she had felt the need to re-evaluate her stance, and now concluded it was a mistake.

Many of the women who were interviewed recalled how their mothers had followed Truby King and had passed on his ideas. Claire was educated at Cheltenham Ladies' College and Oxford University and lived in North Oxford when her children were young. When asked why she followed a routine with her first baby she explained it was on the advice of her mother.[33] Maxine lived in Shipton-under-Wychwood and had three children in the late 1950s and early 1960s. She had grown up in Lancashire and attended Bolton Grammar school followed by Manchester College of Housecraft. She also reported being influenced by her mother. When asked if she followed the advice of any childcare experts she replied: 'My mother followed the Truby King routine and gave me many tips.'[34] Middle-class mothers may have been the first to embrace Truby King's advice but they also seem to have been the first to abandon it as well. His ideas had a longer resonance with the working-class mothers interviewed, who were slower to adopt the more child-centred approach of later experts, perhaps because they continued to rely on their own mothers' advice. Gloria had gone to Dorchester secondary modern and then technical college in Oxford and had her children in Benson in the mid-1960s. She strongly believed in the need for babies to have regular time outside the house: 'Don't matter if it was winter, or whatever, during the day for her sleep she'd be outside, both my babies. Wouldn't be in here, wouldn't be in her cot, she'd be in her pram, outside, under the plum tree, wrapped up snugly and warm if it was winter.' When asked why she thought it was important, she answered: 'It was something my mum used to do I suppose.'[35]

However, as noted above, women increasingly questioned Truby King's approach as the post-war period progressed. The aspect the women interviewed were most sceptical of was his insistence that children should not be 'spoiled'. Truby King had warned mothers that, "'spoiling" may be as harmful to infants as callous neglect or intentional cruelty'. He stated: 'To save a lusty, honest cry she will pacify an infant with a "comforter", or with food given at the wrong times, and may thus ruin the child in the first month of life, making him a delicate, fretful, irritable, nervous, despotic little tyrant who will yell and scream, day or night, if not soothed and cuddled without delay.'[36] But, many women objected to this require-ment that they be physically distant from their babies. Siobhan, who had two children in the early 1970s, described how she had decided this advice was wrong and hence chose to ignore it: 'I went against the rules of the time with my own children, because you were told if they were crying to let them cry, but I just couldn't bear it if they were crying. I thought they were not happy. And so I used to pick them up and try and find out what the matter was. And I used to conclude that if they weren't wet and they weren't hungry then they were bored, so I used to play with them.'[37] And, as Siobhan's response indicates, there was also a change over time. Several interviewees recalled how Truby King became seen as outdated. Yvonne, who had her first child in the early 1960s, associated Truby King with her parents' generation. She said her mother-in-law had followed Truby King but she 'found it difficult to observe it, to go by the book because it was so stern.' Her own mother was also 'very clear that you needed routines and you must have time without the baby, and you had to look after yourself as well as your baby, which I think you'd get in Truby King to some extent.'[38] When asked if there was more of a stress on routines when she had her first baby in the 1940s than with her subsequent children Phoebe explained how her husband, who was ten years older, was more influenced by Truby King than she was. She felt he was already going out of fashion amongst her contemporaries.[39] Sarah also described how Truby King's popularity was waning during the years she had her children. She had four children between 1940 and 1950. Her first baby was 'a perfect Truby King baby', but she changed her approach with her later children, explaining 'we'd got rather beyond this completely rigid way of feeding.'[40] Influenced by the new approaches to child development which were appearing during the period, women had begun to doubt whether such a strict routine was really necessary or desirable.

Interviewees who had been children in the 1940s and 1950s, with mothers who had employed Truby King's routines with them as babies, recalled how this could lead to conflict between them when their own children were born. Carmel was born in 1949 and she had three children in 1977, 1982 and 1985. She felt that the difference between her own approach and that of the older members of her family caused a significant degree of conflict between them. She explained how:

> Even my sister whose children were I suppose a good ten years older than our lot, you know, she'd had a completely different [style] and they felt, my mother probably less than anybody, but they did feel a bit challenged by it all and tended to say 'Oh you can't. Breastfeeding on demand. Don't do that'. And my mother-in-law – I mean we lived in a very small flat in Kensington – my mother-in-law had a huge garden. She used to wheel [her daughter] down to the bottom of the garden and leave her there for four hours and then go back you know and ignore her.[41]

While women felt their mothers had been misguided they could still feel uncomfortable in criticising them too. Pippa was born in 1955 and her children were born in the 1980s. Recalling the difference between her own and her mother's approach to baby care she told me: 'she has said things to me like, "Oh, you were expected to sort of just leave you crying", you know, from that regimented view of childcare.' In contrast Pippa said: 'I never could. I had to pick him up.' However Pippa wanted to defend her mother and stated: 'But I think she was, she was and still is a very loving mother.'[42] The Oxfordshire interviewees were turning away from Truby King's advice as the post-war period progressed. Although they continued to approve of some elements of his guidance, such as regular fresh air for babies, they were also looking for a more relaxed experience for both mother and baby.

Donald Winnicott

Donald Winnicott was one expert who was advocating a less authoritarian and regimented approach. A paediatrician and psychoanalyst, Winnicott's views were extremely influential during the 1940s and 1950s through his radio broadcasts and in the press.[43] Winnicott was supportive of mothers and unlike Frederick Truby King, who often seemed severe, he addressed them in a friendly tone: 'I would like to talk to mothers about the thing that they do well, and that they do well simply because each mother is devoted to the task in hand, namely the care of one infant.'[44] Rather than criticising women for their failings as mothers he was keen to demonstrate what an important contribution a woman made to society through being devoted to her infant, and the respect that should be accorded to a mother's own knowledge and wisdom. Winnicott's belief that mothers knew best held resonance with many of the women interviewed. Phyllis lived in Shipton-under-Wychwood and had seven children between 1946 and 1959, only three of whom survived past infancy. When asked if she tried to follow the advice of childcare experts Phyllis replied that ultimately she put faith in her own abilities. 'I tried, but of course you do feed a bit, you do break the rules, I mean is there a rule? No. You've got to use your own common-sense really.'[45] Bethany, who had two children in 1969 and 1971, recalled a similar experience. She also treated the advice of childcare manuals with scepticism, doubting their use, and instead 'muddled along'.[46] Siobhan had two children in the early 1970s and recalled how she decided to trust her own instincts rather than trying to follow the book. She had become disillusioned with the existing manuals, which seemed to offer contradictory advice, none of which suited her babies. She said, 'it was at the cusp between when you were told that feeding was strictly every four hours and, you know, that you had to have a routine for your baby, which I think is fair enough, I don't think that babies necessarily need to run your life for you. And there was the other strong school of thought that everything was demand led by the baby, but I couldn't really see that you could live life, entirely being dictated to by your baby.' In the end she abandoned trying to follow either practice relying on what she thought was best. 'I didn't really take too much notice of them, cos after a short while you realise that he's just a little person and you get on with getting on with it.'[47]

Donald Winnicott's endorsement of mothers and their inherent aptitude for caring for their babies could be empowering to women. Interviewees were keen to emphasise motherhood was an interesting and important job and felt society should do all it could to enable mothers to care for their children. For example Carla explained: 'it's incredibly hard work to produce good, kind and law-abiding children.'[48] Similarly Elizabeth Roberts found her Lancashire interviewees endorsed Winnicott's stress on the importance of good mothering even if they did not specifically attribute this theory to him.[49] However Winnicott could also be censorious towards those women who could not meet this ideal of selfless devotion or did not want to. Winnicott thought being a mother of a small baby should be all absorbing for a woman – 'to a large extent she is the baby and the baby is her.' Mothers should therefore want to care for their babies on a continuous basis and enjoy doing so. He believed that mothers laid down 'the foundations of the individual's strength of character and richness of personality', which meant that any imperfections necessarily had severe consequences: 'failure of mothers at the Ordinary Devoted Mother level is one factor in the aetiology of autism. It is felt to be an accusation when one really goes on logically and refers to the effects of Ordinary Devoted Mother failure. But is it not natural that if this thing called devotion is really important, then its absence or a relative failure in this area should have consequences that are untoward?'[50] The women interviewed did articulate some support for the view that poor mothering has negative effects upon children. Glenda unfavourably compared the daughter from her son's marriage, whose mother returned to work shortly after she was born, with the children of her own daughters who were both full-time mothers until their children were at secondary school. She considered the conduct and character of her son's daughter to be inferior. 'I can see the difference, she's not a bad girl but I can see the difference in her behaviour.'[51] Her view was likely influenced by the difficult relationship that existed between mothers- and daughters-in-law, but also reveals the contemporary negative stereotyping of working mothers. Indeed Patsy, whose children were born in the early 1970s, said she was 'a bit worried about even telling my mother that I was thinking of getting a job', even though both her children were school age.[52]

Decades after he first developed them, Donald Winnicott's theories remained influential on understandings of motherhood. Lynne's only child was born in 1973 and discussing Winnicott she felt his influence had waned by the 1970s when she was raising her son. However, reflecting back from her current perspective of the 2000s she was now ambivalent over whether this was a good thing and was trying to reconcile her different views on the subject in the course of her interview. Her uncertainty was clear as she endeavoured to articulate her feelings.

> Winnicott and whoever ... suddenly that was absolutely pushed away with I think, you know, monetarism, sort of economic theories, individualism and, although I sort of take it for granted and I believe that feminism is good you know by and large, that became something that sort of pushed the psychological welfare of children a bit to the back, it was as if women's interests and making a living was so important and somehow important, I don't know ... It will probably be a long time before we can tell how negative or not the effects of so many tiny children going into nurseries and things [are] you know, it will probably be hard to quantify but these things always are aren't they?[53]

Furthermore, Winnicott's 'good enough mother' remained a powerful trope throughout the second half of the twentieth century and into the twenty-first; for example there was a special edition of BBC Radio Four's *Women's Hour* on the subject in 2005.[54] Winnicott's hypothesis on the crucial role mothers played had entered into contemporary discourse and the women echoed his views. While his theories did have a strongly prescriptive message, his emphasis that mothers knew best also encouraged women to have confidence in their own ability and experience.

John Bowlby

Although Donald Winnicott was an influential figure in the post-war decades, his contemporary John Bowlby, with his theory of 'maternal deprivation', was perhaps more notorious.[55] Trained in psychology, psychiatry and psychoanalysis, Bowlby's report on the mental health of homeless children in post-war Europe, *Maternal Care and Mental Health*, was published in 1951 and brought his work to a wider audience. It was then reissued in 1953 as a popular penguin edition, *Child Care and the Growth of Love*, which became an instant best-seller, selling 450,000 in the English edition alone, and was translated into ten languages.[56] The view that maternal care in infancy was crucial for the physical development of the child had long roots stretching back to the late nineteenth century, with poor maternal care acknowledged to have a detrimental effect. What was new was Bowlby's idea that mere physical separation from the mother was a pathogenic factor in its own right. He stated: 'a child is deprived if for any reason he is removed from his mother's care.' Bowlby argued the close relationship between mother and child was not only natural but essential for a child's development.[57] This hypothesis was particularly demanding for mothers because it implied that only their care was good enough. Bowlby's influence was evident in the opinions of medical professionals in Oxfordshire and there was a clear association between poor mothering and problem families in contemporary discourse.[58] The Medical Officers of Health of both Oxford and Oxfordshire constantly expressed the belief that nursery care should only be provided in exceptional cases. Attitudes towards nurseries had hardened as the period progressed which may indicate that Bowlby's theories were gaining ground. At the end of World War Two, in 1945, there were 11 nurseries in Oxford with 530 places. Oxford's Assistant MOH in charge of Maternity and Child Welfare, Mary Fisher, wrote, 'There is no doubt that the nurseries were much appreciated by the parents, and their continuation in some form after the war is necessary.'[59] Only a year later, however, her tone had significantly changed. A re-organisation of the War-time Day Nurseries took place on 1 April, 1946. Mary Fisher stated: 'It was decided as a matter of principle by the Maternity and Child Welfare Committee that children under two were better left at home, and as a result nurseries should be provided only for those mothers who for various reasons had to go out to work.'[60] Nursery attendance was only considered suitable where there were unusual circumstances. In 1968 the priorities for attending Oxfordshire's Local Health Authority day nurseries were: where there was only one parent; where the mother was ill; where day-care could prevent breakdown of the family; and where the child was seriously affected by the lack of opportunity to play with others.[61]

John Bowlby's theories seem to have been influential upon many women in the years after World War Two. In her oral history interviews with London women Stephanie Spencer found that her interviewees were clearly aware of Bowlby's childcare theories, even if they did not mention his name directly.[62] Likewise although only one of the Lancashire women interviewed for Elizabeth Roberts' study mentioned the work of Bowlby, a simplified version of his ideas was absorbed by many of the mothers and they believed that only they should look after their children if they were not to grow up with some psychological damage.[63] Bowby's theories were widely diffused within popular culture. Karen had her first child in 1967. At the time she was a student at Somerville College, Oxford and she returned to university after her son was born to complete her degree. To enable her to do this, her son was looked after by a childminder. Discussing how she felt about leaving her baby, she explained: 'Well my biggest memory was that just around about the time we were, I was about to start doing that and have him minded, there was a television … play … Well this was about a terrible childminder who had babies stacked along the couch in rows … and so that made me feel dreadful.'[64] When Polly was asked if she returned to work after her children were born in 1968 and 1970, she emphatically replied she did not. She disapproved of those women who did work and thought children needed maternal care in infancy to become well-behaved, law-abiding adults. She explained: 'I think it's fantastic that in those days we were actually there because I was always brought up to understand that the first five years of a child's life are their actual development years … And I think today because parents are working they're off in pre-schools or whatever and they're not getting the discipline or the bringing up.'[65] In addition the women discussed their unhappiness with the phenomenon of 'latch-key' children. Both Tania and Gail recounted how their mothers had condemned the mothers of 'latch-key' children, and they also shared this view. Tania 'never went home to an empty house'. She believed this was a principal cause of behavioural problems in children, stating: 'I think it all sort of stems from there.'[66] Gail said her mother felt very strongly about latch-key children, 'she would never ever do that because she thought that was something very bad for the children. They like stability and someone there who is responsible. And if they get left on their own well they will wander around and get into mischief and she did not agree with that at all, and neither did my husband or I so ours were not latch-key children either. Never. Never latch-key children.'[67] The women were supportive of the idea that it was important for young children to be brought up in stable, secure environments in order to develop into successful adults. They were also of the opinion that working mothers created delinquent children.[68]

The belief that children needed continuous care from their mothers therefore had resonance with the women interviewed. When discussing the changes between how they raised their children and how children were being raised in the 2000s many referred to the growth of nurseries. Women echoed John Bowlby's pronouncements that infants could not receive the same quality of care in nurseries as from their mothers. Florence worked as a nurse when her children were young but made sure she only worked shifts during evenings and weekends so her husband could look after them when she was not there. When asked how she had managed to combine work and motherhood she replied:

> we didn't have nursery schools in those days, in fact I was one of the mums that didn't really believe in nursery schools for a long time, I thought that if you had babies they were yours to look after and you shouldn't expect anyone else to look after them ... I know they started a small nursery school in our old scout hut, back when [my sons] were tiny ... and [the teacher] came and said, 'Would you send your two?', and I said, 'No, I wouldn't even consider it ... I don't believe in them, I think mums should look after them.' I'm still a bit like that I suppose.[69]

These ideas crossed class and educational background. Ruby was born in 1939 and grew up in Benson. She left school at fifteen and had worked in the dispensary at the local surgery before her two children were born in the early 1970s. It was her opinion that 'if you've got a husband who's out working then you look after your children. That's what you had 'em [sic] for. Not to send them off to early, pre, playschools and people like that.'[70] Rose was born in 1932 and grew up in Yorkshire. She did her undergraduate degree in Oxford and then undertook further research before leaving to have her first child in 1959. While she had enjoyed academic life she thought it was important that she had been a full-time mother when her children were young. She explained: 'I have a strong aversion to the notion of packing a child up like a parcel at seven o'clock in the morning in order to take it to the nursery in order to go to your job, I don't think that's good for the child.'[71] Ingrid was an Oxford graduate who worked as a teacher. She had been involved in helping look after her grandchildren while her daughter went back to work and interestingly she thought this situation was also inferior to her daughter providing full-time care. She described how she had done 'an immense amount of fetching and carrying, I don't mind at all, I love it and they treat this as much as their home as their own, but it's not the same as just being able to be really at home you know. So I think … they have lost out.'[72] Deirdre thought there could not be the same bonding between a baby and its mother when she spent long hours at work.[73] These women were not arguing that mothers needed to remain at home throughout the whole of their children's upbringing nor that doing so would be unproblematic, but they did think that very young children who were not cared for by their mothers missed out.

Women also felt that the quality of the relationship between mothers and their children could be compromised when mothers were employed outside the home. Marilyn's own mother had worked throughout her childhood and she was looked after by her grandmother. She regretted this state of affairs and believed her relationship with her mother suffered because of it. She had therefore decided not to work when her children were young, explaining, 'I didn't want them to be like myself with my mother working.'[74] Linda's father had died when she was four, meaning her mother had to go out to work to support the family. Linda said that in consequence she was determined that she would not work when she had her own children.[75] Likewise Alma's mother also returned to full-time work when Alma was four. Then when Alma was seven her mother went away to college. Alma said that for two years she barely saw her mother and like Linda did not want to repeat this with her own children.[76] The Oxfordshire interviewees raised another tenet of John Bowlby's hypothesis, here, namely that a close, continuous relationship with their baby was also important for mothers.[77] Indeed Enid thought that it was mothers who were deprived rather than their children. Discussing the effects of women going out to work Enid provided the example of her grandson's wife who worked full time. She explained that she did not think the situation was a problem for her great-granddaughter because: 'She's not going to say, "Well I was only two and I remember my Mummy not being there all day". And she's been to nursery you see, and the nursery's been good for her, and [my granddaughter-in-law] is wonderful with her when she's with her. But I think [my granddaughter-in-law's] lost out, because there's all those hours you know, mummy's lost out more than the baby's lost out.'[78] Similarly, when asked why she was opposed to nursery care and whether she thought this was because the children missed out, Florence replied, 'Yes I'm sure they did, or parents miss out on children, because … like the first steps and that sort of thing, if you're not there when they take them they're never repeated are they?'[79] From the interviews it is clear the women were uneasy about the mothers of young children working, partly because they were concerned about the effects of nursery care on the children but also, and they laid great stress on this point, because they thought women who were not at home with their children lost out on perhaps more than they realised. This was also a widely shared attitude. Mrs Morrison, a Lancashire resident who had two sons in the late 1950s, said: 'I think … a lot of women don't want to be at home. They want to get out to work as soon as they can. I can't understand them, being as I am. I can't understand people wanting to go out just after they have had a baby and go straight back to work. I think they miss such a lot, with their baby; because you can't capture those moments again can you?'[80] Those women who did work also felt that this may have been the case. Amelia had to return to work after the birth of her son in 1974 for financial reasons. She still remembered her sadness that her son had been with his childminder when he gave his first smile.[81]

Therefore while the women interviewed did indicate support for many of John Bowlby's hypotheses those who did not meet Bowlby's ideal of maternal care could be left feeling guilty and inadequate. Phoebe was a psychiatrist and when asked how influential she thought Bowlby's work was in the post-war decades she replied, 'I think very important. Very important. It's obviously very biological isn't it that when the child becomes mobile they should have this attachment and I think that work was very important.' However she also recalled how this stress on the importance of attachment made it worrying when she had to leave her own children to go to work, and she had tried to minimise the time she spent away from them.[82] Similarly Siobhan described the feelings of guilt she felt when she tried returning to work and which eventually led her to leave her job. She explained: 'these two small boys came to me one day and said … "could you stop what you're doing please," so I did, and he said, "we've been thinking, and we think you should be at home, looking after us properly and making proper food for us not going out to work and then giving us things like fish fingers." How to make somebody feel really guilty.'[83] Hannah had three children in the 1950s but continued working as a research assistant at Oxford University. When asked if she had read any childcare manuals she answered, 'the book that was all the rage was Bowlby. Yes. And that of course was another, yes that was very worrying, and that is what people kept referring to, deprivation.'[84] Georgie's relationship with Bowlby's theories was also complex. She was a teacher and returned to work when her first daughter was a few months old. She did not think working had harmed her relationship with her daughter and said her daughter thought she had an excellent childhood. However she also argued that parents in the 2000s did not spend enough time with their young children and stressed the importance of the mother–child relationship in a child's first years. Moreover, during another part of the interview Georgie expressed doubts about her mothering ability, saying she believed her daughter's eating disorder was a result of her problems feeding her when she was a baby. There clearly were anxieties – perhaps not fully explored – about how she had related to her children in infancy.[85]

Moreover, despite the criticism that John Bowlby received, particularly from feminists, his theories have remained influential. Commenting on the changes that had occurred between the time when her own children were born, between 1979 and 1982, and the experience of mothers at the beginning of the twenty-first century, Sonia stated: 'Well I would think probably there's a lot more mothers who have to go out to work now so there's a lot more children who, you know, are in childcare from a very young age which I think well is quite sad.'[86] Jean brought up her two children in the 1990s and explained why she did not return to work until her children were school age, and then only part time:

> I was always home for them and they always came first. There's no way I would have not been here for them, not gone to school events, and picked them up and all stuff like that. I feel that it's really important that if you make the decision to have kids then you should actually be around to look after them. I think, you know, these poor kids that go to school or … nursery at half seven/eight in the morning and then [are] picked up at six in the evening, you know, it must be really hard on them. They can't possibly get the same sort of care when there's a ratio of one to six or one to eight that a kid does at home when it's just him and his mother. Even the best nursery in the world just can't care for them with the same values.[87]

Cynthia was a clinical psychologist, and her only child was born in 1993. While she did return to work she was still influenced by Bowlby's concept of separation anxiety in her timing. However, interestingly, it encouraged her to return to work earlier. She explained: 'I'd seen the experience of how people who'd postponed it then hit the whole sort of separation anxious [sic], you know, period when their babies were sort of eight or nine months. So the advice seemed to be, you know, it's better to do it younger on than not.' However, at several points throughout her interview Cynthia mused on whether this had been the right decision. While she enjoyed her work and was pleased to return to it she also said, 'you know, sort of years after the event you do think "Well, you know, maybe I did miss out on stuff"'.[88] Women who did not meet Bowlby's high standards of care for their infants could be left feeling anxious and guilt-ridden, fearing that they could be harming the development of their children, but also that they themselves had missed out on the satisfaction that Bowlby claimed mothers gained from a close and continual mother–child relationship. There was great pressure on women in the post-war decades to conform to the model of good mothering that child psychologists such as Bowlby deemed essential for the health of their children. To women who had left paid work and careers when their children were young these pronouncements served as an endorsement of their choices and validated the role of full-time mother. However for women who could not meet this ideal these theories appeared as distressing and censorious.

Benjamin Spock

However, it was another of the mid-century experts, Benjamin Spock, who was the most important figure to the women interviewed in Oxfordshire. Spock, an American paediatrician who was also trained in psychoanalysis, was referred to by women who had their children throughout the whole of the period 1945–2000, and the majority had seen his book *Baby and Child Care*.[89] First published in 1946 as the *Common Sense Book of Baby and Child Care* the book is one of the best-selling works of non-fiction of all time. By the time of his death in 1998 it had sold more than fifty million copies and had been translated into thirty-nine languages. The book was still in print at the beginning of the twenty-first century.[90] Christina Hardyment argues that while Spock was neither the first nor the only paediatrician to challenge the regimented approach to childcare of earlier experts, *Baby and Child Care* was easily the longest and most comprehensive book of its type and Spock had the knack of putting across complex information in the simplest of terms.[91] Spock proved popular with the Oxfordshire interviewees from the beginning. Phoebe was born in 1921 and had five children, the first of whom was born in 1948. She studied medicine at Oxford and worked as a psychiatrist. When asked if she had read any of the childcare literature that was around at the time she answered, 'Yes. I think was it Mr? Dr Spock came along and that was pretty sensible.'[92] Marjorie was also an Oxford graduate who lived in North Oxford when her first child was born in the late 1950s. She declared that, 'Dr Spock was sort of the source of all knowledge then.'[93] Spock was not the preserve only of highly educated women, however, but had universal appeal. Eve was born in 1927 and grew up in Lancashire before moving to Cowley. She had left school at sixteen and worked as a typist, but also stated that, 'Dr Spock was the man who we all followed in those days.'[94] June, who lived in Cowley throughout her life and had four children in the 1950s and 1960s, turned to Spock for advice after her sister-in-law in America sent her a copy.[95] Moreover Spock remained popular. Marilyn left school at sixteen and worked as a secretary before having two children in Benson in the early 1970s. When asked if she consulted any childcare experts she replied, 'Yes. In our day Dr Spock.'[96] Carla, a secretary from Banbury who also had her children in the early 1970s, believed the only childcare manual at the time was Spock.[97] More educated women were still consulting Spock too. Ellen was born in 1947, held a Master's degree, and had six children in the 1970s and 1980s. When asked if she had any books on childcare she replied, 'I have, I've got a copy of Dr Spock.'[98] And Bonnie, a teacher who had her three children in 1978, 1981 and 1987, recalled being told (although she did not say by who) to read Dr Spock, indicating that his book was still considered to be recommended reading.[99]

Benjamin Spock was therefore positively remembered by a diverse range of women. His popularity cut across social background, locality and age, and many interviewees recalled him as being the only childcare expert they knew of. Part of the reason he was so well-liked was because in contrast to the strict routines advocated by earlier childcare manuals, such as those of Frederick Truby King, he urged parents to be flexible and to see their children as individuals. In addition he delivered this advice in a reassuring and common-sense manner. Many of the women commented upon this difference. Camilla compared the advice she and her mother-in-law had respectively followed. She explained that her mother-in-law's generation had been 'brought up in the old-fashioned style of you leave the baby to cry, you know the pram down the garden, it's got to learn. In a way, the way I brought up my children was pretty novel at the time, and I think Dr Spock has [made] a great contribution to that, huge. Totally outdated now, but at the time he was right at the forefront of thinking about child upbringing.'[100] Spock entreated women to trust in their own judgement. In his opening line of *Baby and Child Care* he told mothers, 'You know more than you think you do.'[101] Women who turned to Spock found he gave them confidence. Rose was an Oxford graduate married to a university lecturer and had two children in 1959 and 1961. Discussing why she consulted Spock she said:

> of course the great confidence boost of Dr Spock was as [a] mother you'll know, this notion that [you have] some sense of competence. But I don't quite know how he elaborated it now, but I know that was a genuine message that came out, and I certainly was willing to take the view if I had enough information and paid attention it could be possible, that I as me and my child as him could work our way along and I think that was before the time.[102]

Rose thought Spock was ahead of his time in his thinking.[103] Likewise Rebecca thought Spock was helpful because 'basically it was do what the mother wants, it was lovely, very nice, from then on I stuck with Dr

Spock really.'[104] Again women thought this was a positive aspect of Spock's advice which they favourably compared with Truby King. Emily had three children in the mid-1960s and claimed that for her generation 'Dr Spock was our bible and that was that really, it was Dr Spock at all times.' She thought 'he was very refreshing because basically he thought mothers were okay you know, you felt good about what you were doing. So I think that must have been quite refreshing because my mother had Truby King, oh dear … that was a disaster.'[105] Women turned to Spock because in contrast to other experts they felt his advice was encouraging and supportive.

Benjamin Spock told mothers to have faith in their own abilities and feel comfortable in disregarding others' advice. He told them, 'Don't take too seriously all that the neighbours say. Don't be overawed by what the experts say. Don't be afraid to trust your common sense.'[106] Several of the women confirmed that they put their faith in Spock rather than seeking advice from their mothers. Camilla stated that she 'was the Spock generation' and therefore 'didn't believe in old wives' tales'. She felt that both she and her peers were consequently better parents: 'my generation was quite lucky in being given a bit more advice in the upbringing of their children rather than listening to mother.'[107] Similarly Lindsay preferred to follow the advice of Spock rather than her mother, even though her mother was a doctor, because she thought her mother was too old-fashioned: 'Mother was a strong advocate of potty training from I think three months. I was going by Spock and took the view there was no point in trying to potty train before the child knew what the hell was going on.'[108] However Spock was so successful in conveying the principle that mothers knew best that some women decided to disregard the advice he did give about raising children. Emily was a supporter of Spock but confessed she did not always follow the book. She joked: 'we soon got used to the idea that Benjamin Spock would be saying one thing about children having to drink a pint of milk and do this and do that and do the other, but we had the evidence of our eyes … They seemed to live on water and dried biscuits for weeks on end and then maybe they'd have an egg or two … and yet they appeared to be fine.'[109] In addition some women did not feel that Spock's suggestions were useful to them. Jill felt that Spock's American perspective reduced the applicability of his advice. His book 'all seemed to be about something mysterious called formula.'[110] Agnes was more scathing and when discussing literature on childcare said, 'Spock, I threw that out the window. I'm not joking. I thought this is stupid.'[111] And even in the late 1960s and early 1970s there were already some indications of a reaction against Spock's approach, perhaps anticipating the later success of Gina Ford. For example, Hilda, who had two children in 1967 and 1970, explained: 'my cousin, my age, [we] grew up together, she brought up her two girls by Spock. They turned out to be absolute horrors. And she admits it. She said, "I wish I'd thrown Dr Spock out the window years before".[112]

There was also an interesting trend amongst some of the women who had their children in the later decades of the century to conflate Benjamin Spock with the routine-based advice that he had in fact reacted against. For example, describing her own upbringing, Hermione, who had her three children in the late 1970s and early 1980s, said: 'So we were raised in the 1950s, we were raised on Dr Spock, who said, put them down but let them scream for four hours, put them out in the fresh air whether it's snowing or raining, and let them yell, because it won't do them any harm at all.'[113] Hermione saw Spock as being the preserve of her parents' generation and an old-fashioned childrearing style that her generation had disowned. She was equating Spock with Frederick Truby King. Shula had three children between 1968 and 1973. Discussing Spock she said, 'We all used Dr Spock in those days, yes, you know, and if you weren't sure of something you just refer to Dr Spock. But I mean I wasn't a great one … it said you had to have a routine, but I was flexible within the routine.'[114] Again Shula associated Spock with a routine based advice. This divergence may indicate more than simply women misremembering. By the third edition of *Baby and Childcare*, published in 1968, Spock had revised a great deal of his earlier advice. For example he retreated from his earlier permissiveness and advocated much stricter disciplining of children. He now argued that spoiling, even in the first few weeks, was clearly possible.[115] These contradictions within Spock's own books highlight the complexity of the advice literature that mothers were faced with and the mixed messages they could receive.

Overall though, Benjamin Spock was seen as an easy-going and reliable source of advice. Unlike figures such as Frederick Truby King or John Bowlby, he had not become tainted in their eyes by later criticism, although they acknowledged that he was probably now considered out of date. Few women levelled the complaints against Spock that they did with other experts, even when the message he gave was similar. For example Rose said, 'Spock was before Bowlby wasn't it [*sic*] and these very much more demanding messages about attachment and so on.'[116] In reality, Spock was (at least initially) as insistent as Bowlby in his assertion that infants needed full-time care from their mothers. Spock offered women both freedom and constraint. He gave them confidence to follow their own instincts and care for their children how they saw best, but within a traditional model of the woman as full-time mother. Fiona highlighted this tension, explaining, 'Dr Spock, I went to him a lot, who was great because he believed that parents had to have rights as well as children.' However she went on to argue, 'I don't know quite why everybody thinks that Dr Spock was so incredibly permissive, he was about feeding on demand, but [not] in things about expecting children to have attention all the time.'[117]

Penelope Leach

Benjamin Spock was highly influential on the writers who have followed him. Penelope Leach's work shared many similarities with that of Spock and was also a reaction against the rigid regime advocated by those such as Frederick Truby King. Leach herself has been one of the most important authorities on child development during the late twentieth and early twenty-first century. Indeed, in April 2010 she reignited the debate over controlled crying by arguing that leaving babies to cry could damage their brains.[118] Her best-known book, *Your Baby and Child: From Birth to Age Five*, was first published in 1977 and sold over two million copies. In it she told parents that, 'Rearing a child "by the book" – by any set of rules or pre-determined ideas – can work well if the rules you choose to follow happen to fit the baby you have. But even a minor misfit between the two can cause misery.'[119] Moreover she thought that following such a strict routine was futile as it made caring for infants harder. 'All babies demand, but the babies whose needs are met or anticipated do not demand more than the others, they demand less.'[120] She told parents not to worry about doing things the wrong way, and that feelings of guilt and self-reproach would be counter-productive and of no benefit to their children. She argued that she was not attempting to lay down rules but instead was 'passing on to you a complex and, to me, entrancing folklore of child-care which, once upon a time, you might have received through your own extended family.'[121] Rather than positing herself in opposition to the traditional methods of childcare that women may have learnt from their mothers, she was offering herself as a substitute if their mothers were not able to fulfil this role. However Leach also felt that she was doing something innovative and told parents that the novelty of her book lay in the fact that it was written from the baby's point of view.[122]

Women who were aware of Penelope Leach felt that her explanations of how their babies felt in given situations, why they did so, and how mothers should respond to them were helpful. Karen had the first of her four children in 1967, her second in 1970 and then had a longer gap before having the next two in the 1980s. She did not remember reading any useful books on childcare when she had her first two children but thought

Leach's books had been a significant development and were useful to her when she had her later babies.[123] Carmel had her three children in 1977, 1982 and 1985 and explained that she relied heavily on Leach's advice. She felt unprepared for motherhood and that 'it was a very steep learning curve'. She said, 'what really helped me was a book called *Baby and Child* by Penelope Leach. That really helped me.' Carmel felt that Leach was an ally in her desire to reject the routine-led baby care of previous generations and follow demand-led care instead. Leach's book, 'gave me confidence and courage, because of course a lot of people, particularly members of the family, felt very threatened by this … I think people get very into what they did themselves and of course if somebody does something completely different it's a bit of a challenge, and so I had all that to deal with.'[124] However while being generally positive about Leach's advice and finding it helpful, some interviewees found that trying to follow certain aspects of it led to difficulties. For example Kaye, a midwife who had two children in the early 1980s, thought, 'Penelope Leach was pretty good', and that there were 'a lot of useful things' in her book. However she also said that, 'I think her weight charts, the percentile charts, they've been shown not to be accurate for breastfed babies and so really, you know, that worried me more than it should have.'[125] Amelia had her only son in 1974. She recalled having copies of the books of both Leach and Benjamin Spock. However she also added that Leach's advice was not always helpful. When her son was about eighteen months he started waking up at four in the morning. She consulted Leach's book which said it was very common, especially for boys, to start this early waking but that they invariably grew out of it on the eve of their fourth birthday. Amelia said that she excitedly looked forward to her son's fourth birthday expecting he would sleep through till morning. He did not, and she joked Leach raised her hopes before they were dashed.[126]

There were also some women who felt Penelope Leach's stress on trying to always meet their child's needs may have been ideal in theory, but in practice was unworkable and they therefore modified her advice to suit their needs. For example Harriet, who had twins in 1986, said Leach was her 'bible' but she also had some reservations:

I mean hers was definitely you know … feed them on demand. Don't pander to these set routines where you've got to do things. And you followed what the child wants. And I thought some of this was quite good but then I did actually think they and I somehow also needed a bit of a structure too. So … we kind of interweaved a sort of a route, somehow, that saved everybody's sanity and the boys seemed to be sort of thriving and growing quite well.[127]

A few of the interviewees took a positively critical stance against Leach's work. Hermione felt that the whole notion of trying to respond to a baby's every need was inherently flawed. She explained how Leach 'was all demand feed, can't spoil a baby, and of course you can, because at what point do you stop? … Then you never, ever denied a child anything, and suddenly realise you've raised this monster, and you start saying no, [and] you've got a child that simply doesn't understand.'[128] Leach's style also alienated women who thought she focused too much on the child's needs and not enough on the mother's.[129] For example, as Rebecca explained, 'I didn't take to the later gurus at all … Penelope Leach … worked for children's rights, but I think, I preferred mothers' rights.'[130]

Gina Ford

The reaction that some women showed against the child-centred experts such as Penelope Leach perhaps explains the popularity of an expert such as Gina Ford. Ford came to prominence in the 1990s through her work as a maternity nurse, and her first book, *The Contented Little Baby Book*, was published in 1999. Evoking the earlier advice of figures such as Frederick Truby King, Ford stressed the need for a daily routine for both the baby and its parents. She posits herself in direct opposition to the style of childcare advice that Penelope Leach and others had been advocating. For example, in *The Contented Little Baby Book* she states:

> The dozens and dozens of baby care books I have read are all in agreement on one aspect: that in the first few weeks it is impossible to put a small baby into a routine. The implication is that if you even attempt to put your baby in a routine you could seriously damage him. Having successfully spent many years teaching parents how to put their new-borns into a routine that results in a happy, thriving, contented baby, I can only assume that the authors of these books have not personally worked with enough babies to know that it is possible.[131]

It is noteworthy that Ford questioned the expertise of medical professionals who have written books about baby care, arguing that her experience of working with over three hundred babies and their families (although interestingly she is not a mother) better equipped her to dispense advice.

> Most of the books about small babies on the market at present are written by doctors, psychologists or people of that status. Their information is based on their own children, or parents and children who have participated in research studies. While the medical information and developmental text can be interesting, one would have to query how

much help it can be to the average first-time mother getting to grips
with the never-ending demands of a new baby.[132]

Some women who had themselves followed a demand-led approach
now wondered whether they might have in fact been better following a
routine-based system such as Gina Ford's. Anna, herself a doctor, had her
three children between 1967 and 1973. At the time she had her children
she had been influenced by the then belief that babies should dictate their
own timetable and had not attempted to follow a routine. Looking back
from her current perspective in the 2000s she now wondered whether
this had been the best course of action. 'I'm interested in how my own
children, particularly learning from sort of manuals like … Gina [Ford],
do sort of controlled crying. And you know don't just pick them up all
the time. So it's quite interesting that I wonder if, you know if I had done
that we wouldn't have had these months and months of you know fretful
baby in the evenings.'[133] Anna was not alone in noting how her children's
generation had returned to a more regimented approach to childrearing.
Hermione was born in the late 1940s and had her children in the late 1970s
and early 1980s. She recalled an exchange she had overheard between her
daughter and her daughter's eldest child, who had been born in the 1990s.
'She did say "it's not [in] my job description for you to like me. It's in my
job description to raise a decent person", and I thought that's exactly what
my mother said to me, not in those words, but that [idea] … And also
now when they are born, they don't demand feed, they swaddle and leave
them for four hours and all that sort of thing.'[134] Jean's two children were
born in 1987 and 1990 and she explained that she believed it was important to instil children with a strong sense of discipline and lamented that:
'I often watch Super Nanny and there's these stupid people that don't tell
their children off and don't put them to bed at sensible times and they
wonder why their children are so badly behaved, because they're tired and
they've got no sense of right and wrong. I've always been very strict about
bedtimes and pretty strict on discipline as well.'[135]

However not all women were happy with this move back towards a
routine. Fiona's children were born between 1966 and 1970. Comparing
her own experience with that of her daughter who had a baby in the early
2000s, she said:

> I saw [my daughter] had got that book about the routine, by whatever
> her name is … Gina [Ford], it is or something and she knows everything,
> six forty-five baby is ready to feed. I thought where have I seen this
> before, this was in the parenting magazines when [my first son] was a
> baby, and I used to say six forty-five Fiona goes to sleep, you know. The

baby's not interested in a feed at six forty-five and he's damn well not getting one, you know ... And I read this thing and I said really, you know, in my experience babies don't behave like this.[136]

Nonetheless, it is interesting that even Fiona thought that some element of routine may be beneficial and said of her daughter, 'I think she's more sensible than I was about feeding and routine, they definitely have their bedtimes.'[137] It seems many women were unsure about what was the best way to care for young children. When reflecting back upon the changes that they had seen from when they were babies, to when they had their children, and then watching their children raising their own families, they were unsure of what had really been the best approach. They felt some degree of routine may have been beneficial, but then again, also felt that too regimented an approach was detrimental to both baby and mother. Indeed Kaye explained that mothers got caught in the middle of conflicting advice, such as between experts like Penelope Leach and Ford. She said, 'I still think it's very difficult for mothers to know what to do, cos you've got the Gina Ford school of rigidity which suits some people and then you've got the opposite [school] of sort of "Do what you like" and I think it's very hard for mothers to know what to do.'[138]

Conclusions

Women recalled childcare experts in an ambivalent manner and indeed held contradictory feelings about their advice. There was a conflict between the confidence the experts' guidance gave women and the anxiety it brought for those who felt they did not live up to the standards expected of them. Frederick Truby King, and then later Gina Ford, offered women a model where their time was deemed valuable. Babies were supposed to adapt to their mothers' wishes, not the other way around. The downside of this approach was that women could feel torn between their desire to meet their babies' needs, such as feeding a baby who seemed to be hungry, and the strict routines they were supposed to be following. The consequences of failure were also severe, with 'spoiled' children becoming flawed adults. In contrast the theories of experts such as Donald Winnicott, John Bowlby, Benjamin Spock and Penelope Leach could be liberating for women. They encouraged women to take pleasure in motherhood and gave them the confidence to believe that they knew best. The stress they placed on the importance of the mother role legitimised the decision of many women to care for their infants on a full-time basis: they were doing a worthwhile and rewarding job. Yet full-time motherhood could also be restricting for women. Many mothers felt anxious or blameworthy whenever they had to leave their children. Women who had to work for financial reasons or chose to pursue careers were left feeling guilty that they could be damaging their children's future emotional and physical wellbeing and that their children were 'missing out'.

In addition it is notable that despite both the content and the tone of the childcare 'bibles' altering over time there remained striking similarities in the way experts presented their advice. Whatever the message, and despite the changes in accepted beliefs of what was best practice, the advice given to women was offered in a consistently prescriptive manner. While the way they addressed mothers may have been more or less friendly, all the authors discussed here employed the imperative mood, so their recommendations took the form of orders – for example 'let the baby sleep' or 'feed them on demand' – rather than suggestions. The experts also highlighted the extreme consequences they believed would result if mothers did not follow the methods of childrearing that they advocated, exacerbating the guilt that mothers could face. And the levels of behaviour they set for both mothers and babies were often unattainably high, meaning women could be left feeling like failures when these targets were not achieved. Therefore while women could find supportive messages within childcare literature, some also found the advice more troubling. Moreover these ambiguities within women's accounts of their relationship with the experts mirrored the conflicts within wider society about the best way to care for small children and the role of mothers within this.

Notes

1 Anna Freud, *The Writings of Anna Freud, Vol. 3: Infants without Families* (London: Hogarth, 1973); John Bowlby, *Maternal Care and Maternal Health* (Geneva: World Health Organization, 1951); D.W. Winnicott, *Deprivation and Delinquency* (London: Routledge, 1990).

2 Riley, *War in the Nursery*, p. 11.

3 Ferdinand Lundberg and Marynia F. Farnham, *Modern Woman: The Lost Sex* (New York: The Universal Library, Grosset and Dunlop, 1947), p. 71.

4 Anderson Oakley, *Challenge to Heritage*, pp. 26–7.

5 Michael Rutter, *Maternal Deprivation Reassessed* (Harmondsworth: Penguin, 1972), p. 15.

6 *Ibid.*, p. 119.

7 Lawrence Casler, 'Perpetual deprivation in institutional settings', in Grant Newton and Seymour Levine (eds), *Early Experience and Behaviour: The Psychology of Development* (Springfield: Charles C. Thomas, 1968), 573–626, p. 612.

8 H.R. Schaffer, *The Growth of Sociability* (Harmondsworth: Penguin, 1971), p. 160; Bruno Bettelheim, *The Children of the Dream: Communal Child-Rearing and Its Implications for Society* (London: Paladian, 1971); Simone Yudkin and Anthea Holme, *Working Mothers and Their Children* (London: Michael Joseph, 1963); Ronald Davie,

Neville Batter and Harvey Goldstein with the assistance of Eva Alberman, Euan Ross and Peter Wedge, *From Birth to Seven: A Report of the National Child Development Survey* (London: Longman, 1972), p. 46.

9   Mary D. Salter Ainsworth and John Bowlby, *Child Care and the Growth of Love* (Harmondsworth: Penguin, 1965), p. 202. Emphasis in original.

10 Robert G. Andry, *Delinquency and Parental Pathology: A Study in Forensic and Clinical Psychology* (London: Staple Press, 1971, revised edn), p. 30. Emphasis in original.

11 Barbara Ehrenreich and Deirdre English, *For Her Own Good: 150 Years of the Experts' Advice to Women* (London: Pluto Press, 1978), p. 203.

12 Riley, *War in the Nursery*, p. 11.

13 E.J. Goodacre, *Teachers and Their Pupils' Home Background* (Slough: National Foundation for Educational Research in England and Wales, 1968), p. 50.

14 Jay E. Mechling, 'Advice to historians on advice to mothers', *Journal of Social History*, 9 (1975), 44–63.

15 Gina, SA8, pp. 8–9.

16 Frederick Truby King, *Feeding and Care of Baby* (London: Royal New Zealand Society for the Health of Women and Children, 1913).

17 *Ibid.*, p. 33.

18 Frederick Truby King, *The Expectant Mother and Baby's First Month* (London: Macmillan, 1924), p. 13.

19 Frederick Truby King, *Feeding and Care of Baby* (Christchurch: Whitcombe and Tombs Limited, 1940, revised and enlarged edn), p. 230.

20 Maud, WY4, pp. 10–11.

21 Mavis, EW10, p. 14.

22 Winifred, CO4, p. 16.

23 Sarah, NO2, pp. 8–9.

24 Truby King, *The Expectant Mother*, p. 55.

25 Many mothers interviewed by Pauline King and Rosalind O'Brien also reported putting their babies outside for 'a good airing'. Pauline King and Rosalind O'Brien, 'You didn't get much help in them days, you just had to get on with it': parenting in Hertfordshire in the 1920s and 1930s', *Oral History* 23 (1995), 54–62, p. 56.

26 Phyllis, WY3, p. 9.

27 Celia, WY5, p. 26.

28 Ellen, EW3, p. 12.

29 Truby King, *The Expectant Mother*, p. 25, 39, 75 and 103.

30 Janice, NO11, p. 7; Cherie, CO9, p. 12; Jackie, WY10, p. 10.

31 Olive, OX6, p. 17.

32 Esther, OX1, p. 6.

33 Claire, NO1, p. 6.

34 Maxine, WY6, pp. 7–8.

35 Gloria, BE14, p. 18.

36 Truby King, *Feeding and Care of Baby*, 1940 edn, pp. 12–13.

37 Siobhan, BE1, p. 16.

38 Yvonne, NO3, p. 11.

39 Phoebe, SO8, p. 7.

40 Sarah, NO2, p. 8.

41 Carmel, NO16, pp. 8–9.

42 Pippa, CO13, pp. 17–18.

43 D.W. Winnicott, *The Child and the Family: First Relationships* (London: Tavistock, 1957); D.W. Winnicott, *The Child, the Family, and the Outside World* (Harmondsworth: Penguin, 1964).

44 Winnicott, *Babies and Their Mothers*, p. 3.

45 Phyllis, WY3, p. 9.

46 Bethany, EW4, p. 14.

47 Siobhan, BE1, pp. 16–17.

48 Carla, BA4, p. 10. Sarah Aiston found similar views among the Liverpool graduates she studied. Sarah Aiston, 'A maternal identity? The family lives of British women graduates pre- and post-1945', *History of Education*, 34 (2005), 407–26, p. 425.

49 Roberts, *Women and Families*, p. 150.

50 Winnicott, *Babies and Their Mothers*, pp. 5–6 and 24–5.

51 Glenda, BA2, p. 13.

52 Patsy, BA15, p. 8.

53 Lynne, OX14, p. 12.

54 'Woman's Hour', *BBC Radio Four* (20 December 2005).

55 Bowlby's most renowned works were his WHO study *Maternal Care and Mental Health* and the Attachment trilogy: John Bowlby, *Attachment and Loss: Volume I, Attachment* (Harmondsworth: Penguin, 1971); John Bowlby, *Attachment and Loss: Volume 2, Separation, Anxiety and Anger* (Harmondsworth: Penguin, 1975); John Bowlby, *Attachment and Loss: Volume 3, Sadness and Depression* (Harmondsworth: Penguin Education, 1981).

56 Jeremy Holmes, *John Bowlby and Attachment Theory* (London: Routledge, 1993), p. 27.

57 Bowlby, *Maternal Care*, pp. 10–11 and 67.

58 Discourses surrounding problem families were prominent in the post-war period and often focused on the capacity of the mother. Women's Group on Public Welfare, *The Neglected Child and His Family* (Oxford: Oxford University Press, 1948), p. 22. For the secondary literature on the subject see, for example, Pat Starkey, 'The feckless mother: women, poverty and social workers in wartime and post-war England', *Women's History Review*, 9 (2000), 539–57; and John Welshman, 'In search of the "problem family": public health and social work in England and Wales 1940–70', *Social History of Medicine*, 9 (1998), 447–65.

59 Oxford MOH, 1945, p. 69.

60 Oxford MOH, 1946, p. 67.

61 Oxfordshire MOH, 1968, p. 22. The priorities were in line with a Ministry of Health circular of the same year.

62 Stephanie Spencer, *Gender, Work and Education in Britain in the 1950s* (Basingstoke: Palgrave Macmillan, 2005), p. 162.

63 Roberts, *Women and Families*, p. 150.

64 Karen, SO4, p. 18.

65 Polly, BE7, pp. 19–20.

66 Tania, EW8, p. 13.

67 Gail, BE11, pp. 17–18.

68 Bowlby made an in-depth analysis of the relationship between deprivation and delinquency, in John Bowlby, *Forty-Four Juvenile Thieves: Their Characters and Home-Life* (London: Ballière, Tindall and Cox, 1946).

69 Florence, BE8, p. 11.
70 Ruby, BE5, p. 9.
71 Rose, NO12, pp. 19–20.
72 Ingrid, SO11, p. 12.
73 Deirdre, BA1, pp. 12–13.
74 Marilyn, BE13, p. 12.
75 Linda, TH2, p. 30.
76 Alma, TH7, p. 30.
77 Bowlby, *Maternal Care*, p. 67.
78 Enid, BE12, pp. 22–3.
79 Florence, BE8, p. 11.
80 ERA, Mrs M. 12. B., p. 68.
81 Amelia, CO15, pp. 17–18.
82 Phoebe, SO8, p. 13.
83 Siobhan, BE1, pp. 9–10.
84 Hannah, SO7, p. 6.
85 Georgie, OX2, pp. 15–16.
86 Sonia, SA11, p. 7.
87 Jean, EW14, pp. 7–8.
88 Cynthia, WY12, pp. 9–10.
89 Benjamin Spock, *The Common Sense Book of Baby and Child Care* (New York: Duell, Sloan and Pearce, 1946).
90 Benjamin Spock and Robert Needlman, *Dr Spock's Baby and Childcare* (New York: Pocket Books, 2004, 8th edn), p. i.
91 Christina Hardyment, *Dream Babies: Childcare Advice from John Locke to Gina Ford* (London: Frances Lincoln Limited, 2007), p. 216.
92 Phoebe, SO8, p. 8.
93 Marjorie, NO10, p. 15.
94 Eve, CO8, p. 2.
95 June, CO2, p. 6.
96 Marilyn, BE13, p. 10.
97 Carla, BA4, p. 9.
98 Ellen, EW3, p. 11.
99 Bonnie, CR14, p. 19.
100 Camilla, SO6, p. 11.
101 Benjamin Spock, *Baby and Child Care* (London: The Bodley Head, 1958, new and enlarged edn), p. 15.
102 Rose, NO12, pp. 6–7.
103 *Ibid.*
104 Rebecca, OX10, p. 12.
105 Emily, NO8, p. 13.
106 Spock, *Baby and Child Care*, p. 15.
107 Camilla, SO6, p. 11. Lucinda McCray Beier has also referred to this generational shift in attitudes with reference to the oral history interviews she and Elizabeth Roberts conducted in Lancashire. McCray Beier, 'Expertise and control', p. 409.
108 Lindsay, OX12, pp. 14–15.
109 Emily, NO8, p. 13.

110 Jill, SO3, p. 6.
111 Agnes, EW1, p. 13.
112 Hilda, BA11, p. 14.
113 Hermione, NO15, pp. 1–2.
114 Shula, BA12, pp. 9–10.
115 Daniel Beekman, *The Mechanical Baby: A Popular History of the Theory and Practice of Child Raising* (London: Denis Dobson, 1977), p. 195.
116 Rose, NO12, p. 7.
117 Fiona, BE10, p. 27.
118 Sarah Boseley, 'Leaving baby to cry could damage brain development, parenting guru claims', *Guardian* (21 April 2010).
119 Penelope Leach, *Baby and Child* (London: Michael Joseph, 1977), p. 8.
120 Penelope Leach, *Babyhood: Infant Development from Birth to Two Years* (Harmondsworth: Penguin, 1975), pp. 17–18.
121 *Ibid.*, p. 15.
122 Leach, *Baby and Child*, p. 8.
123 Karen, SO4, p. 11.
124 Carmel, NO16, pp. 8–9.
125 Kaye, WY14, p. 6.
126 Amelia, CO15, p. 36.
127 Harriet, CR8, p. 8.
128 Hermione, NO15, pp. 1–2.
129 Rebecca, OX10, p. 12; Fiona, BE10, p. 32.
130 Rebecca, OX10, p. 12.
131 Gina Ford, *The Contented Little Baby Book* (London: Vermilion, 1999), p. 88.
132 *Ibid.*, p. 9.
133 Anna, NO13, p. 10.
134 Hermione, NO15, p. 9.
135 Jean, EW14, pp. 7–8.
136 Fiona, BE10, p. 32.
137 *Ibid.*
138 Kaye, WY14, p. 9.

6

Working and caring: women's labour inside and outside the home

From the late 1940s married women were being urged to return to paid work. Initially they were needed to fill the gaps in the workforce created by labour shortages in areas such as transport, agriculture and textiles, but later there was a drive to recruit more women in jobs such as teaching and nursing, where there were large numbers of vacancies due to the post-war social reforms. Women's working patterns changed after World War Two. Domestic service, textiles and the clothing industry lost their predominance as employment sectors for women, while the number of women employed in clerical work grew rapidly. As Gerry Holloway argues, this 'increase of married women working led to a debate that began in the 1950s about when, in the life cycle, women should work, how this affected their primary role as homemaker and whether in fact it was possible or desirable for married women to work.'[1] The ambiguities and disagreements within the literature of the period about what the role of women should be illustrate how contested the issue was.[2] Some commentators were conscious of the new demands upon women that resulted from their increasing participation in the workforce. Richard Titmuss described how the typical woman of the 1950s had completed her mothering role by the age of forty, and thought the tendency for married women to engage in paid work was a response to this. Titmuss believed it brought a new conflict for women between 'motherhood and wage-earning.'[3] Proposals on how to solve these difficulties were also put forward. Criticising the current education of girls in the 1950s and 1960s, which they felt did not address the realities of women's lives, Judith Hubback and Hannah Gavron argued changes were needed to better prepare women for their roles as mothers and workers.[4] Moreover, by the 1960s there were concerns that women were not meeting the needs of the economy. In 1963 the Committee on Higher Education, under Lord Robbins, reported: 'We should greatly welcome a tendency for more girls to stay on at school, if only from the national point of view of making better use of what must be the greatest source of unused talent at a time when there is an immediate shortage of teachers and of many other types of qualified person.[5]

Women did not enter the labour market on equal terms to men, however, because their domestic role was considered to be of paramount importance. Dolly Smith Wilson suggests that 'men and women existed in two separate labour markets, one for men, considered the real workers, the other for women, considered low-paid auxiliaries working on the side, unrelated to their real role as wives and mothers.'[6] Considering the post-war welfare reforms, Jane Lewis proposes that women's role in William Beveridge's conception of society was quite specifically to redress the decline in the population and provide domestic support for men in full-time employment. She believes that this narrow conception of women's role came at the expense of women's interests because 'the needs of race and nation for women's work as wives and mothers' came before 'the needs of women as individuals.'[7] Beveridge can be seen as raising the status of women, though, in as much as he assigned to them a crucial role in the nation's future. Jennifer Dale and Peggy Foster contend that the domestic role was not necessarily perceived as oppressive in the 1940s and 1950s and that women's role as mother was awarded a high status – the Beveridge Plan acknowledged housewifery as a profession. They conclude it has only been with later feminist analyses that dependence and low esteem have been assumed to characterise the role of housewife.[8] Not all women were afforded such an opportunity, though. Immigrant women, in particular, were disadvantaged because of the official view that they had entered the country as workers. The result of this connection between immigrant women and work was that they were not associated with family or domesticity.[9] Consequently they were criticised in their attempts to combine both roles. They were condemned for leaving their children with relatives in their home countries, but also censured if their children had accompanied them.[10] The sociologist Sheila Patterson wrote that, 'Upbringing in a single room, in a cold climate with no outside playground but the street, with a working mother and no male parent other than a succession of "uncles", is hardly more desirable.'[11] In the post-war decades when white women were still being encouraged to stay at home and embrace domesticity and consumerism, the state was not prepared to offer any childcare support to those non-indigenous women who had to work.[12]

A significant transformation in attitudes towards women's work was occurring during the second half of the twentieth century, however. The number of women in work in the United Kingdom as a whole rose from 7 million in 1951, to 9 million in 1971, to just over 13 million in 2000, an average growth rate of 1.3 percent per year.[13] Whereas in 1951 less than a quarter of married women were in the workforce, by 1991 this had increased to half of all married women.[14] At the end of the century there was also an enormous rise in the number of women with young children returning to work. Between 1988 and 1998, the employment rate for women with children under five rose from 36 percent to 50 percent.[15] The types of work women undertook remained distinct from men's however. At the 1981 census three-quarters of all female workers were in just four of the sixteen occupational categories of the census: personal services (such as cleaners and hairdressers); clerical; professional workers in health, education and welfare; and selling (mainly shop assistants).[16] Moreover women's patterns and hours of work were different from men's too. Duncan Gallie notes that the growth of female part-time jobs was one of the most striking changes in the labour market in the second half of the century. At the mid-century only a very small proportion (about 11 percent) of women's jobs were part time, but by 1971 part-time work represented approximately a third of female employment. The overall number of part-time jobs then nearly doubled from 2,750,000 in 1971 to 5,168,590 in 1998.[17] It was women with dependent children who made up this growing number of part-time workers. However, a Labour Force Survey conducted in 2000 revealed that the presence of dependent children still sharply reduced women's participation in full-time work. Mothers were only half as likely to be in full-time work as women without dependent children. Conversely, mothers were substantially more likely to work part time than women without dependent children (44 percent compared to 27 percent). For women without dependent children, looking after family or home had almost disappeared as the major activity. Among mothers, however, the number of full-time homemakers was only marginally smaller than the number in full-time employment. Just fewer than 30 percent were in full-time employment as opposed to about a quarter looking after family.[18] As Sara Connolly and Mary Gregory have concluded, at the end of the twentieth century motherhood was the 'dominant influence on women's employment status.'[19]

But while motherhood was undoubtedly decisive in determining women's working lives, there were also variations between mothers along the lines of class, region and ethnicity. Before the war middle-class women overwhelmingly left work upon marriage and did not return. While many working-class women also aspired to fully withdraw from the labour force, they would often take paid work after marriage when household finances required it. From the late 1940s the numbers of working-class women returning to the labour force after having children climbed, and from the 1960s they were joined by middle-class women. During the 1980s a significant improvement in female access to certain professional occupations started to occur and by the closing decades of the century middle-class, professional women were more likely to be working than their less well-qualified counterparts. Moreover middle-class mothers with successful careers were increasingly returning to work before their children were of school age.[20] There were also differences in the employment opportunities for urban and rural women with women's involvement in paid work lower in rural areas. Those women who were employed were more likely to be in part-time work, and the quality, pay and conditions of work for women were poorer in rural than in urban areas.[21] Other regional differences existed too. In her 1968 survey of women's employment, Audrey Hunt found that regions which had traditionally been those where women did not work, particularly after marriage, were still those where the proportion of women at work was lowest. For example only about two-fifths were at work in the north of England.[22] As noted above, migrant women had been viewed as workers rather than mothers when they first came to England in the post-war decades. However, rates of labour market participation differed between immigrant groups and were higher among African-Caribbean and lower among Pakistani and Bangladeshi women. In addition, while all women's employment has been characterised by confinement to a limited range of occupations, most non-indigenous groups were concentrated in an even narrower spectrum – predominantly in low-paid and low-status work, and in the lower grades of most jobs. While there was some change towards of the end of the century with increasing numbers of non-indigenous women entering into sectors like banking, retailing and local government, even into the 1980s and 1990s ethnic minority women were more likely to work in low-status jobs in the health services and were less likely to be employed in relatively high-status clerical work.[23] Nonetheless this does not mean such women did not take pleasure from their work. In her study of Jamaican migrants to London conducted in the early 1970s Nancy Foner found that: 'women often seem to receive great intrinsic satisfaction from their employment. Many nurses' auxiliaries and ward orderlies talked with enthusiasm and pride about their dealings with hospital patients and the services they provide for the old and sick.'[24]

The rising rate of female employment seen in the second half of the twentieth century was reflected in the experiences of the women interviewed. All the Oxfordshire interviewees had been engaged in some kind of paid or voluntary work after their children were born. However, the older women interviewed did give precedence to their domestic role in their narratives. It was common for them to say they had not worked after having their children when initially asked, but then later in their narratives to reveal that they had.[25] In part this may have been a legacy of the lack of emphasis on careers they received at school, which meant they had grown up expecting to become full-time mothers. It may also have been due to the lack of status ascribed to women workers. Women who had their children at the end of the period more often identified themselves with work outside the home. Nonetheless, for most women, throughout the second half of the century, work was something to be fitted in around their children, hence the popularity of part-time work.[26] Only a small number of women, albeit an increasing one, presented their working lives as a central feature of their accounts. This trend reflected the fact, as Jessie Bernard has noted, that, 'The gifted mothers who pursue professional careers represent only a relatively small proportion of all working mothers who are gestating the future. Far more are simply mothers who have jobs.'[27] This chapter will therefore assess the attitudes towards work of the women interviewed in the context of national debates surrounding women's employment. It will examine three models of work for mothers. The first is professional motherhood and the ideal that full-time housewifery could provide women with a career in itself. The second model is the woman who 'worked on the side', with paid work being supplementary to her principal role as mother. The third model is the working mother who combined motherhood with the pursuit of a career, and for whom both aspects of her life held equal weight. Women's understandings of these models were derived from watching their mothers' generation, their contemporaries and their daughters' generation, and therefore perceptions of change over time will also be considered.

The profession of motherhood

The belief that women should contribute to society through marriage and motherhood was entrenched within post-war thinking. In 1942 William Beveridge had argued, 'In the next thirty years housewives as mothers have vital work to do in ensuring the adequate continuance of the British race and of British ideals in the world.'[28] The same year a Mass Observation Directive asked: 'What do you feel about the position of women in this country to-day?' One correspondent replied: 'the right place of a married woman is in the home because marriage is a career, and if it is going to clash with a career already embarked upon, a choice should be made between the two.'[29] Rose had two children in 1959 and 1961 and recalled how she and her contemporaries were influenced by such views:

> after the war ... everybody was having children, lots of people [were] having children and families ... so I think without necessarily examining ourselves we assumed that at some stage we'd do the same ... and it seems preposterous to me now that at one stage I even had the thought, 'Well I really should have children it would be selfish not to.' You know, you mustn't leave it to everybody else, you must make some sort of contribution, you must all have some place in society.[30]

However after her children were born Rose's attitudes changed. 'When I had the children I realised just to keep them going was as much as I can manage, you know keep them out the hands of the police and the social services is as much as you can hope [for], I'm not sort of making a gift to society.'[31] Rose's account of her optimism at contributing to society through motherhood when she first had her children and subsequent disillusionment indicates that she had come to question the glorification of motherhood which characterised post-war thinking. She now wondered whether it was such an invaluable job. Her re-evaluation of her attitudes with the passing of time may also reflect the later feminist reappraisals of the mother role, as her doubts set in during the later 1960s.

Women could also be left disenchanted if they did not find full-time motherhood to be the satisfying experience celebrated by the contemporary ideal. The feminist historian Sheila Rowbotham believes that many, 'Young, middle-class, educated mothers found the contrast between their assumption of equality and the reality of their domestic confinement was acute.'[32] The dissatisfied, educated mother was a stereotypical figure during the 1960s. The issue of how important a woman's level of education was in determining her attitudes towards motherhood was hotly contested. The letter pages of newspapers, such as the *Guardian* women's page, ran many letters from unhappy, graduate mothers.[33] Suzanne Gail, a London housewife, described her life in Ronald Fraser's book *Work: Twenty Personal Accounts*, first published in 1965. She found housework monotonous and unrewarding: 'When something happens to stimulate me to my former awareness – an enjoyable social occasion, or the tutorials which I still give once a fortnight in the university – I feel I have come back to life. I am ashamed to admit that quite frequently I come home afterwards in a mood of savage rejection.'[34] Moreover Gail was not alone.[35] Ina Zweiniger-Bargielowska has posited that during the 1960s and 1970s 'full-time housewifery and motherhood was a stressful experience for middle-class women who – in contrast to their mothers' generation – had no domestic help and whose aspirations in career terms were frequently thwarted.'[36]

Middle-class women in Oxfordshire who had grown up seeing their mothers employ servants to take care of the house did comment upon the difference in lifestyle they and their mothers enjoyed. Louisa was born in 1939. Her mother was a dentist and worked throughout her childhood. Louisa tried to explain why her mother had been able to combine work and motherhood while she had not: 'My mother worked you see, but she had childcare, there was no problem. We're the sort of the part-time generation because there was no childcare. I mean it was bad enough finding a baby-sitter. I just couldn't go out because I was let down so many times.' Louisa thought this was a common experience for educated women of her generation. She recalled that only one or two of her friends had careers.[37] Camilla, who had her children in the 1960s, thought she belonged to a 'lost generation' who came between 'my mother's generation with the nanny and somebody who came to do the washing and my daughter's generation who send out the laundry and send them to the crèche. We had to do it all.'[38]

Full-time motherhood therefore provoked an ambivalent response amongst a section of educated, middle-class women. By the late 1960s and 1970s women were trying to gain public recognition for the difficulties mothers could face and make it acceptable for women to articulate them. The women interviewed in Oxfordshire benefited from such campaigns and felt able to talk of the loneliness and frustration they had experienced as mothers to young children. Lindsay was an Oxford graduate who had two children in the early 1960s. She explained how she found it difficult to adjust to full-time motherhood: 'I mean having children absolutely, as happened to a lot of graduates, really threw me. I was totally unprepared for not only the sheer drudgery, but what it does to one's feelings, including, occasionally, the feeling that I could quite cheerfully kill this child.'[39] The isolation that mothers of young children faced was frequently referred to. For example Hayley, a graduate from Bedford College, London, also found that being at home all day with small children could be wearisome. She recalled that 'children drive you up the wall after a bit they really do.' Significantly the interviewees explained the ways in which they tried to counter this unhappiness rather than accepting the situation. Hayley thought it was imperative that women had an opportunity to 'get out of the house'. She did not think this necessarily need be for paid work and undertook voluntary work herself.[40]

In Oxfordshire, however, it was not only educated middle-class women who talked about their frustrations as mothers. Cherie had left school at sixteen and worked as a secretary before having her children. She lived in Cowley when her three children were born in the 1960s. Like

Hayley, she thought it was very easy for women to feel isolated and 'a bit sort of shut off at home if you're not careful.' She also made the point of leaving the house everyday even if this was only for a walk around the park.[41] Hilda lived in a small north Oxfordshire village when she had her two children in 1967 and 1970. She recalled feeling depressed when her children had reached school age and she was left alone in the house. Her mother-in-law encouraged her to take a temporary job and Hilda said she was still working twenty-five years later.[42] Despite not being highly educated or middle class Tina, a Benson mother who had three children between 1964 and 1971, was one of the women who spoke most powerfully about her profound difficulties of coping with the expectations placed on her in the role of wife and mother. Tina had left school at fifteen and got married at eighteen to a man who worked at the car works in Cowley. She recalled how she had felt trapped and depressed by her circumstances – 'I'd just had enough of everything.'[43] It is clear from the Oxfordshire evidence that difficulties in adjusting to motherhood and reconciling society's expectations with the reality of their lives was not the preserve of middle-class mothers. Indeed Marilyn, who had attended a secondary modern and left school at sixteen, argued that it was a unifying experience for women at this time. Marilyn also expressed her discontent with the housewife role. 'I didn't find it easy because you know all you're doing is housework and cleaning and things like that'. However, she felt this situation was alleviated by the fact that there were 'quite a lot of people in the same situation' who provided one another with friendship and support.[44]

Women recalled this time spent in the company of other women as being not only helpful but also enjoyable. Karen had four children between 1967 and 1985. Her account of the close relationship that mothers of young children enjoyed encapsulated the views of many of the interviewees about the importance of this community of women:

> when you have children, it may not be the same for everybody but it is for lots of people, you're often at the end of your tether, but not in any desperate way, but you often have to do things that you're not good at doing, you have to do things when you're very tired. You have to clean up mess, you would not have contemplated clearing up in cold blood. And all those kind of things, and the, other mothers are people who are living in that kind of place with you. So in some ways it's a kind of very comfortable relationship. Because people joke about, 'Oh I scream at my children.' But actually they know that they do sometimes scream at their children, but it's ok, and if you got worried that you were screaming at your children too much you would have people, you could actually talk to people who would actually understand the context …

So there's that kind of comfortable thing, you know. And being able to talk to people when you've got sick down your back, because actually they know it's not really that slobby it's because you haven't looked in the mirror since you put your baby over your shoulder ... you haven't necessarily got anything in common apart from that, and people laugh at that kind of baby thing, but it's very good, it was a good part of my life.[45]

Karen's views echoed those of the feminist philosopher Sara Ruddick who in her book *Maternal Thinking* challenged the negative portrayals of motherhood that had been common in much 1970s feminist writing, stating that, 'Many mothers, whatever their other work, feel part of a community of mothers whose warmth and support is hard to match in other working relationships.'[46] It is clear that while women may not have enjoyed all aspects of the mother role there was much that was a good experience.

Not all women found marriage and motherhood restrictive. Some interviewees said they found it liberating, especially if they had not enjoyed their jobs or were keen to cease employment. While women sometimes felt frustrated with the tedium that looking after small children could bring they also found that motherhood imbued them with a sense of fulfilment. Mary Boulton interviewed fifty London women in the late 1970s. In their accounts of their daily lives the women she spoke with reported that they experienced a wide range of feelings about looking after children. While they did include feelings of frustration, irritation and boredom, they also included feelings of delight, pleasure, enjoyment, meaningfulness, personal worth, and significance as mothers.[47] The Oxfordshire interviewees offered similar descriptions in their narratives. Barbie had two children in the late 1970s. She really enjoyed her time at home with the children and was sorry when the youngest one went to school.[48] Geraldine had two children in 1987 and 1989 and thought that staying at home with them was 'the best thing that I've ever done.'[49] Moreover it is of note that some of the Oxfordshire interviewees who voiced the strongest desire to leave work were actually educated and middle class. Sharon referred to marriage as a 'wonderful escape' from doing a PhD which she was not enjoying.[50] In a similar vein, when Grace, an Oxford graduate, was asked if she had always wanted to get married and have a family, she replied, 'Yes I think, I think I had, yes. Partly because of status I think. I mean I wasn't earning, I was living in a bed-sitting room not earning very much money and not very happy, and I was jolly lucky I met him.'[51] Cassie had been a civil servant working in the War Office before marriage and worked as a tutor in Oxford before having her first child in 1946. When asked whether she ever returned to work she replied, 'having earned my living for ten years before I married I didn't feel the urge to go back.'[52] Responding to the esteem with which professional motherhood was held at this time it was possible for women in the post-war decades to believe that marriage and motherhood could offer them the chance of achieving status and indeed independence.

However, there was a generational difference in women's attitudes towards full-time motherhood. Women who had their children from the late 1960s onwards and who chose not to return to paid work, or only did so when their children were past school age, did seem more apologetic in their accounts of why they did not go back. Educated women seemed to feel particularly guilty that they had not fulfilled the potential their education gave them. In part this resulted from a changing attitude towards mothers who did not return to paid employment. Discussing 'stay-at-home' mothers in their study of middle-class couples in the late 1960s, Jan and Ray Pahl concluded that: 'society places a heavy burden of guilt on these women: though many enjoyed being housewives, they felt when their children had all started at school that this role alone was not really enough and that they had to make excuses for being so "lazy".'[53] The women interviewed expressed some of these same dilemmas. Siobhan had two sons in the early 1970s and compared herself negatively to her brother and sisters:

> In fact I think I consider myself to be the least successful of my siblings. My brother is a professor of optometry … and my middle sister was in charge of remedial teaching, she was responsible for the education of handicapped adults in Surrey. My sister who's seven years younger than me was a senior crown prosecutor, she actually doesn't do that anymore, but she's doing all kinds of interesting work in the legal profession, and then my youngest sister runs her own medical PR business. So I'm kind of the dunce of the family.[54]

Claire was an Oxford graduate who had five children between 1960 and 1972. Like Siobhan she felt inferior when comparing her achievements with those of her contemporaries. When asked whether she would have liked to return to work, she answered, 'Well the only difficult thing was that everybody else had important jobs, that I felt that I should be doing something.'[55] Moreover, this seemed to be a national trend. Mrs Wheaton had two children in Lancashire in the 1960s. She did not work outside the home after having her children although she investigated doing paid work at home. She explained: 'I wasn't desperately keen, but I felt guilty that other people should be going out to work and I wasn't; and therefore I wasn't doing my bit. It was guilt. It wasn't a desire to go to work at all. I was quite happy in the environment I was in. I had no spare time. I was completely happy with my lot so I felt guilty.'[56] Such women were also keener to demonstrate that they did pursue intellectual stimulation too. Ellen, who had her first child in the mid-1970s, recalled how she became an Open University tutor after her third child was born: 'A friend said to me, "you ought to be an Open University tutor", she said, "stop you getting intellectually stale while you're at home with your children." So I applied to become a tutor for the Open University, and I got the job in November 1978, and I've been a tutor for the Open University ever since.'[57]

It seems to be generation rather than education alone that shaped this need for justification. Marilyn, who left school at sixteen, expressed similar feelings. She also had her children in the early 1970s and stressed how getting involved in playgroups meant she was more than simply a stay-at-home mother: 'I was involved with playgroups when they were young and that kept me out of the house and gave me something to do, so I didn't work when they were young but went back when they were at school.'[58] The general trend amongst the interviewees as the century progressed was to return to work when their children were at younger ages. While even in the 1980s and 1990s only a minority of the women interviewed returned to full-time work before their children were school age, those who were not engaged in paid work could feel they were looked down upon. Josie had four children between 1985 and 1991. She had not returned to paid work after her children were born because she felt that the cost of childcare did not make it financially possible. However she found that when her youngest children, twins, started school, people started asking her when she was going to get a job.[59] Similarly Jemma, who had two children in the mid-1980s, remembered how, 'my next door neighbour said to me when my daughter was three years old and she was going to nursery for three days a week. She said, "Are you going to go and get a job now, then?" I said, "I beg your pardon?" I said, "Who's going to look after the kids?".'[60]

Women who had their children earlier in the century also commented upon this change. A correspondent to Mass Observation writing on the subject of 'Women and Men' in 1991, stated: 'I feel that women today are pressurised to start earning money again as soon as their children are old enough to be left in a crèche or sent to school. I noticed this with my daughter and her contemporaries, there was a feeling of guilt because just "homemaking" is no longer considered a fulfilling occupation as it was in my early married life.'[61] Reflecting on the changes over the second half of the century, Hermione mused:

I think again, my generation had the magic, magic period between my mother's generation, who weren't expected to work, and were almost not allowed to work in the middle class, and today's women who have to work … We could, or not, which was terrific, it was work if you want to … I think the 1970s and 1980s were the perfect decades for women having absolutely the monopoly on choice. And I don't think they do now. I think if women don't go back to work they're regarded as second-class citizens.[62]

Therefore rather than gaining status through motherhood in the latter decades of the century women could feel that they were losing it. Kaye had two children in 1981 and 1984. Before having her children she had worked as a midwife. She explained that, 'the one thing I really missed when I had the children was the loss of status, because when I was a community midwife, you know, you felt you were a sort of an important person in the community and then suddenly you're just a mother which sounds terrible but … you just feel you're, I suppose not very important.'[63]

Mothers and paid work

It was often assumed in the post-war decades that growing affluence meant fewer women had to take jobs in order to support their families and that those who did were working in order to afford luxuries rather than necessities. For instance Patsy, who had two children in 1970 and 1972, explained, 'we just looked upon it as pin money, we weren't looking about pensions and all this, we just looked at it as a bit of money to supplement our incomes … most people of our age weren't looking [at it] as a career, you might say, we were just going out and earning a bit of money and helping out the family.'[64] Using elements from the post-war discourse that 'good' husbands should be able to support their families, combined with later feminist ideas about women's need for a satisfying career, Sharon recalled that the only women she knew who had paid employment when she had her children in the early 1970s were those who needed the money. She said, 'There were lots of women working at that stage, but they were working-class women who needed the money desperately, not career-minded, aspiring women.'[65] Many working-class mothers did need to work for financial reasons. Peggy, a resident of Middleton Cheney, had four children between 1951 and 1965 and explained how she had to take a job throughout her children's upbringing. Although her husband was employed he spent most of his wages in the pub and she had to make up the shortfall in order to support her family. She said, 'I've always had to work, I've never had a time that I could sit back and say, "Well I don't have to work".[66] Peggy felt she was forced to work. She implied that it was not something she wanted to do, and she would have preferred to remain at home. Indeed several of the women interviewed who worked when their children were young recalled feeling they had missed out through not being at home with them. Lily, who lived in Ewelme, had five children between 1946 and 1961. Although she had left work when her first baby was born she had to return after her first husband died. She stated: 'I had to go back to work. First of all there used to be a honey factory in the village … I went there for two years. I can't say that I thoroughly enjoyed it but it helped.'[67] However while paid work could be a necessity for women rather than an active choice, many women did recall that they took pleasure in their jobs. Rita also had to find employment after she was widowed. She was happy to resume her work as a seamstress which she had left upon the birth of her first child. In part her satisfaction derived from the flexibility her trade brought her as she could work from home. In consequence she did not feel her ability to care for her children was compromised.[68] Paid work could remain supplementary to Rita's role as mother and she did not have to challenge contemporary perceptions of womanhood. There were some parallels here with the popularity of home-work among South Asian women later in the century. Home-work was perceived as being more suitable for women to undertake than paid labour outside the home because it did not seem to conflict with their domestic responsibilities.[69]

Another group of women who had to work were farmers' wives as their labour was crucial to the farm economy. While census statistics have shown the number of female agricultural workers had been in sharp decline over the first half of the century, it was clear from the interviews with Oxfordshire farmers' wives that they were still engaged in farm work.[70] Women's employment in rural areas was probably under-recorded in the post-war decades, perhaps due to the fact that farm labour was not seen as a suitable job for a woman at this time. Furthermore, as Hilary Callan has highlighted, the work undertaken by wives assisting their husbands in professions such as farming was taken for granted. The 'hidden services' wives provided only became visible when they were withdrawn.[71] Maud reported that as a farmer's wife she was expected to care for the prisoners of war stationed on her husband's farm during World War Two. While she told this as a humorous story, recalling having to quickly learn how to cook pasta, she also spoke of the arduous work she faced as a result.[72] Daisy and her husband bought a smallholding in Shipton-under-Wychwood in the early 1950s on which they kept chickens and pigs. Her husband worked full time so she was responsible for the animals and recalled, 'I had two children to look after and chickens and pigs so I tell you it was quite tough really.' Running the smallholding was associated in Daisy's mind with hardship and she highlighted this by telling a traumatic account of an incident when her son was attacked by one of the pigs. In 1955 she and her husband took on a milk-round because they were struggling to pay their mortgage and needed a new source of income. Again Daisy was left in charge of this as her husband still worked outside the village. She explained: 'I had to take the little boy of three … and he had to sit in the van whilst I delivered milk.'[73] Daisy clearly felt this responsibility was a burden to her rather than an exciting employment opportunity.

Later in the century farmers' wives were still playing an important role. Alice was twenty-two when she married a farmer in 1961. When asked what she did on the farm Alice replied, 'Oh driving tractors, I used to do most of the hay and straw-bailing in the summer … I'd work at school in the morning then go home, pick up some sandwiches, take them up the fields and probably stay up there the rest of the day.'[74] Zoe recalled what it was like when she and her husband took over his family's farm in the early 1970s:

> Of course in those days, also, there were lots and lots of farmers' reps, so a lot of people were calling on business and phoning because we had a phone line then, so there was an awful lot of seeing to people and dealing with things, and of course this was all fairly new to me. Reps would come and say 'I want to talk to the husband', or 'the man of the house' and I would say, 'Well, try me first', and that was a challenge because I needed to learn all about the farm and what was going on really. Yes, we were kind of, we went straight in.[75]

It was notable from the interviews with these farmers' wives that they conceived of their work as simply part of life on the farm. They described it as their duty. Although they may have also found satisfaction from the work, they did not stress this fact in their accounts.

There were also middle-class women who needed to work for financial reasons. These women were their families' only financial providers. In the years after 1945, and particularly from the 1970s, increased social security and housing benefits became sufficient to facilitate the autonomous existence of lone mothers (whether through widowhood, never-married motherhood or divorce), albeit at a low level.[76] Nonetheless women recalled that the difficulties of being a single parent were still acute. Jessica, who was a doctor, had to return to work in the late 1940s when her husband left her with three small children. She explained: 'I wasn't intending to practice, I was intending to bring up the children and then think again. But when he left me … he took any money we had, so

I'd got by that time three little children and no income, I had a house and a car but I had nothing else, I had twenty pounds in the bank, so I put my plate up on the wall, and gradually I built up a practice.'[77] Faith experienced a similar situation to Jessica over twenty years later. Faith's husband left when their daughter, born in 1971, was six weeks old. She explained that she had to return to work 'because we had to pay the rent. And so it was really quite difficult. And I was in trouble with my doctor, who said I shouldn't have gone back to work so soon. So I couldn't really say, "Well I just have to, I don't really have a choice".'[78] Sophie's two children were aged ten and twelve when she got divorced in 1980. She also recalled that she was compelled to seek full-time employment in order to support the family.[79] These women spoke somewhat ambivalently about their need to return to work. They were reticent, and almost defensive about their situation, but also talked with pride that they had been able to support their families. Although under change, the ideal throughout much of the second half of the century had been that women would not have to be financially responsible for their families. In consequence those women who were single mothers due to widowhood or divorce, or who were never married, faced acute difficulties in trying to reconcile their roles as mother and worker.

Norms were changing however. Increasing numbers of mothers were returning to paid work as the second half of the century progressed. In response, women developed a variety of approaches to combining work and motherhood. In her 1957 book, *Wives Who Went to College*, the writer (and later analytical psychologist) Judith Hubback argued that individual methods were always necessary:

> What is needed is to work out the individual combination or compromise which achieves the best possible relationship between the three sides of a married woman's life, the woman as wife, as a mother, and as an individual. No-one can do this piece of work for another woman, for each must find her own compromise ... to come to certain conclusions. And these conclusions can only be temporary ones, because the years will not stand still, and what works at the age of twenty will no longer be satisfactory at forty.[80]

The most common course of action for women throughout the second half of the century was to seek part-time work, usually once their children were of school age. This trend towards part-time work was prevalent amongst women of all classes and educational backgrounds. Indeed Pat Thane has noted how few married graduates of Girton College, Cambridge, spent their adult lives in full-time paid employment; instead many of them had career patterns similar to less-educated contemporaries.[81] Such a pattern was also the experience for the majority of the women interviewed in Oxfordshire. For example, Jill graduated from Oxford University in the mid-1950s and remained at work in the university both before and after her two children were born in 1966 and 1970. She explained that she was able to do so because she worked part time, sharing childcare with a colleague's wife: 'she was a teacher in fact, and she had a baby at almost the same time, and we used to swap babies.'[82] Shift-work was also a common solution. For instance Melanie took part-time work in the evenings so her husband would be able to care for the children while she was a work.[83] Similarly in their history of black women in Britain, Beverley Bryan, Stella Dadzie and Suzanne Scafe conclude that night- and shift-work were also the most commonly employed solutions by black women to enable them to combine their responsibilities as mothers and breadwinners.[84]

These private arrangements were the most popular methods of childcare with the women interviewed. Few women recalled using state-provided nurseries. Sadie had two children in 1970 and 1975. She returned to work as a speech therapist part time when her first child was three but left when her second child was born. She then returned to work part time after his birth, returning to full-time work when he was nine. She said that she could not have returned to full-time work earlier because she did not qualify for state nursery provision and there were no private nurseries.[85] Sadie's experience reflected national trends. Audrey Hunt's survey of women's employment in the late 1960s found that little use was made of day nurseries or nursery schools by mothers of children aged from birth to four: only about one-sixtieth of these children were looked after in establishments of this kind. However she found that more mothers would have made use of such facilities had they been available, and some mothers said they would have returned to work sooner if their children could have been looked after in this way.[86] For the middle-class mothers of Oxford (particularly north Oxford) during the 1950s and 1960s, au pairs were a common source of childcare.[87] Their prevalence may have been encouraged by the fact that Oxford attracted young, foreign, female workers because it was a famous university city. The women interviewed displayed some uncertainty in their attitude towards au pairs, and their narratives revealed ambivalence. Phoebe had eight au pairs and recalled that she had enjoyed living with all but two. Nonetheless she thought 'it comes apart when you give an untrained au pair too much responsibility, leave them too long alone with the children.'[88] For Michelle these doubts extended to unhappiness. She recalled: 'I had a French au pair girl who was absolutely hopeless and didn't understand any English and it was all very traumatic.'[89] Furthermore the opportunity to have an au pair was limited to women who could afford one and was therefore an option outside most women's reach.

From the 1970s onwards, though, the popularity of au pairs seemed to diminish somewhat with childminders or nannies being preferred instead. Interviewees who used childminders said they liked the intimacy that a childminder could offer. Bev had two children in 1987 and 1990 and she returned to work after her maternity leave. She explained:

> I wanted … to have a childminder because, because I thought that would create a family atmosphere like I was used to. And I'd looked for a childminder before the birth … So, that was a little bit of anxiety, which you probably can't avoid … it was unusual for a lady to go back to work. And certainly to go back full time … and there was family pressure not to do it. But financial pressure was such I was the main breadwinner, so [pause] there was no alternative.[90]

Cynthia also returned to work after taking the minimum maternity leave when her daughter was born in 1993. She said her childminder was brilliant: '[my daughter] was always terribly happy to go and it did feel like, yeah, [my childminder] was part of the family so there was never any problem.'[91] Alexa and Anna referred to their children's carers as nannies rather than childminders, although they were not residential, because the children were looked after in their own homes rather than at the minders'. Alexa had originally wanted her daughter to attend a nursery but there were no places available so she looked for a nanny instead. However Alexa said she was subsequently pleased she had used a nanny as it enabled her daughter to grow up seeing normal 'womanly' things and that the nanny was a 'substitute me'.[92] Indeed it is interesting that some women felt that their nannies or childminders may have been better suited to caring for small children than they were. Discussing her nanny Anna said:

> [She] was lovely, very sensible and I learnt a lot from her. She was just very commonsensical and I mean the thing [pause] the area that I didn't really know about with children – and again I can see my own children [are] much better at it than me – was, it was just the whole area of play with children. Knowing what kind of things children like to do and how to entertain them. I mean the first year that I was at home with [my son] there was sort of long stretches of time where I didn't know what I should be doing with him.[93]

However, while they were spoken of positively by the women interviewed, the figure of the childminder in fact demonstrated the low status often ascribed to women's work. For example writing in the 1980s, Bryan *et al.* noted that, 'Because it was women's work, childminding was, and still is, grossly undervalued.'[94] Women themselves could also hold such views. In her study of school leavers in the early 1980s Christine Griffin found that because of its association with the domestic sphere, the young women she spoke to did not assign childminding 'the status of *real* work.'[95]

Working mothers

Some young women had grown up with higher expectations of women's work, though. They had witnessed at first hand, through the example of their own mothers, that it could be possible for women to combine motherhood with a successful professional life. Carol Boyd has suggested that mothers' occupations and work orientation had a profound influence on their daughters' employment.[96] For the sample of graduate women interviewed whose own mothers had often been professionals – such as teachers, medical professionals (including doctors and dentists as well as nurses), academics and writers – the expectation was that they too would have a career. Lindsay's mother was an eye specialist who had returned to work when Lindsay and her sister were still young children in the late 1930s. Lindsay's parents took it for granted that she too would have a successful career, which in fact caused distress for Lindsay, who struggled to meet this ideal.[97] Hannah, who was born in 1924, talked more positively about her mother's influence and indeed credited her mother with her own successful academic career. Her mother was a teacher and Hannah felt she was a 'wonderful model for me, absolutely, and tremendously encouraging. I mean she always made me feel I was the ant's pants and I think that you know it gave me tremendous self-confidence, I owe that to her ... I always felt I could do anything.'[98] There were also mothers who did not feel they had fulfilled their own potential and therefore encouraged their daughters to succeed where they could not. Anna's mother was a Jewish refugee whose own career ambitions had been thwarted. Anna explained:

> I think there was probably a lot of, I mean not pressure from my mother, it would be quite unfair to call it pressure, but she herself had desperately wanted to be a doctor. And she had gone to university very young in Moscow and then they had had to emigrate and they went to Germany and in Germany she couldn't get a place at medical school, so she did biochemistry instead and then she was a refugee from Germany as well and couldn't, you know any idea of career was sort of finished by then. So I think there was a very strong assumption around [that] both boys and girls in the family should be going to university.'[99]

Many of the graduate women in Oxford described following in their mothers' footsteps and thought it was their mothers' generation, rather than themselves, who were the pioneers.

The mothers of these women could act as role models because they had been 'working mothers' combining motherhood with a career. It was important to women to have role models who did not jeopardise their domesticity.[100] This reflected wider ideals of femininity in society at this time. In her study of graduate women Judith Hubback wrote:

> The early pioneers for the higher education of women thought of themselves mainly in terms of future salary-earners and as competing with men in the professions, which were (thanks largely to them) gradually opened to women. They sometimes seem, to one of my generation, to have overstressed the incompatibility between the intellectual and biological sides of women's lives. Or, as we owe them so much, should we perhaps say instead that they were more willing to sacrifice the biological aspects of womanhood than we are?[101]

Reminiscent of Hubback's words Sharon, who left school in the early 1960s, said her teachers acted as 'anti-role models' because she considered them to be 'a lot of rather dingy spinsters.' She recalled how she had resolved that, 'I'm not going to be like her. I'm going to get married. I don't want to be like her.'[102] Moreover, these attitudes were slow to change. Tara left school ten years later in the early 1970s but recalled how unmarried teachers were still often regarded with pity: '"Poor Miss So-and-so. Maybe her fiancé died in the war, maybe that's why she's a spinster." It was not, "Lucky Miss So-and-so. She's earning a very good wage and has got loads of freedom".'[103] Women were not seeking role models who rejected a woman's traditional role as wife and mother, but instead those who offered an example where family and career could be successfully combined. For the group of Somerville women interviewed for this study their most admired figure was Janet Vaughan, the College Principal. The interviewees held her in esteem because she managed to combine an academic career with marriage and motherhood.[104] Camilla attended Somerville in the late 1950s and thought Janet Vaughan was 'fantastic'. The weight she placed on Janet Vaughan's domesticity was seen in an anecdote she told about seeing 'the nappies hanging out outside the principal's lodgings' when her grandchildren came to stay, which Camilla felt highlighted the maternal side of Janet Vaughan's personality.[105]

Several of the women who were interviewed spoke of their desire to have children, but also to continue working after their children were born. They were aware, however, that it would be a fight to do so. Monika was an undergraduate and postgraduate at Oxford in the late 1940s and early

1950s. When asked whether university-educated women were expected to have careers she replied, 'it wasn't very easy in the 1950s for people to do that. So the expectation wasn't there. But the personal expectation was there, and my husband's support was very strong.'[106] Yvonne had her first three children in her late teens and early twenties, as soon as she left school. At first she was content to be a full-time mother, but recalled how when they were school age she realised, 'I'd got to go to university, I really needed to do something.'[107] While Yvonne did not become conscious of her need to have a career until after her children were born, Georgie always knew she wanted to be a teacher. Indeed one of the reasons why she married her husband was because he understood how important this was to her. 'I had quite a lot of boyfriends as well as him … I had one who said, "Marry me, and then you don't need to be a teacher", I thought, "You don't understand me, I am a teacher, first and foremost", and my husband never ever tried to stop me teaching, quite the reverse he was totally supportive of me.'[108] It was not only educated middle-class women who wanted to pursue careers. Enid grew up in Benson and left school at fourteen. She had her first baby at eighteen in 1943. Like Yvonne, it was after she had her children that Enid felt the desire to pursue a new interest and so she and her husband bought a shop which she managed.[109] Similarly Tina started to question her life when her three children, born between 1964 and 1971, started school, concluding that, 'I haven't done anything with my life, and I want to sort of do something.'[110] Work outside the home was also valued for the financial independence it brought. Doris, Tina's sister-in-law, had two children in the early 1960s but worked throughout their childhood, usually in part-time domestic work. Unlike more educated women who valued employment because it brought intellectual stimulation, Doris prized the financial independence that work brought. She said, 'it's just nice to have that little bit which is mine sort of thing. And if I want something I don't have to ask [my husband] if I can have it, I can get it myself.'[111] Indeed this was a common attitude. A Jamaican woman in London interviewed by Nancy Foner in the early 1970s stated: 'Here you work for yourself. In this country we do as we like. I have my own pay packet and don't wait on my husband for money.'[112]

There were women who did report that they went on to have interesting and successful careers from which they took great satisfaction on returning to the labour market. It is also noteworthy that women who felt they had done poorly at school and in their pre-marriage careers were amongst those who felt they had accomplished the most. Enid left school at fourteen in 1939 and Tina left school at fifteen in 1959. Both had only worked in temporary, low-skilled jobs for a few years before marrying at eighteen. However, as noted above, Enid subsequently ran her own shop, and Tina had her own business.[113] A small number of Oxfordshire respondents who were older mothers and did not have their children until they were in their thirties, and as a result had worked for fifteen or so years before having children, felt they had already achieved all they could in their careers and were happy to now give priority to motherhood. For example Cassie had worked as a civil servant in the War Office, which delayed marriage and motherhood for her. Although she had enjoyed the work she was relieved when the chance to start a family finally came and she had her first child aged thirty-three in 1946.[114] Ruby worked as a dispenser in the surgery in Benson and was happy to leave work when she had her first and much longed for baby in 1972 at the age of thirty-two.[115] Finally, the group of women in Oxfordshire whose accounts indicated the greatest feeling of success in combining work and motherhood were school teachers. It seems likely that several factors were at work here to produce their satisfaction, but it was surely significant that teaching was presented in popular imagery as a profession that could be combined with motherhood. Indeed some women embarked on teaching as a second career after their children were born precisely because they felt it was 'family friendly'. School working hours and holidays meant that difficulties in providing childcare, at least for school age children, were reduced. For instance Olive, who returned to teaching when her youngest child started school, recalled that the only day when she was not available at home was staff inset days, when her eldest daughter babysat her younger brother.[116] There was little social disapproval of women teachers because teaching, particularly primary school teaching, was constructed as a female profession. Consequently there was less conflict for women who taught than those engaged in many other occupations between their identities as mothers and workers.

In her study of two thousand male and female graduates of the late 1930s, Carol Dyhouse found the women who wrote most confidently about the ways in which they had combined child-rearing with professional work were married to successful professional men, whom they described as having been supportive of their careers, and co-operative in domestic arrangements.[117] The fact these couples could also afford childcare must have been important. Both Hannah and her husband had successful academic careers. Hannah recalled that her daughter 'was born in 1952 and I was determined to go straight on, in fact I took six weeks off and went back into the Physiology Department … and the way we managed is that we had au pair girls living-in and [my husband] agreed to completely share looking after her.' However, even when husbands took an equal part in child-rearing compromises still had to be made. When asked if she felt having children affected her career Hannah answered: 'Oh yes, I mean certainly, certainly. As I say they were the centre of my life and I didn't, for instance, I didn't think of going on sabbatical leave abroad, I didn't travel to conferences until they were much older, yes. But that applied to both of us ... I mean we sacrificed, we went very much more slowly than we would have done otherwise.'[118] Hannah and her husband had to be prepared for their careers to advance at a reduced pace in order to successfully combine work and parenthood. Moreover while many interviewees described their husbands as helpful, it was rare for them to take an equal share in housework and childcare and these women had to find other strategies.

Indeed women reported the many difficulties that working mothers faced. Janice enjoyed an academic career in Oxford, but felt that she was unusual, asserting: 'No it was very rare to be a working mother even in Oxford. You needed to have money.'[119] Molly, an Oxford graduate, also discussed the hurdles that existed for women in her account of why she did not return to full-time work. It is interesting that rather than recalling this as an experience personal to her, she defined it as the common experience for women at the time:

> It always seemed such a big expense. So unless you were earning quite a bit it didn't work out. So you would just get a job for hours when they were at school. I mean I did try at one time doing something in the evenings when my husband would be there with the children, but only after they were in bed. I would always be there when they'd come home from school to put them to bed, that sort of thing. So it didn't, we weren't the sort of couple who were equally sharing. And talking to people, other people my age, you know they quite often say that the husbands weren't as helpful as they probably became later on. And you felt it was really difficult to get more training and have a job. I mean I once wanted, well right away really, I wanted to do some other courses and different things and it was, 'Who's going to look after the children if you're doing that?'[120]

Amanda, who was a nurse, reported that her husband was a hindrance rather than a help to her career ambitions. Before she had her first child in the mid-1960s she had 'wanted to do health visiting ... I was due to do my degree, but my husband wasn't keen ... cos I had to be resident or something. And I sort of, I don't why, but I sort of agreed not to do it, which was crazy.'[121] Similarly Tasha, who had her children in the 1970s, said that her husband 'had the view that his own career was important and nothing was allowed to disrupt his career. So there was no way he was going to [help].[122]

However, even with supportive husbands the perceived hardships of combining work and motherhood dissuaded women from trying. Fiona described how it would have been physically impossible for her to combine work and motherhood when her children were young: 'There was no question of being able to work, absolutely no question. I mean I had thought there might be. But there was no formal childcare to be had anyway … And actually when it came to it I felt so tired you know with a new baby and getting up at night, and broken nights and that sort of thing. I don't think I could possibly have managed it.'[123] Ellen initially continued at work as a researcher when her first child was born in the late 1970s but it also proved physically difficult. 'I thought oh I'm going to be at home all day, I can do this, that and the other, I'll be out in the garden, but I couldn't even do what I had done, what I was doing when I was at work full time once I'd got this baby that was so demanding … So it was, you know, a big change.'[124] Such feelings were common nationwide. When asked if she considered going back to work after her first baby was born in 1955 Mrs Barlow, who lived in Barrow, Lancashire, said, 'No I didn't, not at all, no. No I don't think I could have done. I don't think I could have coped, they are very overwhelming, the first one.'[125]

Mothers who did try to pursue careers also experienced significant discrimination in the workplace. Hannah was an academic at Oxford University. Initially a research assistant she later became a university lecturer. When asked whether the university was sympathetic to women with children she emphatically answered, 'Oh totally no. No. In fact in 1956 the head of department said to me that I had to leave … he said, "You have a husband and children, I don't think you should be here," and he threw me out.' She was only able to resume her position when there was a change in personnel.[126] Kelly reported the prejudice she faced as a lecturer at Manchester University in the 1960s and 1970s. She declared, 'There was a great deal of discrimination in Manchester. I didn't realise how extensive it was, I was discriminated in payment, I was discriminated in every respect, and in promotion, and I intensely objected to that.'[127] This inequity was not limited to academics. As a civil servant Ivy had to cease work upon her marriage in 1946. Although she was later allowed to return to her position when the marriage bar was removed, she became pregnant soon after and again had to leave.[128] Olive was a teacher and should have stopped work when she married but was allowed to carry on due to the shortage of men in wartime. However she said, 'I can always remember them saying, "We shall have to examine you every so often to see that you're still fit enough to teach."[129] Sarah was also a teacher. She and her husband moved from Leeds to Oxford because married women were not allowed to teach in Leeds but were in Oxford due to the different rules of the two authorities.[130]

Increasingly women were expected to give up work on pregnancy rather than marriage, but conventions were still strictly adhered to. Tania worked as a cashier in a cinema and explained that she gave up work when she had her first child in the early 1950s because 'once you became pregnant, it was basically you gave up work. They didn't want to know you then.'[131] Patsy worked at the Children's Department in Oxford when she had her first child in 1970. She said: 'in those days within six months you left work and, of course you couldn't get your job back, you couldn't go back, you left didn't you.'[132] The situation for women workers did improve as the period progressed. The campaign for equal pay had been ongoing throughout the post-war period. However it was not until 1970 that comprehensive legislation in the form of the Equal Pay Act was steered through Parliament by the then Secretary of State for Employment Barbara Castle. The Act entitled women to equal pay for like work (although it was not implemented until 1975). The Sex Discrimination Act was then passed in 1975 which made it unlawful to discriminate on grounds of sex in relation to employment, education and provision of services. The Employment Protection Act, also passed in 1975, gave employees a right to return to work, providing unpaid maternity leave for eleven weeks before the birth and twenty-nine weeks after. It became automatically unfair to dismiss an employee on grounds of pregnancy. Nonetheless, despite such legislation discrimination in the workplace remained routine. While the Equal Pay Act did effect some narrowing of the pay gap, men continued to be paid more than women. Heather Joshi states that in 1978 there was an unexplained excess in men's pay over women's, which was about 30 percent for the average thirty-two-year-old employee.[133] Women's experiences reflected these trends. Jean left school at eighteen and went to work for a bank in the late 1970s. She said:

> It was dire. I only lasted nine months. I mean the thing then you quickly learnt that men would get ahead and women didn't. I joined at the same time as a man. He went straight onto the tills and I was shoved in this room out the back. His was seen as obviously a more prestigious job than mine. I was just what was called a REN clerk, which meant I was processing work, and he was being trained. We both did the day release course but it was just obvious from the start that he was going to get on faster than I did. Then I changed branches and the second branch I worked at there was a girl ... who was doing security, and she'd

been doing the job I don't know how many – six months, a year – in a temporary capacity because the last man had left, and then she was told that she couldn't be given the promotion to do that job permanently. A man was coming in to do it. I thought this is ridiculous. There's no point wasting my time here.[134]

Moreover while the earnings gap for women in full-time work did narrow substantially in the years between 1970 and 2000, this has not been the case for women in part-time work. The relative pay of women in full-time work compared to men rose from 62 to 85 percent of hourly earnings. However, even in 2000 the hourly earnings of women working part time were only 59 percent of that earned by men working full time.[135]

There were also social and cultural expectations which reinforced the view that women with young children should not work. Siobhan remembered that when she and her husband applied for a mortgage in the late 1960s she was 'the one with the steady income … But the bank would not take my earnings into account at all. And in fact looking back on it, that was in fact, although it seemed sexist at the time, it was actually beneficial to the family because as one could only get a mortgage based on one salary, house prices were based on one salary.'[136] It is interesting that Siobhan felt this discrimination in some ways advantaged women. She thought that it freed them from having to work as families could live on one, namely the husband's, income. Viv left work when she had her first child in 1968. Like Siobhan she also talked about the continuing acceptance at this time of the notion of a family wage paid to the man. She said: 'Most people at that time gave up work when they had children. One or two, I think there was a couple of people I knew who were nurses who carried on doing part time and things, but most people right that I knew didn't work. Yeah, we didn't have careers as such. I was a shorthand typist. But it was just assumed that you … were living on one lot of money.'[137] This belief that a woman's 'real' role was in the home while men went out to work meant that sometimes women were discouraged from pursuing careers at all. Pippa recalled visiting the Careers Office at University College London in the early 1980s. She said: 'I do remember very distinctly – I had done, you know, got a first in my first degree and then a distinction in my MA and such, it wasn't as if I was failing academically – this career, the female career's officer saying to me I should go home. I should go home and have babies first. And I was really shocked by that.'[138] Moreover the part-time nature of many women's work meant their terms of employment were poor. Martha had three children in 1969, 1971 and 1973. She took a part-time job as an alumni officer in an Oxford college in the 1980s. It had previously been one of Oxford's women's colleges. While she enjoyed the work, she felt the college was a poor employer as she was kept at a low grade and was paid for too few hours to gain a pension. She recalled hearing the college's 'treasurer and a don talking about recruiting somebody for the crèche. And they said, I mean I was standing there it was really awful they could feel so unashamed. But they said, "I think we'll have to get a married woman, because we can't afford to pay anybody who's actually wanting to make her own living." And if you think that that's an institution dedicated to women's education. It's not right.'[139]

The difficulties for mothers in the 2000s who endeavoured to combine paid work with child-rearing were also frequently referred to by interviewees of all classes, educational backgrounds, localities and ages. Some women spoke admiringly of those who did manage. Hilda said, 'I have great admiration for these people that have a career, whether it is a very high flying one or a very mundane one, that have a young family and go to work with babies.'[140] Similarly Tina spoke positively about women's growing autonomy: 'I think we were more independent [than her mother's generation], but I think today they're more independent.' However she also discussed how these increased opportunities for women were not without their consequences. She contrasted the life of her mother-in-law, who she felt was confined to the home 'twenty-four seven really', with women of the 2000s who have the chance to both raise families and pursue careers:

> I feel sorry for career women, because you think when's the right time to give up, and who's going to step into my shoes, and will I be able to get back onto the ladder again? So I think although there's a lot more opportunities for women I think it's still very scary and I think it's quite frightening. Cos before, because I'd had my children young I didn't feel I'd had to give much up, and I did what I wanted after … But I think for career women it's very hard to give up something. When you've got to a certain standard in life and you've got to the same level as a man. There comes a time when you've only got so many eggs and you've only got so many years to breed children. And I think that's a bit unfair and I don't really know what the answer is.[141]

Indeed several women made the same point as Tina, namely that it must be hard for women to leave long-established careers. For example Sharon had been happy to abandon her PhD and become a full-time mother, but felt 'if you've actually got an interesting job, to leave it for years and years is not a good idea, and so … to me the compromise would be to keep your foot in the labour market, to keep your job going, but not work full time … But to have kids and work full time and never see them, what's the point of it really? But some people are caught in that.'[142]

Enid thought that women of the 2000s had been brought up with higher expectations of their professional lives than when she was growing up in the 1920 and 1930s:

> [They] need more these days than what we did, we didn't know any different but they've had so much by the time they get married haven't they? You know a young person today, by the time she starts a family, she's had far more out of life than I did, we'd had nothing really, so there was nothing to give up. You see you know no different … you hadn't had money, cos you hadn't earned big money. But if you've a good job and it's an interesting job and you love it, and then you're going to be at home all day, and you're going to miss all that money, it takes a lot of thinking about, it's a lot to give up.[143]

Enid's suggestion that it was harder for these women to forego their incomes than it had been for her generation was also an issue that many of the Oxfordshire respondents commented upon. Bethany thought that 'now with the cost of housing … people just can't afford not to go out to work.'[144] She believed that this dual-income came at a price with women losing the 'more leisurely' life she had enjoyed. Gloria also lamented that couples in the 2000s felt they could not manage without the wife's earnings; she thought working mothers 'miss an awful lot.'[145] Lindsay explained that she felt this situation must be especially hard for those women who do not even like their jobs, stating: 'I suppose the pattern which there is now, is simply that it's the norm for women to go back to work because they'll be in dire trouble if they don't, the need to work is being hung over women as a threat, and it seems to me that women who have not got satisfactory jobs, I think the pressures must be appalling.'[146]

The overwhelming impression that emerged from the interviewees was that the women were rather ambivalent about the changes that had occurred over the half century. For example Shula was clearly trying to reconcile her mixed opinions on the subject as she spoke. Comparing her own and her daughter's experiences she said:

> See people think you're a bit weird I think sometimes, you know, what about your career? Well people didn't used to bother about those things quite as much years ago and I think people are more protective of their careers now. I think it's a good thing for women. I'm not saying [pause]. I mean to be aware [of] their careers and I think there should be equality in the structure for women. But I don't think, I mean I don't think the children have suffered. It's just been different. And I … and my friends who were like me had time out, we feel privileged. We feel as we were really lucky. And it was, you had that freedom which I don't think they have now because I mean they had, like everybody else they

had such a high mortgage that she [her daughter] needed to contribute. And you know this is the way it is, but everybody's doing it now so it's, I don't know whether it's right or wrong but it's just different really.[147]

The interviewees felt that both full-time work and full-time motherhood could be stressful for women. Moreover they were not sure if there were any easy solutions to the problems they felt existed for mothers of the 2000s.

One area the Oxfordshire interviewees did believe could be improved, however, was the availability of part-time work for women. Indeed the provision of part-time employment was one of the areas they were most concerned to see progress in and felt strongly about. For example Bertha had returned to part-time teaching when her children, born in the early 1960s, were school age. She felt that working part time had enabled her to combine her work and home commitments but said, 'I don't think I'd be able to cope full time, I really don't. I don't know how these mums do it. They must do somehow. I mean I feel quite sorry for people really who have to, you know, well I can understand them wanting to keep their careers going but I think it's an awful lot of stress.'[148] Ellen, also a supporter of part-time work, explained her stance:

> I've always been a great advocate of part-time work for mothers, really. Because it gives you an interest outside, and brings you some income. I think we've got a very bad situation in this country, where work tends to be very all or nothing, certainly from a financial point of view. If you've got a full-time job you get well paid, but you get worked off your feet and not a lot of time for yourself and your family. If you have a part-time job you don't get paid anywhere near as well, by and large, and you feel a second-rate person in the workforce if you like. And I think that's a shame, I mean I think you ought to do more in the way of job-share. I think it's coming gradually, but we ought to do more of it really. So that people get the best of both worlds.[149]

Women like Ellen were not being conservative or reactionary in their attitudes to women working outside the home, but argued that they should do so on their own terms. Many Oxfordshire respondents thought the increased opportunities for women had to some extent been negated by the increased pressures upon them. They concluded that mothers of the 2000s were suffering because they had simply adopted male patterns of work when what was needed was a revision of working conditions for everyone to provide a better work- and home-life balance.

Conclusions

The uncertainties and inconsistencies which existed in post-war thinking about the relationship of mothers to employment outside the home were reflected in the Oxfordshire interviewees' own experiences of work at this time. They expressed some ambivalence in their attitudes to paid work and whether they thought it was beneficial for women.[150] Women who did combine paid employment with motherhood described the difficulties in doing so, the worry and guilt it brought, and the discrimination and disapproval they faced. While many enjoyed working before their children were born, and some were pleased to return once their children reached school age, very few took a job when their children were under five, although there were signs this picture was beginning to change by the end of the century. However the reality of being a full-time mother was not always easy for women and they expressed conflicting feelings about their domestic role. While the interviewees did not recall the blissful, uncomplicated relationship with their babies that childcare literature and popular culture portrayed, neither did most remember the levels of discontent and unhappiness which characterised the stereotype of the dissatisfied mother that existed at the time. There was no evidence that educated women suffered in their adjustment to motherhood any more than their less-educated contemporaries; instead they may have simply been more capable of bringing their concerns into the public sphere.[151] Indeed writing in the early 1970s Lee Comer argued, 'The only difference between Suzanne Gail and the working class housewife – the pattern of their daily lives is almost identical anyway – is that she has articulated what they know and feel.'[152] Motherhood was a contradictory experience for many women, bringing pleasure and enjoyment, but also feelings of loneliness and constraint.[153]

The theme of independence was also a prominent feature of women's accounts of their attitudes towards work inside and outside the home. Irrespective of their class or educational background the interviewees' narratives were united by this quest for autonomy. The Oxfordshire respondents were perhaps influenced by the discourses of second-wave feminism which prioritised women's ability to take control over their own lives. However there was a general belief that women achieved this autonomy in different ways and that these could also change during the course of their lives. For example many interviewees, particularly those from working-class backgrounds, talked of being keen to leave school to gain independence through work. They felt that work would offer status, socialisation into the adult role, and the right to determine their own lives. For those who felt that the reality of their work-life did not meet these aspirations, marriage and motherhood offered an alternative way of achieving these goals. They hoped to find freedom through being 'mistress' of their own household. However women also reported that they then sought independence, particularly financial independence, through paid work, most often once their children had reached school age. It is interesting that the Oxfordshire respondents characterised both work and motherhood as ways in which status could be gained for women in the post-war period. By the early 1970s it seems women were becoming increasingly doubtful about whether their domestic role alone could be sufficient to provide this approbation, and women who had children after this time felt compelled to stress they were more than full-time mothers. Those who did not return to work felt guilty for not doing so. However, it is clear from women's discussions of their daughters' generation that they were also uneasy about many of the changes taking place at the beginning of the twenty-first century. Interviewees were trying to reach conclusions during the course of their narratives about how women's roles as workers and mothers could be reconciled, but the overriding impression to be gained from the interviews was the real difficulties they found in doing so.

Notes

1 Gerry Holloway, *Women and Work in Britain since 1840* (London and New York: Routledge, 2005), pp. 186–7, 191 and 197.

2 See Alva Myrdal and Viola Klein, *Women's Two Roles* (London: Routledge and Kegan Paul, 1956), p. 149; Rosser and Harris, *Family and Social Change*, p. 208; Ann Oakley, *The Sociology of Housework* (Oxford: Martin Robertson, 1974), p. 77.

3 Richard Titmuss, *Essays on 'The Welfare State'* (London: Unwin, 1958), p. 93 and 102. Young and Willmott also detailed the difficulties that working, married women faced. Michael Young and Peter Willmott, *The Symmetrical Family: A Study of Work and Leisure in the London Region* (Harmondsworth: Penguin, 1975) p. 117. Tilly and Scott believe changes in the work patterns of married women observed by Titmuss were a continuum from pre-war trends. Louise Tilly and Joan Scott, *Women, Work and Family* (London and New York: Methuen, 1987), p. 3.

4 Gavron was primarily interested in working-class women, and Hubback in 'really intelligent girls'. Gavron, *Captive Wife*, pp. 146–8; Judith Hubback, *Wives Who Went to College* (London: Heinemann, 1957), pp. 12–13.

5 Committee on Higher Education, *Robbins Report* (London: HMSO, 1963), p. 66.

6 Dolly Smith Wilson, 'A new look at the affluent worker: the good working mother in post-war Britain', *Twentieth Century British History*, 17 (2006), 206–29, p. 225.

7 Jane Lewis, *Women in Britain since 1945* (Oxford: Blackwell, 1992), p. 92.

8 Jennifer Dale and Peggy Foster, *Feminists and State Welfare* (London: Routledge, 1986).

9 Webster, *Imagining Home*, p. 39.

10 Christopher Brocklebank-Fowler, Christopher Bland and Tim Farmer, *Commonwealth Immigration* (London: The Bow Group, 1965), p. 24.

11 Patterson, *Dark Strangers*, pp. 339–40.

12 Beverley Bryan, Stella Dadzie and Suzanne Scafe, *The Heart of the Race: Black Women's Lives in Britain* (London: Virago, 1985), p. 25.

13 Sara Connolly and Mary Gregory, 'Women and work since 1970', in Nicholas Crafts, Ian Gazley and Andrew Newell (eds), *Work and Pay in Twentieth-Century Britain* (Oxford: Oxford University Press, 2007), 142–77, p. 144.

14 Duncan Gallie, 'The labour force', in A.H. Halsey with J. Webb (eds), *Twentieth-Century British Social Trends* (Houndmills: Macmillan, 2000), 281–323, pp. 291–2.

15 Anne Mooney, 'Mother, teacher, nurse? How childminders define their role', in Julia Brannen and Peter Moss (eds), *Rethinking Children's Care* (Buckingham, Quebec: Open University Press, 2003), 131–45, p. 131.

16 Pat Thane, 'Women since 1945', in Paul Johnson (ed.), *20th Century Britain* (Longman: London, 1994), 392–410, p. 407.

17 Gallie, 'The labour force', p. 296.

18 Labour Force Survey 2000 as cited in Connolly and Gregory, 'Women and work', p. 153.

19 Connolly and Gregory, 'Women and work', p. 153.

20 Thane, 'Women since 1945', p. 395 and 408; Carol Vincent, Stephen J. Ball and Soile Pietikainen, 'Metropolitan mothers: mothers, mothering and paid work', *Women's Studies International Forum*, 27 (2004) 571–87.

21 Shen Cheng and Keith Hoggart, 'Women's pay in English rural districts', *Geoforum*, 37 (2006) 287–306, p. 288.

22 Audrey Hunt, *A Survey of Women's Employment* (London: HMSO, 1968), p. 9.

23 Wendy Webster, '"Race", ethnicity and national identity', in Zweiniger-Bargielowska (ed.), *Women in Twentieth-Century Britain*, 292–306, pp. 297–8; Holloway, *Women and Work*, p. 209.

24 Foner, *Jamaica Farewell*, p. 69.

25 Martin and Roberts found a similar pattern. Jean Martin and Ceridwen Roberts, *Women and Employment: A Lifetime Perspective. The Report of the 1980 DE/OPCS Women and Employment Survey* (London: HMSO, 1984), p. 19.

26 Such views are also representative of national trends. Martin and Roberts, *Women and Employment*, p. 183.

27 Jessie Bernard, *The Future of Parenthood* (London: Calder and Boyars, 1975), p. 181.

28 H.M. Government, *Social Insurance and Allied Services (The Beveridge Report)* (London: HMSO, 1942), p. 52.

29 MOA, DR 2466, reply to September 1942 Directive.

30 Rose, NO12, p. 6.

31 *Ibid.*

32 Sheila Rowbotham, 'To be or not to be: the dilemmas of mothering', *Feminist Review*, 31 (1989), 82–93, p. 83.

33 Educated women's dissatisfaction with housewifery was not new to the 1960s, however. See Jenna Bailey, *Can Any Mother Help Me?* (London: Faber and Faber, 2007), p. 7.

34 Susan Gail, 'The housewife', in Ronald Fraser (ed.), *Work: Twenty Personal Accounts* (Harmondsworth: Penguin, 1968), 140–55, p. 144.

35 Similar descriptions are prevalent in Michelene Wander's collection of the life stories

of women who attended the first Women's Liberation conference in 1970. Michelene Wander (ed.), *Once a Feminist: Stories of a Generation* (London: Virago, 1990).

36 Ina Zweiniger-Bargielowska, 'Housewifery', in Zweiniger-Bargielowska (ed.), *Women in Twentieth-Century Britain*, 149–64, p. 162.

37 Louisa, SO5, p. 5.

38 Camilla, SO6, p. 17.

39 Lindsay, OX12, p. 10.

40 Hayley, NO5, p. 8.

41 Cherie, CO9, p. 11.

42 Hilda, BA11, p. 7.

43 Tina, BE3, p. 24.

44 Marilyn, BE13, p. 16.

45 Karen, SO4, pp. 24–5.

46 Sara Ruddick, *Maternal Thinking: Towards a Politics of Peace* (London: The Women's Press, 1990), p. 30.

47 Mary Georgina Boulton, *On Being a Mother: A Study of Women with Pre-School Children* (London: Tavistock Publications, 1983), pp. 53–4.

48 Barbie, TH4, p. 29.

49 Geraldine, CR9, p. 5.

50 Sharon, EW9, p. 7.

51 Grace, NO7, p. 5.

52 Cassie, NO6, p. 13.

53 J.M. Pahl and R.E. Pahl, *Managers and Their Wives: A Study of Career and Family Relationships in the Middle Class* (London: Allen Lane, 1971), p. 139.

54 Siobhan, BE1, p. 4.

55 Claire, NO1, p. 4.

56 ERA, Mrs W. 5. B., p. 80.

57 Ellen, EW3, p. 12.

58 Marilyn, BE13, p. 6.

59 Josie, TH6, p. 29.

60 Jemma, SA13, pp. 12–13.

61 MOA, T540, 35: Autumn Directive 1991, part 1 'Women and Men'.

62 Hermione, NO15, pp. 10–11.

63 Kaye, WY14, p. 6.

64 Patsy, BA15, pp. 14–15.

65 Sharon, EW9, p. 15.

66 Peggy, BA9, p. 14.

67 Lily, EW6, p. 7.

68 Rita, BA6, p. 3.

69 Verity Saifullah Kahn, 'Work and network', in Sandra Wallman (ed.), *Ethnicity at Work* (London and Basingtoke: Macmillan, 1979), 115–33, p. 116.

70 Edith H. Whetham, *The Agrarian History of England and Wales: Volume VIII, 1914–1939* (Cambridge: Cambridge University Press, 1978), p. 213.

71 Hilary Callan, 'Introduction', in Hilary Callan and Shirley Ardener (eds), *The Incorporated Wife* (London: Croom Helm, 1984), 1–26, p. 4.

72 Maud, WY4, p. 6.

73 Daisy, WY9, pp. 3, 4, and 10.

74 Alice, WY2, p. 14.

75 Zoe, BA16, p. 8.

76 Kathleen Kiernan, Jane Lewis and Hilary Land, *Lone Motherhood in Twentieth-Century Britain: From Footnote to Front Page* (Oxford: Oxford University Press, 1998), p. 277.

77 Jessica, BA8, p. 7.

78 Faith, SO12, p. 10.

79 Sophie, TH12, p. 20.

80 Hubback, *Wives Who Went to College*, p. 144.

81 Pat Thane, 'Girton graduates: earning and learning, 1920s-1980s', *Women's History Review*, 13 (2004), 349–58.

82 Jill, SO3, pp. 10–11.

83 Melanie, CO16, pp. 20–1.

84 Bryan *et al.*, *Heart of the Race*, p. 31.

85 Sadie, CO14, p. 19.

86 Hunt, *Women's Employment*, p. 15.

87 The women who had au pairs were Michelle, OX8; Megan, OX11; Yvonne, NO3; Juliet, NO9; Janice, NO11; Anna, NO13; Hannah, SO7; Phoebe, SO8; Bella, SO9; Ingrid, SO11.

88 Phoebe, SO8, p. 5.

89 Michelle, OX8, p. 9.

90 Bev, CR10, pp. 12–13.

91 Cynthia, WY12, pp. 9–10.

92 Alexa, SO13, p. 4.

93 Anna, NO13, pp. 10–11.

94 Bryan *et al.*, *Heart of the Race*, p. 30.

95 Christine Griffin, *Typical Girls: Young Women from School to the Job Market* (London: Routledge and Kegan Paul, 1985), p. 37.

96 Boyd, 'Mothers and daughters', p. 295. See also Henrietta O'Connor and John Goodwin, '"She wants to be like her mum?" Girls' experiences of the school-to-work transition in the 1960s', *Journal of Education and Work*, 17 (2004), 95–118.

97 Lindsay, OX12, p. 8.

98 Hannah, SO7, p. 11.

99 Anna, NO13, p. 6.

100 Sarah Aiston found similar results in her survey of women who graduated from Liverpool University between 1947 and 1979. Aiston, 'A maternal identity?', p. 417.

101 Hubback, *Wives Who Went to College*, pp. 25–6.

102 Sharon, EW9, p. 4.

103 Tara, SO15, p. 12.

104 Camilla, SO6, p. 17; Hannah, SO7, p. 13; Phoebe, SO8, p. 3; Bella, SO9, p. 3.

105 Camilla, SO6, p. 17.

106 Monika, SO1, p. 10.

107 Yvonne, NO3, p. 15.

108 Georgie, OX2, p. 7.

109 Enid, BE12, pp. 17–20.

110 Tina, BE3, p. 5.

111 Doris, BE2, p. 7.

112 Foner, *Jamaica Farewell*, p. 67.

113 Enid, BE12, pp. 17–20; Tina BE3, p. 5.
114 Cassie, NO6, p. 13.
115 Ruby, BE5, p. 10.
116 Olive, OX6, pp. 21–2.
117 Carol Dyhouse, 'Graduates, mothers and graduate mothers: family investment in higher education in twentieth-century England', *Gender and Education*, 14 (2002), 325–36, p. 333.
118 Hannah, SO7, p. 6.
119 Janice, NO11, p. 3.
120 Molly, NO4, pp. 13–14.
121 Amanda, BE9, p. 7.
122 Tasha, SO14, p. 6.
123 Fiona, BE10, p. 7.
124 Ellen, EW3, pp. 7–8.
125 ERA, Mrs B. 3. B., p. 37.
126 Hannah, SO7, p. 6.
127 Kelly, SO10, p. 9.
128 Ivy, BE4, p. 7.
129 Olive, OX6, pp. 9–10.
130 Sarah, NO2, pp. 13–14.
131 Tania, EW8, p. 5.
132 Patsy, BA15, p. 6.
133 Heather Joshi, 'The changing form of women's economic dependency', in Heather Joshi (ed.), *The Changing Population of Britain* (Oxford: Basil Blackwell, 1989), 157–76, p. 168.
134 Jean, EW14, pp. 2–3.
135 Connolly and Gregory, 'Women and work', p. 160.
136 Siobhan, BE1, p. 10.
137 Viv, EW12, p. 1.
138 Pippa, CO13, p. 7.
139 Martha, NO14, pp. 17–18.
140 Hilda, BA11, p. 7.
141 Tina, BE3, p. 37.
142 Sharon, EW9, p. 16.
143 Enid, BE12, p. 23.
144 Bethany, EW4, p. 20.
145 Gloria, BE14, p. 14.
146 Lindsay, OX12, p. 19.
147 Shula, BA12, p. 14.
148 Bertha, EW11, p. 11.
149 Ellen, EW3, pp. 12–13.
150 Dyhouse found a similar stance amongst the university graduates she questioned. Dyhouse, 'Graduates, mothers and graduate mothers', p. 333.
151 In the words of the Women's Group on Public Welfare they were a, 'small but vocal group of disgruntled housewives with professional training'. Women's Group on Public Welfare, *The Education and Training of Girls* (London: National Council of Social Service, 1962), p. 99.

152 Lee Comer, *Wedlocked Women* (Leeds: Feminist Books, 1974), p. 117.

153 These views were articulated by women around the country. See Thane, 'Girton graduates', p. 355; and Aiston, 'A maternal identity?', p. 425.

7

Breadwinners and homemakers: ideals of men and women in the family

D
ramatic changes occurred in conceptions of motherhood and the family over the second half of the twentieth century. During the 1950s femininity was viewed as intimately associated with domesticity, both by contemporaries and in subsequent accounts. The ideal mother figure at this time was a full-time homemaker dependent upon her breadwinner husband, with two, three or four children, living within a nuclear family. In his comparative study of the St Ebbe's and Barton regions of Oxford in the early 1950s, John Mogey stated: 'the family as we saw it consists of husband, wife, and their children. Occasional families may be called incomplete in that one parent is missing or that there have been no children. These are accepted as deviations from the normal state of the family, both by us as investigators and by our informants.'[1] Marriage was linked with children in popular understandings of the family.[2] The nuclear family was a norm in British culture and society and it was widely experienced. It was also assumed that the contemporary model of family life would strengthen and continue, and many of the women interviewed recalled holding this belief when they entered into marriage and motherhood. However, in reality significant changes occurred. While at the end of the century the majority of men and women still married, non-marriage was on the increase; those who still married did so later; and about one in three marriages ended in divorce.[3] Cohabitation had become increasingly common, usually preceding or following marriage but, for some couples, replacing marriage. The most visible outcome of these changing patterns of family formation and dissolution was the growth in the number and proportion of families headed by a lone parent. At the end of the century lone-parent families formed about 23 percent of all families with children in Britain and numbered about 1.7 million families with about 2.8 million children.[4] However, many of these lone parents went

on to form new partnerships, and in some cases to have more children. Patterns of family formation and dissolution also differed along the lines of class and ethnicity. For example, Caribbean men and women were less likely to be married or cohabiting than their white counterparts, while South Asians had higher rates of marriage and lower rates of cohabitation and marital breakdown.[5]

The relationship between ideals of the family presented in popular culture and the changing reality of people's lived experience is a complex one. Dennis Dean believes that in the desire for post-war reconstruction 'a strategy had been evolved to present the home and family as the agents of social cohesion in a world of chance. This was promoted in schools, cinemas and magazines.'[6] While it is difficult to quantify the ways in which films or magazines affected how women viewed themselves as mothers, they clearly did provide images of the ideal woman at this time. Marjorie Ferguson argues that women's magazines are pervasive in the extent to which they act as agents of socialisation – 'They tell women what to think and do about themselves, their lovers, husbands, parents, children, colleagues, neighbours or bosses.'[7] Magazines were a potent source of information for women on how a woman was expected to behave and what was considered 'good' mothering practice. However, the interviewees spoke ambivalently about popular culture. While some did report reading magazines and finding pleasure in doing so they were reluctant to admit that they were influenced by their content. For example Hayley said she subscribed to *Good Housekeeping*, but 'didn't take any notice of it really.'[8] The women liked to construct themselves as being unaffected by outside influences such as television and magazines. This ambivalent response seems to have been widespread and not just a result of the passing of time. A correspondent to a Mass Observation Directive in August 1943 on the question 'What book are you reading now?' replied: 'August number of "Housewife" – gosh awful. Crochet dinner mats. Appliqué for tots. Babycraft which should only be given by fully responsible people in actual contact with the "client".'[9] It is interesting that women who chose to read such magazines were nonetheless dismissive about their content. Their negative attitude may have been partly encouraged by the belief that women should not spend their time reading, watching television or listening to the radio as it meant they were reneging on their other duties as wife and mother. Tina remembered how her mother-in-law thought reading books and magazines was an 'absolute disgrace'. She said that if her husband came home and caught her reading he would complain to his mother that 'there was a sink full of washing-up and she had her head in a book.'[10] Nonetheless the interviewees did refer to portrayals of motherhood they saw in popular culture and held a clear image of how a mother was supposed to behave.

The expectations of the women interviewed did vary, however, according to when they were born. The oldest interviewee was born in 1912 and the youngest in 1962. The first child born to the interviewees was born in 1938 and the youngest child in 1996. More than one generation was therefore represented amongst the Oxfordshire respondents, as well as those who grew up before the war, and those who reached adulthood in the decades after. While substantial continuities were revealed in the interviewees' experiences, for example they all grew up with the assumption that motherhood was the adult woman's primary role, there were notable differences in the constructions of womanhood with which they were familiar. Describing girls who grew up in the 1930s, Pearl Jephcott noted how:

> Girls are accustomed to read in the evening paper such an advertisement as this: 'Girl age 14 wtd. for warehouse. Wages to commence 14/-'; and to see in the next column, 'Boy wanted; just left school, for warehouse – to commence 20/-wk.' They grew up in the knowledge that the boy does not have to do any housework, and that he has a better wage and more pocket money than they have and they accept its concomitant that the woman is an inferior person to the man. Many of them also accept the belief, still prevalent in a great many working-class families, that the woman's responsibility ends with the home.[11]

Twenty years later aspirations were changing. Referring to girls growing up in the 1950s, Liz Heron states: 'It seems also that as little girls we had a stronger sense of our possibilities than myths about the fifties allow. There was a general confidence in the air, and the wartime images of women's independence and competence at work lingered on well into the decade in the popular literature and the girls' comics of the day.'[12] However, despite these positive developments growing up a girl remained fraught with tensions and contradictions. Discussing the 1970s Sue Sharpe argued:

> their position has been changed and complicated by developments in women's role and attitudes. Like all girls, they confront a situation that is the product of historical change – embracing economic, technological and ideological developments. For instance middle class girls have come to accept and expect their right to work. They take their choice from a better selection of jobs than working class girls, but are still barred from easy entry to men's jobs or high positions. This may provide conflict for some girls, but other contradictions particularly affect working class girls. The idea of job involvement for example, which is so implicit in school careers teaching, clashes with the routine

and monotony of most jobs open to them. It clashes too with the deep investment that many of their own mothers have made in family life.[13]

As Judy Giles has shown, when women remember their lives they do so in ways that draw on cultural and linguistic resources available to a particular social group and a specific historical moment.[14] This chapter will explore the relationship between public conceptions of mother-hood and women's private understandings of their identities in order to examine how women's narratives were shaped by the ideals of mother-hood with which they were confronted. It will investigate the different understandings of the family that existed during the period 1945–2000 and how women related to these constructions in their accounts. It focuses on three models of family life that were dominant at the start of the period: the ideal of the 'nuclear family'; the associated figure of the 'homemaker wife'; and that of the 'breadwinner husband'. The chapter will consider how these ideals were refashioned in the context of the changing attitudes towards marriage and motherhood that occurred as the century progressed; whether women embraced or rejected these developments; and how they reassessed their own attitudes towards marriage, the family and motherhood with the passing of time.

The nuclear family

In the years immediately after the war there were clear ideals of how families were supposed to behave. Films ranging from *Brief Encounter* (1945), which dealt with a love affair between two middle-class strangers, to *Here Come the Huggetts* (1948), about working-class family life, demon-strated a concern with the state of marriage and the family in the aftermath of the war, but ultimately offered a conservative portrayal.[15] The ideology of companionate marriage and the nuclear family was also a dominant theme of women's magazines, with husbands presented as breadwinners and wives as homemakers.[16] Indeed despite the alarm about the state of the family which emerged in the last period of the war, it was still possible to think of lifelong monogamy as the norm and divorce as the compara-tively rare exception in the years that followed.[17] The women interviewed who reached adulthood in the late 1930s and 1940s spoke powerfully of the pressures they felt existed upon them to marry. Discussing the average marriage age of her contemporaries (she herself married at eighteen in 1943), Enid said: 'From the time you were eighteen onwards, eighteen, nineteen, twenty, most people were married. If you were about twenty-two and not married, I think they were a bit worried. Different now in't [*sic*] it?'[18] For girls from all class backgrounds marriage was viewed as an entrée into adulthood with the benefits, including a sexual relationship, that it would bring. Molly married at twenty in 1946 while she was still an undergraduate at Oxford University. When asked why she had decided to marry so young she replied: 'Well, that's to do with the days when you got married or nothing, you know, and I can remember that we very much wanted to go on holiday together and I remember saying to my parents, 'Well we're going on holiday together, so either you let us get married beforehand or we're going anyway!'[19] Ethel became pregnant when she was eighteen before she was married in 1937. When asked how her mother reacted when she told her of her pregnancy, Ethel replied that her mother was, 'Not very happy, no'. In contrast Ethel was not displeased to find she was pregnant as it meant that she 'had' to marry. Consequently she was able to leave home and her parents' authority, and also a job that she did not enjoy:

> Well we wanted to get married anyway, and even though I was only eighteen I was fed up with being cook, and well sort of in domestic service you're at everybody's beck and call whatever your position is, and I hated it. I loved cooking and having all the nice things to do but I didn't like being tied down. I liked being in the girl guides and all those kind of things, and so that was that. So I told her, 'Well now Mum, you're going to have to let me get married now aren't you?' [laughing]. That didn't go down very well.[20]

Ethel saw her pregnancy and subsequent marriage as offering independence rather than worrying it would bring constraints. Marriage and motherhood were her dream of escape from an unhappy home and worklife.

Until the 1960s getting married was equated with having children. A number of the correspondents to a 1943 Mass Observation Directive which asked, 'How important do you think children are to family life?', answered that they thought children were essential.[21] A similar picture emerged amongst the Oxfordshire interviewees. Camilla married in 1960 and her daughter was 'there on my first wedding anniversary, she was a fortnight old'. She had two further children in 1963 and 1965. When asked if she had planned to have her children so quickly and close together, Camilla replied that she had just assumed when she married that children would follow. She stated: 'I mean obviously at the time if you got married you had children basically. This was the expectation. If you didn't it was either because you were pretty clever or you had a problem.'[22] Lisa married in 1959 and had four children between 1960 and 1967. There were eleven months between her wedding and her first baby. She explained that children were viewed as an integral part of marriage: 'one got married and one was going to have children you know.'[23] The Oxfordshire respondents said they actively intended to have children so soon after marriage rather than simply being resigned to it. Claire had her first daughter fifteen months after her marriage in 1959. In total she had six children over the course of the next twelve years. When asked if the children were planned, she emphatically asserted, 'Oh yes, we'd planned to have children as soon as we got married.'[24] Phyllis married at the end of the war in 1945 and had her first child the next year. She also answered that she and her husband had wanted to have a child straight away: 'Oh yes. Yes, yes, we did.'[25] It is impossible to know whether these women really had intended to have their children so soon after marriage, or if it resulted from ignorance or failed attempts to make use of contraception. However women's portrayal of themselves as wanting children quickly after they had married reflects the strength of the association in their minds between getting married and starting a family.

There appear to have been both class and regional differences in attitudes towards family planning, however. A number of Elizabeth Roberts' working-class Lancashire interviewees recalled how 'you just couldn't plan.'[26] In contrast the largely middle-class correspondents to a Mass Observation Directive on the subject of family planning in 1944 replied that they did.[27] Many of the Oxfordshire interviewees revealed that they entered marriage with an ideal family size in mind, with two or three children being commonly desired, even if this did not always work in practice. Ivy had her first baby in 1947 in Tunbridge Wells but had not intended to have children at all. She explained: 'of course you know contraception wasn't the efficient thing it is these days, and there was something issued by the Kent County Council public health department, [they] issued something called Volpar, which was nothing more than a gel, a lubricant really, but Volpar, "voluntary parenthood". And there were a lot of Volpar babies.'[28] In contrast Oxford was advanced in the provision of birth control advice. A pioneering group of doctors with an interest in the provision of birth control opened a birth control clinic in Oxford in 1926 under the auspices of the Oxford Family Welfare Association. The nearest similar clinics were as far away as Bristol and Birmingham; there were none in either Oxfordshire or Berkshire.[29] Although women in Oxford were fortunate to have benefited from the provision of such a clinic, they did not always speak appreciatively of it. Madge, who attended the clinic in the early 1940s, described it as being 'a little tiny cottage in Jericho, well it was like a slum in those days and they had this little tiny cottage, and I went in and there were, well they seemed like elderly ladies to me, like midwives, I went up a rickety staircase and they'd got no bed, no anything, they just, everything had to be done squatting down, and it was terrible.'[30] In oral history interviews with men and women from Oxford, Hertfordshire, south Wales and Blackburn about the middle decades of the century Kate Fisher found there were significant class and regional differences in the birth control practices couples employed. Urban, industrial, working-class areas revealed a much higher dominance of withdrawal than middle-class suburban regions where condoms, caps and pessaries were more often used. Nonetheless Fisher argues that in all areas traditional methods of birth control, namely coitus interruptus, abstinence and abortion, continued to be important alongside the rise of appliance methods.[31]

Birth control was both more accessible and reliable by the end of the century. The introduction of the contraceptive pill was a turning point. First introduced in late 1961, by 1964 an estimated 480,000 women were taking the drug. Hera Cook argues the pill was novel in two ways. Firstly, it had very high effectiveness, and secondly it was under female control.[32] Then in 1967 abortion was legalised and local authorities were empowered to provide family planning advice and contraceptives free of charge. As a result women's plans surrounding their optimum family size were more often realised. For example, when asked if she always knew how many children she wanted to have Jean (whose children were born in 1987 and 1990) said: 'Yes, absolutely. Two fit in the car, you know, holidays are all catered for families with two adults and two children. It's very sensible.'[33] However for many women the ultimate plan was to have a girl and a boy, and this still relied on luck. Discussing her ideal family, Margaret, who in actuality had two sons, said: 'I was going to have two but they were going to be a boy and a girl. Slipped up there.'[34] Similarly Kim's dream was to mirror her own childhood experience: 'there would be two of us, two children ... and preferably a girl and a boy, but we didn't [manage that], but the two children was optimal.'[35] There remained couples who were less exact in their planning though. When asked if she had known how many children she wanted to have, Carmel, who had three children in 1977, 1982 and 1985, replied: 'Well, we had sort of ideas, but we're Catholics you see, so it was a bit more kind of, well we left it a bit more open than perhaps other couples did.'[36]

While fertility may have become easier to control, however, infertility was not. Medical advances were being made – Louise Brown, the world's first baby to have been conceived by in vitro fertilisation, was born in 1978. Bev felt she had benefitted from such developments. She had suffered from a series of seventeen miscarriages before her two children were born in 1987 and 1990 and said, 'I am grateful for science.'[37]

However many couples still suffered from infertility. Shirley's first baby was born in 1978, after a traumatic delivery. She was unable to conceive again and her second child was adopted.[38] Moreover even at the end of the century infertility treatments were often unpleasant and their success rates remained relatively low.[39]

One of the reasons for women enduring fertility treatments may have been their desire not to have an only child.[40] Interviewees who had been only children were particularly adamant that they did not want to have just one child themselves. Marilyn, Hope and Nancy all stated that they had not minded how many children they had as long as it was more than one; they had been only children and did not want to repeat this.[41] Glenda thought that her contemporaries were consciously trying to break with the past and were 'a generation in revolt against the cult of the only child.'[42] These women felt the ideal family size for their own parents had been very different, with one child being accepted in the inter-war period (particularly amongst the middle classes although not exclusively so). Rose was an only child born in 1932. She said that that in the 1930s 'only children were very common.'[43] But only children were not simply a preserve of the 1930s. Sarah was an only child born in 1912. She felt only children were increasingly prevalent throughout her childhood because she 'grew up in the age when cars were just coming in and you had one baby and a baby Austin you see.'[44] Valerie was an only child born in 1947. She said her father was 'pretty horrified' when she was expecting her second child, as he believed that having one child was the right thing to do.[45] Those women who had only children recalled being aware this was considered unusual. Lynne had her only son in 1973. She said: 'you know there was definitely sort of, [pause] there was a strangeness about it, I'm thinking about people's attitudes in Oxford then where we lived. Whereas now I can imagine people might well think one child is fine and not sort of question it, I think there were a few other mums who sort of thought, "Are you going to have another one? If not, why not?".'[46] By the end of the century a new trend was emerging though. Educated, middle-class women were marrying and having their children later which often meant their completed families were smaller. Women who had prioritised their careers during their twenties and thirties and waited until their late thirties and forties before deciding to have children could find that they were then only able to have one child. For example, when asked if it was her choice to have just one child Cynthia, who had her only daughter in 1993, replied, 'Oh no, I would have been happy – in fact I'm sorry only to have one really. I certainly would have liked to have had two, but given that I didn't actually, I was thirty-six I think when [my daughter] was born. There was a sense in which I'd left it too late then so, so I'm sorry to only have [one] really.'[47] However a demanding work-life could also mean that these women wanted a small family. Alexa also had her only daughter in 1993 in her early forties. While in practice she said she had left it too late to have more children, unlike Cynthia she did not regret this decision. Alexa doubted whether she could have really accommodated another child with her academic career.[48]

However, while a one child family was not seen as ideal, society also held definite ideas about the maximum size a family should be. Penelope Mortimer discussed the subject in her novel *The Pumpkin Eater* (published in 1962). Mortimer's unnamed heroine has an ever-larger family, which everyone – her parents, her husband, and her doctors – see as a problem and leads to her being aborted and sterilised.[49] Large families were viewed as deviating from accepted (English) norms. For example Ann Phoenix has shown how non-indigenous women were stereotyped as having too many children with more health education leaflets on family planning translated into Asian languages than on any other health issue.[50] The Oxfordshire interviewees recalled similar attitudes. Violet had six children between 1953 and 1965. When asked if she had always wanted to have a big family she answered, 'No I think, when we used to talk as children, "Oh I'm going to have three", you know. But no, my mother – there was only two, my sister and I – my mother was sort of shocked.'[51] Ellen had six children between 1975 and 1985. Her mother, Ivy, was disapproving. Discussing large families Ivy said, 'It's so irresponsible isn't it? Just can't understand it, still can't. Well Ellen of course, our Ellen with her six kids has got the answer to all of this.'[52] While Ellen did not say that her mother had made such comments to her directly she was aware of a general social disapproval and recalled that she got 'some quite funny looks when I went on to have my fifth child.' She felt that having four children would have been acceptable but she faced condemnation for having more. She gave the example of a neighbour who had said to her, 'Goodness me why do you want some more?'[53] This social disapproval extended to official practice. Claire had six children between 1960 and 1972. She explained how after her last child was born the staff at the hospital 'came and lectured me on birth control.'[54]

The dominance of the ideal of the nuclear family was also visible when women gave accounts of unmarried mothers. The uncertainty with which women told these stories indicates that they were unsure about the most appropriate way to do so. The interviewees' difficulties may have been a result of the taboo that surrounded the subject of unmarried motherhood for much of the second half of the twentieth century and, indeed, the ways in which single motherhood can still be seen as stigmatised at the beginning of the twenty-first century. Women were aware that legal as well as social sanctions applied to unmarried mothers. For example, referring to the 1940s Sarah said 'you couldn't afford to get pregnant if you weren't married because there wasn't this cosseting of the one parent family as there is these days. You got no maternity, no allowances, you were just a destitute woman really. I mean you were relying on charity if you had a baby before … marriage.'[55] Also discussing the 1940s Tilly recalled that to become pregnant when not married at this time was a fate worse than death. Indeed she thought that attitudes towards unmarried mothers had been one of the greatest transformations seen over the second half of the century.[56] Unmarried motherhood was not an entirely new phenomenon, though. Eunice was born in 1928 in West Sussex. An only child, she said her mother was the original unmarried mother. While her mother did go on to marry in later life, and Eunice remained close to her, Eunice said she was largely brought up by her grandmother, indicating the difficulties that her mother faced.[57] Furthermore, the change in attitudes towards unmarried mothers was a gradual one. Dawn and Bonnie were both teenagers in the late 1960s and grew up in London. They remembered what happened when neighbours they knew had got pregnant outside of marriage. The mother of the girl Dawn knew came to apologise to Dawn's mother for bringing down the reputation of the area.[58] Bonnie's friend was sent by her mother to apologise in person.[59] In a similar vein Ivy told an anecdote of a girl who went to the same Kent grammar school as her daughter in the 1960s. 'She was about seventeen and she got herself pregnant, not married. This was you know, wasn't done. So [her mother] stood by her, I think she had the baby at home. But it was the sort of thing that was kept hush-hush. Especially in that sort of home.'[60] Her phrase 'that sort of home' is revealing as it indicates how she intertwined discourses of class and gender in her narrative. Ivy felt it was particularly shocking for a 'respectable' middle-class girl to have become pregnant. The age of the mother seemed to be a factor in determining the interviewees' response to single parenthood, though, with teenage pregnancies evoking more sympathy.[61] Recalling being pregnant with her first son in 1970 Siobhan said, 'the person I felt sorriest for when I'd had my baby was actually one of my students from the poly', who was pregnant at the same time. She said her student 'was only a little girl of sixteen' who 'hadn't got a husband and she was on her own'. The image of this girl's plight had remained with Siobhan and she 'often wondered how she managed.'[62]

In the immediate post-war decades the assumption remained that women needed husbands to support them and their children and this meant that many entered into marriage for pragmatic reasons. Working-class women in particular thought it would offer them security. A Mass Observation survey of 100 people about marriage conducted in 1947 found that in the working-class London areas of Poplar, Bermondseay and Shoreditch the women said they married to have a home considerably more often than that they married for love. In the middle-class areas of Hampstead, Chelsea and Marlybone, the emphasis was reversed.[63] However, marriage was often a gamble. Peggy married at eighteen in 1951. In the course of her interview she had explained that her husband was a poor 'provider' who would spend his wages in the pub rather than giving the money to her for the family's upkeep. Describing why she gave up smoking she said that after her husband's death her doctor told her, '"If you don't pack up those woodbines", he said, "You'll be joining him." I said, "I don't want to join him", I said, "I've only just got shot of him", that was it and I packed up my fags.' However, despite her own bad experience she went on to say, 'I believe in marriage'. Peggy was concerned that women of the 2000s were left facing instability and uncertainty in their family lives because they did not marry their partners. She stated: 'you can be living together perhaps a year and you'll have a fallout over the silliest thing [and] he'll be gone, you'll perhaps be left [with] three or four babies, but if you're married it gives you security.' Peggy's attitudes were probably influenced by the situation of her own daughter, who was not married to her partner, and about whom Peggy was clearly worried.[64] Peggy's views were not unrepresentative, with many of the older Oxfordshire respondents regretting the loss of the security of marriage. The value they assigned to marriage may also be the result of hindsight. In their sixties, seventies and eighties the companionship marriage provided was, perhaps, particularly significant to them. They worried their children would not reap the benefits of long marriages in later life that they felt they had enjoyed.

The older women who were interviewed spoke ambivalently about rising rates of cohabitation. Gloria expressed a great deal of uncertainty in her sometimes contradictory account of her daughter who cohabited with her partner in the 1980s and 'started the rot'. While she said 'it doesn't worry me', she later explained that at the time, 'I didn't think that was the right thing to do.' She indicated this was partly because she was anxious about the reaction of family members. 'Certainly my parents didn't think it was the right thing to do and my brothers weren't very happy with it either.'[65] However talking about her daughters cohabiting with their partners Tina explained that she felt she had 'put them off getting married'. While she said she did not explicitly tell her children not to marry, she did warn them men 'change when you got married'. She explained: 'I couldn't let them go through, into the lions' cage, without telling them how I really felt.' Tina herself had separated from her husband for a few years although they had subsequently reunited. While Tina 'always respected him and he's always respected me' she felt she 'just didn't want to be married.'[66] Amongst the younger women cohabitation was not uncommon although for most this was for a few years before marriage, or with a new partner after the breakdown of a previous marriage. Lynne lived together with her partner for several years in the late 1960s before marrying him in 1970. She said that this was 'quite pioneering in those days' and it 'was something which rather agitated my parents.'[67] Parental disapproval was a common theme in the interviewees' accounts of cohabitation. Pippa lived together with her future husband in the late 1970s but she hid this from her family because she did not think they would approve.[68] Tara described what happened when she told her mother she was living with her partner in the early 1980s: 'My mother was totally traumatised! Yeah, she was totally traumatised because I had a very strict religious upbringing and everything. And I think that was bound to be a problem at some stage. She was not at all happy about it.'[69] Some younger women also regretted the changes that had taken place, though. Pam was born in 1947 and had two children in the late 1970s. Discussing the changes that had occurred at the end of the century and why she thought there were 'problems', she said that in the past 'people stayed together', whereas, 'today it's all different. My parents stayed together, and [my husband] and I have been together for thirty-six years, but my niece isn't married and then my daughters live with their partners, but it just wasn't contemplated then.'[70]

The second half of the twentieth century also witnessed a rising divorce rate. Andrea was born in 1952 and had three children in the 1970s and 1980s. She commented on the changes that had taken place: 'I mean if you heard of divorce when I was a child, oh it was the scandal of the area. Whereas now it's not unusual at all. I think that's quite sad that it's got to that.'[71] While dramatic change only occurred after the 1969 Divorce Reform Act, divorce had been present in the lives of women in earlier decades too. Jessica got divorced in the 1940s after her husband left her. She thought that attitudes towards divorce had been one of the most remarkable transformations of the second half of the century. When she had divorced 'it was a very naughty and horrible thing to do, but now it's common, it's uncommon not to have been divorced isn't it?'[72] Camilla who married aged twenty-three in 1960 and Bethany who married at twenty-two in 1966 both thought there had been a generational change in people's opinions of divorce. They felt their contemporaries had been prepared to stay in marriages which may have been at times unhappy in the hope they could work through their difficulties. In contrast they thought the next generation were quicker to end their marriages. Like Andrea they were uncertain, however, whether this was a 'good thing'.[73] Some women were more positive about these developments, though. Carol had been married and divorced twice. Although she currently lived with a new partner, she said, 'I'm not marrying again'.[74] And Lindsay, who was born in 1935, thought that easier divorce was a great improvement and regretted that it had not been possible for her parents' generation. She said her parents were 'unhappy' to the extent that her she and her sister asked them why they did not divorce. She felt in the climate of the 2000s they would have done so thereby preventing the years of dissatisfaction in their marriage they both clearly faced.[75]

While women who had not experienced divorce seemed to feel that it had got 'easier' to divorce in the 1970s and 1980s, those women who had been through a divorce were less certain. They spoke of the social and financial consequences it brought. Moreover for some groups of women these penalties made the costs of divorce prohibitive. For instance Alison Shaw has shown how it was rare for Pakistani women in Oxford to even consider divorce at this time.[76] The families of divorced women could face many difficulties. Sophie and her husband divorced in 1980. She said she was the first person she knew to have been divorced and recalled how a child had said to her daughter that she would not play with her any more as she no longer had a daddy at home. Sophie also talked about the financial problems she faced.[77] Indeed financial hardship was mentioned by several of the women who got divorced. Amelia and her husband separated in the late 1970s when Amelia's son was three. She was left as the sole provider for the family and said that her salary was so low she could still qualify for supplementary benefit.[78] Edna married in the early 1960s and her only son was born in 1966. She and her first husband divorced after fourteen years. She then had to go out to work as a cleaner in some of the Oxford colleges to support the family. Edna then had a brief unhappy second marriage before she met and married her third husband in the early 1980s with whom she said she had been contentedly married ever since. While pleased she had eventually met her third husband Edna seemed somewhat embarrassed that she had been married three times and joked that she felt like Elizabeth Taylor.[79] Furthermore while after the 1969 Act it became legally easier to obtain a divorce the women who did divorce recalled how it was a still a hard decision to make. Tasha explained that she and her husband had a tense relationship after their children were born in the 1970s. The couple stayed together until the children reached adulthood when they eventually divorced but Tasha was unsure whether this had been the right decision or whether they should have separated earlier.[80] The interviewees therefore thought there had been both gains and losses for women due to the increasing prevalence of cohabitation and divorce. Many welcomed the independence it had brought women, particularly those with young children, as it offered the possibility of escape from unhappy marriages, but there were others who were not sure these changes were without costs. Eunice represented this ambivalence. She was born in 1928 and married at nineteen in 1947. Bemoaning the rising divorce rate she said that she felt couples in the 2000s were too quick to split up whereas those of her generation worked at marriage and stuck together. However she then added that she had herself divorced after thirty years of marriage and married again.[81]

Homemaker wives

Post-war society was founded upon the conception that a woman's principal role was in the home. Elizabeth Wilson argues that the state's designation of woman's vocation as motherhood was central to the purposes of welfarism.[82] William Beveridge's report on social insurance and allied services was highly influential and formed the basis of the welfare state legislation introduced by the 1945 Labour Government. Beveridge prescribed a restricted role for married women in the post-war world. He stated: 'The attitude of the housewife to gainful employment outside the home is not, and should not be, the same as that of a single woman. She has other duties.'[83] Beveridge conceived of society in terms of a male citizen as breadwinner with women and children as his dependants. While women were acknowledged as performing a 'vital unpaid service', it was taken for granted that 'the housewife's earnings in general are not a means of subsistence.'[84] It was expected this model applied to all women irrespective of their social background. Stephanie Spencer believes the Beveridge Report clearly presented 'women' as a universal grouping.[85] In the 1940s it was still assumed that wives only worked if their husbands failed in their duty to support them. Women who had married in the late 1930s and 1940s were familiar with such views. Mavis summed up the division of labour as she saw it during these years: 'In those days the men went out to work, and you just sort of stayed and looked after the babies.'[86] Sarah, who married at the start of the war, thought 'it was pretty well supposed that when you married in my day you didn't work anymore, that was it'. She told the story of a conversation she had with her neighbour which exemplified this state of affairs: 'I said to her, "Did you ever have a job?" and she said, "Oh no, my parents could afford to keep me", so she'd never had a job ever, and then she'd married and a husband was supposed to be able to support his wife; if she went out to work it was a disgrace.'[87] Similarly Juliet, who married in 1942, said: 'Before the war if wives worked it looked as if husbands couldn't support them. But even of my friends not many had actual jobs.'[88]

This ideal of the dependent wife was well-established in post-war culture. Women who worked when their children were young were either pitied, because it was assumed they would only do so if they did not have a husband who could provide for them, or condemned for jeopardising the health and happiness of their families. In a letter to the editor of *Woman* magazine in 1958, a reader wrote:

> One of our neighbours, a woman of middle-age, works not only by day, but also at night. 'How awful!' I exclaimed when I first heard this. 'It seems some people are never satisfied where money is concerned.' Then I hear that she supports a crippled husband and disabled son. She never gets more than three hours' sleep a night, and still manages to keep going in spite of this. I felt very remorseful. But is it pride that keeps such a deserving woman from asking for help?[89]

Likewise, the dominant and organising ideology of femininity in 1950s' advertisements was the mother as housewife, always wearing an apron, youngish, smiling brightly.[90] These representations of femininity were influential, and interviewees employed this image of the housewife when recollecting their experiences of motherhood nearly fifty years later. Glenda, who had two children in the 1950s, explained: 'we belonged to a generation that felt you ought to bring your children up and they should come in from school and smell fresh hot cakes cooking and have television with mummy and daddy.'[91] Also employing such images, Eve used the language of housewife as worker in her narrative, stating that, 'the housewife in those days, you sort of did your work in the morning, had your lunch, and husband came home for lunch so you'd got all that to do, it was really hard work, and then husband went back and you got the child ready, got the child in the pram and went out shopping and went to the park and met your friends and that was the life.'[92] Those women who grew up in the 1950s looked back on the decade as a time of idealised femininity. For example Melanie, who was born in 1944, remembered the cookbooks from the 1950s which required women to spend five hours preparing a recipe.[93] That they would have the time to do so reinforced the assumption that a woman's place was in the home.

However not all women identified with the images of womanhood presented in the adverts in such a positive way. A woman correspondent to a 1951 Mass Observation Directive on housework wrote, 'I like washing least. It is hard work in spite of the advertisements.'[94] A correspondent writing to the Mass Observation New Project fifty years later, reflecting back upon the 1950s and 1960s, expanded on the same theme:

> We certainly saw why serial programmes were called soaps, soap powder being the most widely advertised product, and ideal families were pictured using such products, with the stereotyped wife particularly in evidence with her whiter than white washing also feeding the family with meals incorporating Bisto gravy. Somehow, as a housewife, later a working wife/housewife, one's standards never came up to the TV ones, which seemed unrealistic.[95]

Similarly when discussing adverts Siobhan stated that they:

> all seemed very fairytale, which of course it is because advertising is always showing you the glamorous side of whatever it's trying to sell you … And life's not like that. One of my sisters … I think she's had a tough life emotionally. And I think she's always thought people's lives are like they are in advertisements. And therefore I think it's just been one long disappointment, and one long feeling of failure, because it's not like that. And I think you have to have an eye to reality, and you have to accept your own limitations as well. I think if you don't you end up being very unhappy.[96]

Deirdre thought advertising did 'a lot of harm' by creating a desire for consumer goods which were unaffordable for many people.[97] However while advertising may have made women regret the absence of goods, or feel pressure to obtain them, the impact that labour-saving devices had on women's lives cannot be understated. Their joy on obtaining their first washing-machine was a feature of several interviewees' narratives.[98]

By the 1960s the figure of the dependent wife was beginning to be challenged, as married women were increasingly participating in the labour force. Representations of the family and the role of women within it were also being modified. For instance Brian Braithwaite has noted that the magazine *Nova* was launched in 1965, which proclaimed to be 'The New Magazine for the New Kind of Woman'. That 'new kind of woman' was designated as intelligent, thinking and worldly. She would be well-educated, radical, sceptical and definitely not the typical reader of the woman's weeklies, with their mundane concentration on shopping and cooking.[99] Women reflected upon these changing understandings of the role of women in their accounts. Bethany was born and brought up in Wallingford, moving to nearby Preston Crowmarsh when she married in 1966. She thought that there was a divergence in attitudes between her friends and relatives who married in the 1960s and those who married in the 1970s. Divorce was far more common in the latter group. When asked why she thought this difference occurred she answered, 'I suppose a lot of people would say it's the swinging sixties, but I mean morals did perhaps go out, it was considered fashionable to be divorced and all these things, free sex or whatever, you know you were a bit boring if you weren't into those things.'[100] Emily married in 1962 when she was twenty-four and had three children by the age of twenty-nine. She recalled how she found herself at the end of the 1960s with a husband and three children, and feeling that the social changes of the decade had passed her by. Emily thought this may have been a common experience for women at this time and said 'it wouldn't surprise me if a lot of people didn't think that they suddenly woke up at the age of thirty and thought, "Mmm, there's a life ahead of us, there's things going on out there, this is the 1960s", you know because we were tied up in the 1960s giving birth when everyone else was having a cool time, I just I remember that so vividly you know the Beatles hitting the scene [and] suddenly the world opened.'[101] It is interesting that Emily used expressions made popular in the 1960s, such as 'cool' and 'scene', at this point in her narrative, demonstrating how the period encouraged her to change both how she viewed her life and how she articulated these feelings.

Interviewees recalled how they responded to the changes that they perceived were occurring from the late 1960s. Hannah thought the feminist movement in the late 1960s and 1970s was enormously important to women at that time. While she had always considered herself a feminist she found she was in an isolated position in the 1950s and early 1960s. She explained, 'I've been a feminist as far back as I can remember, a very strong sense about that I was entitled to everything that the boys were entitled to, but I have always lived in a largely male community, I mean you know the Physiology Department [at Oxford] for a long time there was only one other woman on the staff and I was the only married woman in the department.' Hannah had 'always fought for the rights of women and I've always tried to encourage my women students to expect more for themselves. What I found was many of them first of all lacked self-confidence, and secondly had much fewer aspirations than the boys, I mean for years, this is no longer so now, but at the interviews at entrance I used to say, "What do you expect do to with your life?" One said, "I'll work until I get married." I was absolutely staggered.' She believed it was the work of women themselves that had generated this change in attitudes and recalled being actively involved in the feminist movement. 'I belonged to … a group called the women tutors' group here in Oxford, and we agitated for maternity leave, for a change in language, for a great deal that has been achieved.'[102] It was not only educated middle-class women who supported feminist arguments. Tina left school at fifteen, married at eighteen and worked mainly as a cleaner when her children were young, although when they were adults she ran her own business. Throughout her narrative she advocated women's rights, for instance stating: 'As far as I'm concerned I'd give it all to women. I'd like women to do a lot more, myself.' Like Hannah, Tina also thought it was the efforts of women themselves which had led to the increased opportunities that now existed.[103]

A group of women interviewed had been members of OWL – Oxford Women's Liberation – and attended their local Women's Lib group in Cowley in the 1970s.[104] It is interesting that in the course of their discussion about the group they revealed different motivations for their membership. Amelia welcomed the social life it brought. She said that it enabled her to make new friends and gave another dimension to her life in addition to her home and work. She said the thing she valued most about the group was the opportunity it provided the women to share problems relating to their husbands and children.[105] In contrast Sheilagh stressed that the group had political aims and that they believed they could change things. Commenting on the four demands formulated at the initial Women's Liberation Conference held at Ruskin College, Oxford, in February 1970 (for equal pay; equal education and opportunity; twenty-four-hour nurseries; and free contraception and abortion on demand), Sheilagh said considerable progress had been made: in the 2000s reliable contraception was freely available; nurseries were available for people who wanted them; there were women in more senior roles; and the Abortion Act of 1967 had been protected.[106] Many women expressed a more ambivalent relationship to the feminist movement though. Although the older interviewees were generally more conservative in their attitudes, their responses were not simply determined by age. Some older women championed the developments that had occurred while some younger women were more hesitant. For example when asked if she had been aware of second-wave feminism when she had her children in the early 1970s, Sharon replied:

> It didn't impinge on me. It hadn't reached Wallingford. I was aware of the Women's Liberation Movement, but I was under no pressure from Women's Lib. And I actually am a feminist, but it took me a while to become a feminist. And I had a very good friend in Birmingham who was very much in with the Women's Lib. And the doctrinaire, dogma that they used to come out with I used to think, cor, can't do with all that. No I think it was a relief that I wasn't involved. You know, cos they'd have all this angst about oh what toys you were allowed to give boys and girls.[107]

It is also noteworthy that Hannah felt that there had been a 'backlash' against the efforts of the campaigners of the late 1960s and 1970s by the end of the century. 'I mean many women now always say, "Oh I'm not a feminist" as if that's some terrible label.'[108]

Women were also uncertain about the new ideals of womanhood that were being presented to them at the beginning of the twenty-first century. Jemma said:

> I think also there's a lot of pressure on women, you know, from the media. And I buy *She* magazine and, I mean, their slogan is, 'For women who juggle their lives'. And I don't believe that you can be, you know, people say, 'I'm a full time mother and I've got a career'. I don't believe you can have both and do both of them properly. I think you need a hell of a lot of support to do both of them properly and whether that comes from the family or exceptional childcare … you get so many sort of women being portrayed on the television as having it all … And a lot of people probably think, 'Well, I want some of that as well'. Something's got to give somewhere along the way.[109]

Women were conscious that from the late 1960s the position of women in society was beginning to alter. Some were keen to help usher in these changes and celebrated the new opportunities for women that had resulted from them. But it is clear that others found it difficult to adjust to the transformations for women that have occurred over the course of the second half of the twentieth century and addressed them with mixed feelings.

Breadwinner husbands

As Stephanie Spencer has noted, 'the celebration of women's domestic role was only possible if men's breadwinner role was similarly constructed and prescribed.'[110] The breadwinner model which was so dominant in the years after the war depended upon a gendered construction of men's principal role as being in the public rather than the domestic sphere. Indeed being a good father was dependent on a man's ability to provide for his children. In Victorian England, as John Tosh puts it, 'The convergence of fatherhood and breadwinning was widely recognized as a fact of modern life.'[111] The social order in the middle of the twentieth century was still based on the fact that men were breadwinners. In his 1942 report William Beveridge stated: 'On marriage a woman gains a legal right to maintenance by her husband.'[112] As shown earlier, there were social restrictions that prevented women with children from working, demonstrating the conservative attitudes to female workers that still existed in the post-war decades. It was not simply employment structures that assumed a sole male breadwinner. Only the husband's earnings were taken into account when a couple applied for a mortgage, and Tina recalled that if a woman wanted to buy goods through hire purchase she had to have her husband's signature, meaning that 'the men still had quite a big influence on what you had or couldn't have.'[113] This economic reliance of women upon their husbands gives an indication as to why women were often so keen to return to work once their children were of school-age, and so gain some financial independence. Indeed Elizabeth Roberts has noted how in Lancashire working-class women became more dependent on their husbands in the post-1945 years, as increased prosperity marginalised women's traditional management skills, wages were increasingly paid into bank accounts rather than given in cash to the wife, and there was a growing belief that responsibility for the budget should be shared rather than left to the woman.[114]

The women in Oxfordshire were familiar with the ideal of the male breadwinner model and had grown up witnessing the pre-eminent status many men thought they should subsequently enjoy. Madge grew up in Shipton-under-Wychwood between the wars and recalled the authority of her father. She left school at fourteen to work in the local telephone exchange. When asked how she had found this job she explained that her father had obtained it for her; Madge 'didn't have a choice.'[115] Moreover while they may have been in decline, patriarchal fathers were still present in the post-war world. Agnes was born in Berkshire in 1938 and experienced a difficult relationship with her violent and dictatorial father when she was growing up in the 1940s and 1950s. She explained:

> He worked very hard in a factory, he was a store-keeper. We had a council house, and he worked in the garden, and his attitude to life and children was, don't waste your time reading, excuse me, bloody books because he swore profoundly. Because we only had the radio of course, don't read, don't waste your time, do the housework, do the shopping, do the gardening, and so I had to really work, and my brother, and we had a set regime. Thursday morning before I went to school strip beds, get in soak, Thursday night soak the sheets in a big copper, Friday morning get up early, get it boiled, rinsed out, Friday night, dried over the weekend and Sunday was ironing.[116]

Women believed this conception of the man as breadwinner was under modification during the latter decades of the century as women were increasingly entering the labour force. Doris summed up what she felt were the changes: 'years ago you just didn't go to work, you just had to rely on the man's wage didn't you, and then our generation went out to work sort of part time, but now they've got to work full time most of them.[117] However there had always been men who could not or chose not to provide for their families. The ideal of father as the sole breadwinner was a fantasy for many working-class families. Peggy had four children between 1951 and 1965 but although her husband was employed he did not give her his wages, keeping the money for himself, and she went out to work to support the family. She explained that she would have 'loved to have had a bit more money, and a husband that was a better provider. That was my bugbear.'[118] In addition, the economic crisis of the mid-1970s meant that more families suffered from male unemployment in the years that followed. Tina's husband was made redundant from the car works in Cowley and she recalled how she went to work because they needed the money. However Tina also noted that her mother-in-law 'didn't agree with it', believing that women should stay at home.[119]

Therefore, whether or not it was possible for couples to live up to this ideal, men were expected to be breadwinners and the home was viewed as a woman's domain. Sarah recalled the conduct of her male relatives in the inter-war years: 'I can remember, I used to go and stay with cousins and their two little children, they were the only children I really knew before I was married, and [my cousin] would never have wheeled the pram not even up a hill, couldn't have been seen wheeling a pram. And my uncle, my aunt was not very strong and so my uncle had to do a lot of housework but only if it wasn't seen, he wouldn't clean the windows in case somebody saw you were a sissy.'[120] Indeed these attitudes were also seen after World War Two. Theresa found her neighbours in Edgecote were very disapproving when they saw her husband helping her in the home after her first baby was born in 1948. 'They didn't think it was right because my husband filled the copper for me, that was woman's work'. Theresa said it was the older women in the village who were most critical.[121] Although such views were softening, the women who were interviewed revealed how little their husbands helped in the home throughout the period. Tina's husband was incapable of even making his own breakfast. When he was working on a milk-round she used to 'get up at three and cook him breakfast' because if she did not she would be considered 'a bad wife'.[122] It is noteworthy that even in the 1960s she still felt she would be reneging on her obligations in the home if she did not provide her husband with every meal. A similar situation was described by Norman Dennis, Fernando Henriques and Clifford Slaughter in the Yorkshire mining town of Featherstone in the late 1950s. However they had thought such a strict division of labour was a feature of Featherstone's dependence upon heavy industry.[123] The Oxfordshire evidence indicates such attitudes were more widespread than they had thought. Doreen and Peggy were asked if their husbands helped with childcare when they raised their families in the 1950s and 1960s. Doreen replied: 'Not a lot. I don't think my husband ever changed a nappy.' Peggy said her husband did nothing at all. "'Not my job", he used to say, "Not my job, it's yours, yours".'[124] While such beliefs were changing as the period progressed this did not mean there was a wholesale rejection of the gendered division of labour. Sophie had her first child in 1968. She said that the men in her peer group were present at their children's births, but that was then all they did until their children was about five and could kick a ball around.[125]

Not all women accepted that home and family were their responsibility alone, though. Winifred, who married for the second time in 1950 after the death of her first husband, recalled how her new 'hubby was hopeless', but she felt that this was because both his mother and his first wife 'had done everything for him' whereas she would not. Winifred told an anecdote to exemplify how she educated her husband into a new way of behaviour, saying, 'he came in and he put his shoes in the hearth because we had coal fires then, and they stayed there, they stayed there all the week, I used to pick them up clean underneath and put them down again. Of course Sunday morning they were looking a bit grubby, the second Mrs Brown hadn't cleaned his shoes for him to go to church, mmm, that was a bit sad wasn't it? He learnt to clean his own shoes.'[126] Some interviewees had also been determined that their sons would not replicate traditional male attitudes towards housework. Siobhan explained how she brought up her two sons born in the early 1970s 'to regard doing domestic things as being a perfectly normal part of their lives'. Initially she taught them how to cook and then as they got older they started doing their own ironing and washing as well. She thought her ambition to produce domesticated sons was realised because 'my daughter-in-law said to me one day, "it's absolutely wonderful having this person who can wash and cook, and sew".'[127] Florence also ensured her three sons could cook when they left home, although, interestingly, her daughter could not.[128] Moreover many interviewees reported that their husbands were more than happy to help in the home. Queenie married in 1941 and said her husband 'would do anything, he absolutely idolised the children. Oh yeah he'd do anything, especially for them. He'd always help me, round the house.'[129] Hope's husband was responsible for cooking breakfast for their three children born between 1955 and 1960.[130] Tania said her husband was 'very supportive' and 'quite hands on' as a father and would help with cooking and washing when they had their four children, who were also born in the 1950s and 1960s. Doris recalled that she never had to bath her two children, born in the early 1960s, because her husband always did it.[131]

However, implied within these women's accounts was the notion that their husbands were special. Likewise Michael Peplar found that among the Greenwich women he interviewed men who 'helped' with housework were seen as unusual; and in her study of Jamaican immigrants to London in the early 1970s Nancy Foner found that the women she spoke to regarded helpful husbands as exceptional and therefore deserving of gratitude.[132] It was rare for women to say their husbands took an equal share. Nor did they expect them too. In a 1948 Mass Observation Directive addressed at women, correspondents were asked 'Do you feel that the men in your household should be expected to help in domestic jobs, or not?' Most replied that they thought their husbands should help with certain masculine tasks, but should only be expected to do more than this in exceptional circumstances.[133] A similar picture emerged amongst the Oxfordshire women. While they were appreciative of husbands who helped, they rarely thought it was the husband's responsibility to take an equal share. Hannah and her husband had agreed to divide childcare when their two children were born in the mid-1950s. She explained that before she married she and her husband 'discussed this at great length and I said, "Look my career is as important as your career", and I've always had [his] full support, I've kept my own name and so on and I've had really a great deal of independence. I'd say he had a very tough time when [my daughter] was born because his colleagues used to laugh at him because they saw him pushing the pram in the parks and so on, I mean it was very unusual in those days.'[134] Significantly Hannah reported that she did not know any other couples who shared their domestic duties in this manner. While women may have recalled their husbands shared responsibility at a theoretical level, in reality it was women who were left to undertake the day-to-day care. Anna was a doctor and her husband an academic. They had three children between 1967 and 1973. Comparing her relationship with her husband to that of her children and their partners she said: 'So the division of labour ... was much more of the traditional kind. The interest was absolutely equal ... But the expectation was that I was the one who was around. I always sort of you know made the dressing up clothes for the fancy dress party or you know attended the school fete or whatever it was.'[135] As Ann Oakley has argued, it is not accurate to speak of equality when men's role in the home was only that of helping their wives.[136]

The interviewees thought the increasing role men played in the home was in fact one of the most significant changes in family life that occurred over the course of the century.[137] For instance Jessica, who was born in 1914, said:

I've got four great-grandchildren and it's marvellous how the men in the family take at least 50 percent of the baby care and it opens my eyes because my father never did. Although he was a lovely father he didn't even boil an egg and he never did any cooking or anything whereas now the men do just as much cooking as the women. And I've watched my grandson changing his baby's nappy and he was so sweet, he was talking to him all the time and talking to him as if it was man to man and it was really lovely to watch and that's very different.[138]

Similarly Bethany summed up how she felt attitudes had altered between her father's generation (in the 1940s), her husband's generation (in the 1970s), and her son's generation (in the 2000s). 'Men are so different today. My son cooks and my husband is only just beginning to cook a bit really. My father obviously he never cooked or did anything like that.'[139] Enid, who was born in 1925 and had her children in the 1940s, also reflected upon this development. She said, 'fathers are good these days. Although ... fathers were beginning to [get] better when my babies were born. Because I don't know whether the war changed them or what, because my husband would bath the children, push the pram out, do everything. But say when I was a baby, the fathers then wouldn't have done anything.'[140] Enid was not alone in thinking World War Two had proved pivotal. Sarah also thought the war had precipitated a change in attitudes, stating, 'the war was over and men came back and women by that time had started being free and expected to share'.[141] Sarah's comments are interesting as they show the relationship that women felt existed between men's increasing domesticity and women's participation in the labour force. However unlike their uncertainty over the issue of women's increasing participation in the workforce, the interviewees were confident in their belief that men's increasing role in the home was a positive development. This divergence raised an interesting contradiction, because, as Sarah indicated, they often believed that men's increased role in the home was a result of women engaging in paid labour outside of it. Within the generally laudatory discussions of men in the 2000s, there were voices that were more doubtful. Amelia noted that studies of housework have tended to show that while men increasingly say they do more in the home, in reality little has changed since the 1930s or 1940s.[142] Similarly when discussing her son's relationship with his children Lynne sad: 'my son actually only has a four day week and he does an amazing amount with the children you know relatively amazing. It's the kind of thing that still there's a lot of gender prejudice I think, I'm using the word amazing; if he was their mother I wouldn't be saying it presumably, you know what I mean?'[143]

Conclusions

Popular conceptions of motherhood in the decades after World War Two, with the associated ideals of happy nuclear families founded upon the companionate relationship between breadwinner husbands and homemaker wives, were deeply influential upon the ways in which the women interviewed constructed their narratives. When discussing their experiences of motherhood the Oxfordshire interviewees employed the discourses of marriage and family which dominated the post-war social and cultural milieu. However contemporary ideals did not remain static and the interviewees were also influenced by changing attitudes towards the role of men and women within the home. This was perhaps seen most visibly in their views of fathers. Women advocated a more involved role for fathers in childcare than had been celebrated in the post-war years. Instead their attitudes seemed to reflect later calls for men to take a more active role in the home, encouraged by the feminist arguments of the 1970s that the care of children should not be a woman's responsibility alone. However, many of the older interviewees (and indeed some of the younger ones) were less receptive to other changes, as seen by their ambivalent attitudes towards cohabitation and divorce. They had grown up with a strong ideal that marriage and the nuclear family was the best and perhaps only form that families could take. The women interviewed often found it difficult to relate to the other arrangements with which they had been confronted, often through the experiences of their own children, in later life. Many did try to incorporate more recent understandings of the family in their accounts, but when they did so their narratives often became disjointed, reflecting the problems they faced in these attempts.

Some interviewees also faced difficulties reconciling their personal experiences of motherhood with popular discourses. While they interweaved elements of these discourses within their accounts to validate their own life choices, for example that a good mother was one who stayed at home, there are interesting points in the women's narratives where the public and the personal diverge. The ideals women wished to endorse did not always fit their own experiences, and interviewees could struggle to unite the two. For example Polly's portrayal of the 1960s as a golden age for the family was undercut by her own experience of divorce. She compared the past when families got 'together round the table, no television or anything like that just having a quiet meal and talking', with the 2000s when people 'just leave the kids to get on with it.' As she discussed this subject the flow of her narrative broke down. She was forced to address the fact that her own family life did not meet this model. Her husband left her when her children were small and she concluded: 'Yes life can be very, very difficult.'[144] Similarly in her narrative Bethany expressed strong support for the ideal of companionate marriage. She believed that a man's place was at work and a woman's place was in the home, and considered herself 'very lucky' that this had been her own experience. However when she raised her son's relationship with his family as an example of how things have changed for the worse – both he and his partner worked full time and shared childcare – she voiced her regret that her husband had not been similarly involved in the home: 'My husband, he didn't, he didn't sort of change nappies or do anything like that. He was always fond of the children but he wasn't involved in that type of thing really, washing or washing up, he wasn't involved in household duties, I did most of it, whereas I know it's very different today … So I think, there is more of an equality between the sexes, which is probably a good thing.'[145] Women were trying to tell their stories of motherhood using the narrative genres surrounding the family that were available to them. However, portrayals of the family that existed in 1945 were very different to those of 2000. Through an analysis of the interviewees' narratives it seems that they did not always find reconciling these competing ideals to be an easy task, and many struggled to respond to the changing representations of women and men which they encountered.

Notes

1 Mogey, *Family and Neighbourhood*, p. 50.
2 Slater and Woodside, *Patterns of Marriage*, p. 118. Josephine Klein, Ferdinand Zweig and Geoffrey Gorer made similar findings. Klein, *Samples from English Cultures*, p. 154; Ferdinand Zweig, *Women's Life and Labour* (London: Victor Gollancz, 1952), pp. 27–8; Geoffrey Gorer, *Exploring English Character* (London: Cresset Press, 1955), pp. 138 and 161.
3 Lawrence Stone, *Road to Divorce: England 1530–1987* (Oxford: Oxford University Press, 1990), p. 417.
4 John Bradshaw, Carol Stimson, Christine Skinner and Julie Williams, 'Non-resident fathers in Britain', in McRae (ed.), *Changing Britain*, 404–27, p. 404; Jane Millar and Tess Ridge, *Families, Poverty, Work and Care: A Review of the Literature on Lone Parents and Low-Income Couple Families with Children* (Department of Work and Pensions Research Report No. 153) (Leeds: Corporate Document Services, 2001), p. 23.
5 *Ibid.*, p. 23.
6 D.W. Dean, 'Education for moral improvement, domesticity and social cohesion: the Labour government, 1945–1951', in Liz Dawtrey, Janet Holland and Merril Hammer, with Sue Sheldon, *Equality and Inequality in Education Policy* (Clevedon: Multilingual Matters, 1995), 18–30, p. 28.
7 Marjory Ferguson, *Forever Feminine: Women's Magazines and the Cult of Femininity* (London: Heinemann, 1983), p. 2.

8 Hayley, NO5, p. 5.

9 MOA, DR 3474, reply to August 1943 Directive.

10 Tina, BE3, p. 20.

11 Pearl Jephcott, *Girls Growing Up* (London: Faber and Faber, 1942), p. 39.

12 Liz Heron (ed.), *Truth, Dare or Promise, Girls Growing Up in the Fifties* (London: Virago, 1985), p. 16.

13 Sue Sharpe, *"Just Like a Girl": How Girls Learn to be Women* (Harmondsworth: Penguin Books, 1976), p. 45.

14 Giles, 'Narratives of gender, class, and modernity', p. 25.

15 Peplar, *Family Matters*, pp. 68–99; Marcia Landry, 'Melodrama and femininity in World War II British cinema', in Robert Murphy (ed.), *The British Cinema Book* (London: British Film Institute, 1997), 119–26; John Hill, *Sex, Class and Realism: British Cinema 1956–1963* (London: BFI Publications, 1986), p. 159.

16 Janice Winship, *Inside Women's Magazines* (London: Pandora, 1987), p. 50; Janice Winship, *Advertising in Women's Magazines 1956–74* (Birmingham: Centre for Contemporary Cultural Studies, University of Birmingham, 1980), p. 15; Brian Braithwaite, *Women's Magazines: The First 300 Years* (London: Peter Owen, 1995), p. 73; Jill Allbrooke, 'Three hundred years of women's magazines, 1693–1993', *Serials*, 7 (1994), 60–3; Mary Grieve, *Millions Made My Story, Mary Grieve Editor Woman 1940–62* (London: Victor Gollancz, 1964).

17 J.E. Goldthorpe, *Family Life in Western Societies: A Historical Sociology of Family Relationships in Britain and North America* (Cambridge: Cambridge University Press, 1987), p. 42; John R. Gillis, *For Better, For Worse: British Marriages, 1600 to the Present* (New York: Oxford University Press, 1985), p. 233.

18 Enid, BE12, p. 9.

19 Molly, NO4, p. 5.

20 Ethel, BE6, p. 8.

21 MOA, DR 3133, DR 3305, DR 1346, DR 3306, DR 1635, DR 3387, DR 2873, DR 3399, DR 1289, DR 3471, DR 2892, DR 2254, replies to November 1943 Directive.

22 Camilla, SO6, p. 14.

23 Lisa, CO12, p. 7.

24 Claire, NO1, p. 3.

25 Phyllis, WY3, p. 7.

26 ERA, Mrs J. 1. B., p. 11; also Mrs A. 4. L., p. 43; Mrs T. 2. L., p. 86; Mrs W. 4. L., p. 25; Mr and Mrs K. 2. P., p. 115.

27 MOA, DR 3371, DR 3535, DR 2884, DR 3410, replies to March 1944 Directive.

28 Ivy, BE4, p. 6.

29 Parfit, *Health of a City*, pp. 93–4.

30 Madge, WY8, p. 7.

31 Kate Fisher, *Birth Control, Sex and Marriage in Britain, 1918–1960* (Oxford: Oxford University Press, 2006), pp. 127–30.

32 Hera Cook, *The Long Sexual Revolution* (Oxford: Oxford University Press, 2004), pp. 268 and 272.

33 Jean, EW14, p. 4.

34 Margaret, EW15, p. 8.

35 Kim, OX15, pp. 5–6.

36 Carmel, NO16, p. 8.

37 Bev, CR10, p. 18.

38 Shirley, SO10, p. 8.

39 Ann Oakley, *Essays on Women, Medicine and Health* (Edinburgh: Edinburgh University Press, 1993), pp. 171–88.

40 Only ten of the women interviewed had just one child: Vanessa, BA13; Amelia CO15; Thelma, CR6; Edna, OX13; Lynne, OX14; Monika, SO1; Faith, SO12; Alexa, SO13; Cynthia, WY12; Amy, WY13. Women interviewed by Elizabeth Roberts expressed similar feelings. For example: ERA, Mrs B. 2. B., p. 48.

41 Marilyn, BE13, p. 12; Nancy, CO3, p. 1; Hope, CO11, p. 6.

42 Glenda, BA2, p. 14.

43 Rose, NO12, p. 1.

44 Sarah, NO2, p. 18.

45 Valerie, SA4, p. 4.

46 Lynne, OX14, p. 5.

47 Cynthia, WY12, p. 6.

48 Alexa, SO13, p. 4.

49 Penelope Mortimer, *The Pumpkin Eater* (London: Hutchinson, 1962).

50 Ann Phoenix, 'Black women and the maternity services', in Garcia, Kilpatrick and Richards (eds), *The Politics of Maternity Care*, 274–99, p. 277.

51 Violet, BA7, p. 8.

52 Ivy, BE4, p. 20.

53 Ellen, EW3, p. 25.

54 Claire, NO1, p. 7.

55 Sarah, NO2, p. 14.

56 Tilly, CR12, p. 5.

57 Eunice, SA2, p. 1.

58 Dawn, CR13, p. 5.

59 Bonnie, CR14, p. 5.

60 Ivy, BE4, p. 19.

61 For a discussion of teenage pregnancy at this time see Ofra Koffman, 'Towards a Genealogy of Teenage Pregnancy in Britain, 1955–1978' (PhD dissertation, University of London, 2008).

62 Siobhan, BE1, p. 13.

63 MOA, FR 2495 'The State of Matrimony', June 1947, pp. 14–17.

64 Peggy, BA9, pp. 7–8.

65 Gloria, BE14, p. 8.

66 Tina, BE3, p. 24.

67 Lynne, OX14, p. 4.

68 Pippa, CO13, p. 4.

69 Tara, SO15, p. 11.

70 Pam, SA7, p. 3.

71 Andrea, SA9, p. 9.

72 Jessica, BA8, p. 14.

73 Camilla, SO6, p. 15; Bethany, EW4, p. 21.

74 Carol, TH14, p. 14.

75 Lindsay, OX12, p. 18.

76 Shaw, 'Pakistani Families in Oxford', p. 107.

77 Sophie, TH12, pp. 20–1.
78 Amelia, CO15, p. 18.
79 Edna, OX13, p. 10.
80 Tasha, SO14, p. 12.
81 Eunice, SA2, p. 7.
82 Elizabeth Wilson, *Women and the Welfare State* (London: Tavistock, 1997), p. 35.
83 H.M. Government, *Social Insurance*, p. 50.
84 *Ibid.*, p. 50. Elizabeth McCarty has shown how this image of woman as housewife was common across the political spectrum. Elizabeth McCarty, 'Attitudes to Women and Domesticity in England, c. 1939–1955' (DPhil dissertation, University of Oxford, 1994), p. 175.
85 Spencer, *Gender, Work and Education*, p. 24.
86 Mavis, EW10, p. 7.
87 Sarah, NO2, p. 13.
88 Juliet, NO9, p. 11.
89 'Letter to the Editor', *Woman* (1 February 1958), p. 4.
90 Winship, *Advertising*, p. 15; Braithwaite, *Women's Magazines*, p. 73; Cynthia L. White, *Women's Magazines 1693–1968* (London: Michael Joseph, 1970), pp. 65–181.
91 Glenda, BA2, p. 12.
92 Eve, CO8, pp. 2–3.
93 Melanie, CO16, p. 34.
94 MOA, DR 0987, reply to March/April 1951 Directive.
95 MOA, B1475, reply to 69: Spring Directive 2003, part 1 'Images of the 1950s and 1960s'.
96 Siobhan, BE1, pp. 22–3.
97 Deirdre, BA1, pp. 12–13.
98 Theresa, BA10, pp. 8–9; Tina, BE3, p. 15; Ethel, BE6, p. 15; Gail, BE11, p. 7; Ellen, EW3, p. 20.
99 Braithwaite, *Women's Magazines*, p. 79.
100 Bethany, EW4, pp. 21–2.
101 Emily, NO8, p. 6.
102 Hannah, SO7, pp. 17–18.
103 Tina, BE3, p. 38.
104 Sadie, CO14; Amelia, CO15; Melanie, CO16; Sheilagh, CO17.
105 Amelia, CO15, pp. 21–5.
106 Sheilagh, CO17, pp. 21–7.
107 Sharon, EW9, pp. 21–2.
108 Hannah, SO7, pp. 3–4.
109 Jemma, SA13, pp. 12–13.
110 Spencer, *Gender, Work and Education*, p. 5.
111 John Tosh, *A Man's Place: Masculinity and the Middle-Class Home in Victorian England* (New Haven and London: Yale University Press, 1999), p. 85.
112 H.M. Government, *Social Insurance*, p. 50.
113 Tina, BE3, pp. 16–17.
114 Roberts, *Women and Families*, pp. 89–92.
115 Madge, WY8, pp. 3–4.
116 Agnes, EW1, p. 2.
117 Doris, BE2, p. 39.

118 Peggy, BA9, p. 21.
119 Tina, BE3, pp. 32–3.
120 Sarah, NO2, p. 17.
121 Theresa, BA10, p. 4.
122 Tina, BE3, pp. 17–18.
123 Norman Dennis, Fernando Henriques and Clifford Slaughter, *Coal is Our Life* (London: Tavistock Publications, 1969), p. 181.
124 Doreen, BA3, p. 12; Peggy, BA9, p. 12.
125 Sophie, TH12, p. 14.
126 Winifred, CO4, pp. 19–20.
127 Siobhan, BE1, pp. 18–19.
128 Florence, BE8, p. 15.
129 Queenie, EW5, p. 17.
130 Hope, CO11, p. 22.
131 Doris, BE2, pp. 30–1.
132 Peplar, *Family Matters*, p. 110; Foner, *Jamaica Farewell*, p. 75.
133 MOA, DR 0595, DR 1485, DR 0174, DR 1054, DR 1498, DR 1826, DR 1048, DR 0751, DR 1252, DR 1253, DR 1831, DR 0157, DR 1169, DR 0987, DR 0854, replies to March–April 1948 Directive.
134 Hannah, SO7, p. 4.
135 Anna NO13, pp. 20–1.
136 Oakley, *Sociology of Housework*, p. 160.
137 Correspondents to a Mass Observation New Project directive made very similar comments about increased male domesticity as being one of the biggest changes in the second half of the century. MOA, P1637, R451, S2190, B1771, G1483, replies to 35: Autumn Directive 1991, part 1 'Women and Men'.
138 Jessica, BA8, p. 13.
139 Bethany, EW4, p. 23.
140 Enid, BE12, pp. 12–13.
141 Sarah, NO2, pp. 17–18.
142 Amelia, p. 29.
143 Lynne, OX14, p. 11.
144 Polly, BE7, pp. 20–1.
145 Bethany, EW4, p. 9 and 22–3.

8

Conclusions

Motherhood was a contested subject between 1945 and 2000, with mothers being both celebrated and scrutinised. Women were making their choices surrounding motherhood in a new and changing context. Those women who had children in the immediate post-war years experienced welfare reforms, falling maternal and infant mortality rates, the baby boom, and rising numbers of married women in the workforce. Further important social, cultural and demographic changes then took place from the late 1960s. Growing feminist activism encouraged a reassessment of the place of women in the family and society. The Divorce Reform Act of 1969 precipitated a sharp increase in the divorce rate, and the 1970s and 1980s witnessed increasing rates of cohabitation and family reformation. Therefore throughout the second half of the century being a mother was a role fraught with contradictions and ambiguities, and these are reflected in the way women of these generations now articulate their attitudes towards, and experiences of, motherhood. These complexities have been revealed in each of the thematic areas discussed in the preceding chapters.

Firstly the interviews with Oxfordshire women revealed how locality and the type of community in which women lived was a highly significant factor in their experiences of motherhood. It affected the level of support the women received and who it was likely to come from, usually family or friends. Locality influenced how they interacted with other mothers and the degree of isolation they faced – living in supportive communities being one way of combating dissatisfaction with motherhood. It also determined the facilities and services available to them. This study confirms some of the findings of the contemporary surveys. Class differentials could be marked, with the more geographically mobile middle classes less likely to receive support from family. In addition there was a pattern of neighbourliness centred upon a street-based life in traditional working-class communities, whether urban or rural, which was not seen on new estates. However the picture of estate living found in this study, for both middle-class and working-class women, was not the bleak portrayal that was common in contemporary discourse. This finding may indicate that post-war investigators were overly pessimistic about the new estates, tending to over-romanticise the established neighbourhoods. They did not take into account that while different to those seen in the old areas, new community structures could build up in the estates. In particular they did not recognise the agency of women, especially mothers of young children, in striving to form bonds of friendship, and often assumed women were the passive victims of their environment rather than active participants within it. The interviews also indicate that historical interpretations which have seen the women's movement of the late 1960s and 1970s as emerging from a post-war malaise have overlooked the many ways in which women were already organising themselves to improve their lives. Moreover while the formal associations which developed in importance during the latter decades of the century may have added to and augmented these existing networks they did not replace them.

Some commentators believed that due to the perceived breakdown of the extended family, women were no longer being instructed in the arts of motherhood. The question of whether women should be educated for motherhood and where this education should take place was a subject of intense discussion and it was one where a range of discourses met – sociological, educational, psychological and medical. From the interviews with Oxfordshire women it appears their experiences were affected by these national debates – for example women were receiving a domestically orientated education at school, and were increasingly attending antenatal classes. Two principal discursive models emerged – motherhood as innate, and motherhood as a skill that needed to be learnt. Women embraced elements of these discourses and incorporated both their ideas and associated language within their own narratives. They did so in complex ways, however, and borrowed different strands from the various ways of thinking in order to construct a model of motherhood that was acceptable to them. In short, they endeavoured to unite the conflicting ideals of motherhood with which they were confronted. It also seems clear that this debate was intensely bound up with wider questions of how 'normal' women should behave. These were pervasive ideas, with interviewees from all types of background sharing an understanding of what this norm should be. Indeed women's fantasies of being 'natural' mothers demonstrate the pressure women felt in the second half of the twentieth century to fulfil the ideal of the 'perfect' mother.

Women's accounts of the maternity care they received were also revealing of the popular discourses surrounding pregnancy and childbirth that existed during the years between 1945 and 2000. Questions of whether women should be taught about motherhood intersected with debates over whether maternity was a natural part of a woman's life or a medical event. The second half of the century has been characterised as one of increasing medical intervention within the spheres of pregnancy and childbirth, as medical professionals sought to control women's reproductive capacity. The picture that has emerged from this study, however, is a more complex one. There was no unified position amongst health professionals, but rather inter- and intra-professional debates between midwives, GPs and consultants. Developments in national and local policy sometimes took place in harmony with women's desires and sometimes in opposition to their needs and wants. In addition policies determined at the national level could conflict with current local practice leading to rapid alterations in the care offered, but also resistance to change. Moreover when reflecting back upon their experiences from their current perspective it was not the medical interventions that women recalled as being the most decisive factor in determining their satisfaction with their care, but rather the relationships they enjoyed with the medical professionals who attended them. Therefore historical accounts of maternity care which have focused simply on what was being done to women can miss the importance of subjective factors such as their knowing and liking the person who was doing it. Interviewees who objectively had similar birth experiences could recall them very differently, with women who knew and trusted their attendants remembering their care far more positively.

In addition to being responsible for the physical health of their children, mothers in the post-war decades also found themselves answerable for their children's psychological wellbeing. Literature on childcare abounded throughout the twentieth century and ideas of how mothers should behave were hotly contested. Women could also receive contradictory advice from different sources such as their mothers and medical professionals. Definitions of what made a 'good' mother were constantly in flux so women had to adjust to these changing requirements. For example what Benjamin Spock told women was good childcare practice was often in opposition to what Frederick Truby King had asserted a generation before. There was also a cyclical nature to this advice. By the end of the century Gina Ford's championing of routine closely resembled the approach Truby King had taken almost a hundred years earlier. Nonetheless childcare experts were deeply influential in shaping expectations of what mothers should be like between 1945 and 2000. From the interviews with Oxfordshire women it is clear that mothers struggled to reconcile the demands that these experts were making upon them with the reality of raising their children. While they could give women confidence and support and make mothers feel they were doing an important and worthwhile job, the pronouncements of the experts did not always have positive effects. Theories of child development and the role of the mother in ensuring the healthy growth of her children could be oppressive for women in the second half of the century. Those women who could not meet the ideal of 'good' mothering were left feeling anxious and guilty.

Working mothers had long been characterised as a problem for society and after the war childcare experts provided new rationales for why it was important that women remained in the home. Nevertheless during these years mothers were increasingly participating in the workforce once their children reached school age and they were being encouraged to do so. The result was that society was left struggling to come to terms with women who might want to combine motherhood with a career. Women's personal testimony indicates that their own attitudes to work were also complex. Women of all classes and backgrounds could feel the need to rebel against the domestic role assigned to them. At the same time, many interviewees reported that they were more than happy to cease work and devote themselves to full-time motherhood. Their attitudes also changed at different points of their lives, and they were aware they were living through a reconceptualisation of women's work. However they had ambivalent attitudes towards working mothers, just as contemporary commentators had done, and this was clearly seen in their attitudes towards their daughters' generation. While paid work was viewed as offering a means of subsistence, a degree of financial independence, or a break from domesticity, few interviewees conceived of employment in terms of a career and they prioritised family in their accounts. However, perhaps influenced by the discourses of second-wave feminism, women spoke of their desire to gain independence through work, whether this was inside or outside the home. It is interesting that the women interviewed thought that both paid work and motherhood were ways in which status could be gained for women in the post-war world. While this picture was beginning to change by the end of the century it remained true that only a small minority of educated, professional women considered their role as worker to be as, or more, important than that of mother.

In reaching these conclusions women were influenced by the representations of mothers in popular culture. There were clear ideals of how families during the period 1945–2000 were supposed to behave. The model family in the immediate post-war decades consisted of a mother as dependent homemaker, father as breadwinner, and two, three or four children. Couples without children or with only one child were regarded as selfish or abnormal. Families with more than four children were viewed as ill-disciplined and without self-control. Women who worked when their children were young were either pitied, because it was assumed they would only do so if they did not have a husband who could provide for them, or condemned for jeopardising their families' wellbeing. There were some notable changes in this ideal over time, however. Women were increasingly expected to play a more active role in the labour force and men to be more involved in the home. Lifelong marriage became less secure. Feminist analyses of the family had challenged conventional understandings of the mother role. Women tried to respond to these changing representations in their accounts. They were trying to tell their stories of motherhood using the narrative genres surrounding the family that were available to them, and these were shaped by the changing depictions of the family that had occurred. However, the women interviewed had all grown up with a strong image of the nuclear family as being the ideal form that the family should take. They were familiar with this model of the family and felt comfortable when describing it – they had the language to do so. In consequence the interviewees found it more difficult to talk about the changes, often within their own families, that had subsequently occurred.

The preceding chapters have therefore revealed two principal conclusions. The first is that motherhood was a role characterised by ambivalence and contradictions during the period 1945–2000. While women talked of the joy that having children brought them they also revealed the hardships that mothers from all backgrounds faced. Moreover these difficulties were visible in all aspects of their lives. For example in relation to maternity care women often suffered from a lack of information and respect. They faced the arrogance of medical professionals who felt that they, rather than the women they attended, knew best. Interviewees also spoke of their guilt and anxiety if they did not live up to the ideals of good mothering with which they were confronted. In the years immediately after the war it was assumed that fathers would provide for their wives and children, which in turn meant that there was little support for those families who did not meet this ideal. The expectation that all women would want to be full-time mothers meant they experienced discrimination both at school and in work. The adversities which interviewees experienced during these years perhaps encouraged the feminist activity of the 1970s. The younger generation of women reaped significant benefits from feminist campaigns, as seen, for example, in increasing educational and employment opportunities, a new ability to control their fertility, and equality legislation. However, the interviewees did not always think that the lives of women had become easier at the end of the century. The expectations upon women brought new pressures. For example women who did not want to return to work when their children were school age faced increasing disapproval for not doing so.

The second conclusion is that, despite the differences between women, they could use motherhood as a unifying experience. Indeed the stereo-typing of the period between the late 1940s and 1960s as one of conservatism before the changes that began in the later 1960s and 1970s means that women's activism and the ways in which they were already organising themselves to improve their lives has tended to be disregarded. This lack of awareness has possibly occurred because these associations were often established on an informal basis, such as neighbours coming together to share childcare. They were important though, and interviewees recalled them as being extremely significant features of their lives. Throughout the second half of the twentieth century women used their collective experience of being mothers of young children to develop social networks and form communities of women, both to take mutual pleasure in the delight that motherhood could bring them, but also with the aim of alleviating some of the difficulties and inequities that they faced.

APPENDIX I

Typical interview schedule

1 Growing up

Can you tell me when and where you were born?

Do you have any brothers and sisters? Where did you fit into the order?

(If younger siblings) Did you know your mother was pregnant? Did you help look after your siblings?

How many people lived in your house?

Did you live near any relatives?

Did your parents bring you up to consider certain things important in life?

When did you start at school? Where did you go?

Did you like school?

(If relevant) Would you have liked to stay on longer?

Were you taught things like cookery, childcare etc?

Were you taught about pregnancy and childbirth?

2 After school

What were your hopes and dreams on leaving school?

Were you expected to work or get married?

Were you given any careers advice?

(If went to higher education) Where/what did you do?

What was your first job?

Did you stay at work after your first child was born?

(If not) Did you go back when your children were older?

Was there any support for women who wanted to combine work and motherhood?

How did you meet your husband? When did you marry? How old were you both?

How long had you been married when you had your first child?

How many children have you had?

Was this the number you and your husband planned to have?

3 Pregnancy

Where were you living/working when you became pregnant?

How did you feel when you found out?

How regularly did you see your GP/midwife?

Did you enjoy your pregnancy?

Did you suffer from morning sickness etc?

What arrangements did you make for your baby after delivery?

Did you attend antenatal and childbirth preparation classes? What did you learn? Was it useful?

Were there other sources of information like books and magazines, or other mothers?

Would it have been better to know more or less?

4 Birth

Where was your baby born?

Did you know what to expect in childbirth?

What were your sources of information?

How did the delivery go?

Did you know the doctor/midwife who delivered you? What were the medical staff like?

How did you feel after delivery and during the next few days?

What were your main concerns or worries after the baby was born?

Did you breastfeed?

(*If birth in hospital*) How long did you stay in hospital? Did you want to stay this long?

How did you feel when you brought your baby home?

Was anyone there to help you?

5 Parenthood

Did you find things came naturally to you?

Did you worry about doing things wrong?

If you needed advice who did you ask (e.g. mother, friends, doctors, health visitors, clinics)?

(*If relevant*) What were the differences between having your first child and later children?

Did you follow the advice of childcare manuals?

Did you try to be similar or different to your mother?

(If different) What were the differences?

Did you bring them up to believe that certain things are important in life?

Do you have grandchildren?

(If yes) How has your relationship with your children changed?

What are the differences between how people used to raise children and today?

What are the pluses and minuses of these changes? Why do you think the changes occurred?

APPENDIX 2

Oxfordshire interviewees' biographical details

Note: *Individual hospital names are included where known.*

Banbury villages

BA1 *Deirdre*   Born 1927 (Banbury). Two children born 1955 (Banbury, Elms Maternity Hospital) and 1958 (Banbury, Elms Maternity Hospital).

BA2 *Glenda*   Born 1927 (London). Three children born 1952 (London, maternity home), 1954 (London, home) and 1958 (Banbury, Elms Maternity Hospital).

BA3 *Doreen*   Born 1929 (Lancashire). Two children born 1948 (Banbury, hospital) and 1951 (Banbury, hospital).

BA4 *Carla*   Born 1942 (Oxford). Two children born 1971 (Banbury, Horton Hospital) and 1974 (Banbury, Horton Hospital).

BA5 *Nicola*   Born 1935 (Leicester). Two children (twins) born 1969 (Banbury, Horton Hospital).

BA6 *Rita*   Born 1933 (Brackley). Two children born 1961 (Oxford, Radcliffe Infirmary) and 1963 (Banbury, Elms Maternity Hospital).

BA7 *Violet*   Born 1930 (Oxford). Six children born 1953 (Oxford, home), 1954 (Oxford, home), 1955 (Oxford, Radcliffe Infirmary), 1960 (Chipping Norton, hospital), 1963 (Chipping Norton, hospital) and 1965 (Chipping Norton, hospital).

BA8 *Jessica*   Born 1914 (Edinburgh). Three children born 1943 (London, hospital), 1945 (London, hospital) and 1947 (London, hospital).

BA9 *Peggy*   Born 1933 (Redditch). Four children born 1951 (Londonderry, hospital), 1953 (Londonderry, hospital), 1954 (Chipping Wardern, home) and 1965 (Banbury, hospital).

BA10 *Theresa*   Born 1925 (Lincolnshire). Four children born 1948 (Adderbury, home), 1950 (Adderbury, home), 1955 (Adderbury, home) and 1963 (Banbury, hospital).

BA11 *Hilda*   Born 1942 (Sunderland). Two children born 1967 (Hillingdon, hospital), 1970 (Banbury, Horton Hospital).

BA12 *Shula*   Born 1940 (Coventry). Three children born 1968 (Oxford, Churchill GP Unit), 1970 (Oxford, Churchill GP Unit), 1973 (Oxford, John Radcliffe Hospital GP Unit).

BA13 *Vanessa*   Born 1950 (Oxford). One child born 1979 (Oxford, John Radcliffe Hospital).

BA14 *Nellie*   Born 1948 (Buckinghamshire). Two children born 1980 (Oxford, John Radcliffe Hospital) and 1981 (Oxford, John Radcliffe Hospital).

BA15 *Patsy*   Born 1943 (Oxford). Two children born 1970 (Oxford, Radcliffe Infirmary) and 1972 (Oxford, John Radcliffe Hospital).

BA16 *Zoe*   Born 1940 (Oxford). Four children born 1965 (Oxford, Churchill Hospital), 1966 (Oxford, Radcliffe Infirmary), 1972 (Oxford, Radcliffe Infirmary) and 1976 (Oxford, John Radcliffe Hospital).

Benson

BE1 *Siobhan*   Born 1945 (Abingdon). Two children born 1970 (Oxford, Radcliffe Infirmary) and 1971 (Oxford, Radcliffe Infirmary).

BE2 *Doris*   Born 1937 (Watlington). Two children born 1961 (Wallingford, St George's Maternity Hospital) and 1963 (Wallingford, St George's Maternity Hospital).

BE3 *Tina*   Born 1945 (Hayling Island). Three children born 1964 (Wallingford, St George's Maternity Hospital), 1968 (Benson, home) and 1971 (Benson, home).

BE4 *Ivy*   Born 1921 (Walton-on-the-Naze). Two children born 1947 (Tunbridge Wells, maternity home) and 1950 (Tunbridge Wells, maternity home).

BE5 *Ruby*   Born 1939 (Southampton). Two children born 1972 (Oxford, Radcliffe Infirmary) and 1974 (Wallingford, Community Hospital).

BE6 *Ethel*   Born 1919 (Benson). Two children born 1938 (Benson, home) and 1948 (Benson, home).

BE7 *Polly*   Born 1943 (Aylesbury). Two children born 1968 (Wallingford, St George's Maternity Hospital) and 1970 (Wallingford, St George's Maternity Hospital).

BE8 *Florence*   Born 1932 (Benson). Four children born 1953 (Oxford, Churchill Hospital), 1955 (Wallingford, St George's Maternity Hospital), 1962 (Oxford, Radcliffe Infirmary) and 1966 (Benson, home).

BE9 *Amanda*   Born 1940 (Taunton). Four children born 1965 (Bristol, maternity hospital), 1966 (Bristol, home), 1968 (Solihull, hospital) and 1973 (Wallingford, Community Hospital).

BE10 *Fiona*   Born 1941 (Shropshire). Three children born 1966 (Brighton, hospital), 1968 (Brighton, hospital) and 1970 (Oxford, Radcliffe Infirmary).

BE11 *Gail*   Born 1931 (Portsmouth). Three children born 1961 (Wallingford, St George's Maternity Hospital), 1964 (Benson, home) and 1970 (Benson, home).

BE12 *Enid*   Born 1925 (Benson). Two children born 1943 (Benson, home) and 1946 (Benson, home).

BE13 *Marilyn*   Born 1946 (London). Two children born 1973 (Oxford, John Radcliffe Hospital) and 1976 (Oxford, John Radcliffe Hospital).

BE14 *Gloria*   Born 1939 (Benson). Two children born 1966 (Oxford, Radcliffe Infirmary) and 1969 (Wallingford, St George's Maternity Hospital).

Cowley and Florence Park

CO1 *Bet*   Born 1943 (London). Four children born 1968 (Wantage, cottage hospital), 1972 (Oxford, home), and 1975 (twins) (Oxford, John Radcliffe Hospital).

CO2 *June*   Born 1931 (Oxford). Four children born 1959 (Oxford, Churchill Hospital), 1962 (Oxford, Churchill Hospital), 1964 (Oxford, home) and 1966 (Oxford, home).

CO3 *Nancy*   Born 1926 (Wantage). Three children born 1949 (Oxford, Radcliffe Infirmary), 1956 (Oxford, Radcliffe Infirmary) and 1965 (Oxford, Radcliffe Infirmary).

CO4 *Winifred*   Born 1917 (Edinburgh). Two children born 1946 (Hereford, hospital) and 1951 (Oxford, Churchill Hospital).

CO5 *Joanna*   Born 1937 (Royston). Three children born 1961 (Oxford, Churchill Hospital), 1963 (Oxford, Radcliffe Infirmary) and 1965 (Oxford, Radcliffe Infirmary).

CO6 *Deborah*   Born 1930 (Derbyshire). Three children born 1955 (Oxford, Radcliffe Infirmary), 1958 (Oxford, Radcliffe Infirmary) and 1965 (Oxford, Radcliffe Infirmary).

CO7 *Penny*   Born 1937 (Lancashire). Three children born 1955 (Cambridge, hospital), 1957 (Reading, hospital) and 1964 (Oxford, Radcliffe Infirmary).

CO8 *Eve*   Born 1927 (Wigan). Two children born 1957 (Liverpool, hospital) and 1960 (Liverpool, hospital).

CO9 *Cherie*   Born 1936 (Gillingham). Three children born 1963 (Oxford, home), 1965 (Oxford, home) and 1969 (Oxford, home).

CO10 *Judy* Born 1932 (Oxford). Three children born 1959 (Oxford, home), 1962 (Oxford, home) and 1964 (Oxford, home).

CO11 *Hope* Born 1930 (London). Three children born 1955 (Oxford, home), 1958 (Oxford, home) and 1960 (Oxford, home).

CO12 *Lisa* Born 1934 (Leicester). Four children born 1960 (Oxford, home), 1963 (Oxford, home), 1964 (Oxford, home) and 1967 (Oxford, home).

CO13 *Pippa* Born 1955 (Paisley). Three children born 1983 (Oxford, John Radcliffe Hospital), 1985 (Oxford, John Radcliffe Hospital) and 1988 (Oxford, John Radcliffe Hospital).

CO14 *Sadie* Born 1946 (London). Two children born 1970 (Birmingham, hospital) and 1975 (Oxford, John Radcliffe Hospital).

CO15 *Amelia* Born 1943 (United States). One child born 1974 (Oxford, John Radcliffe Hospital).

CO16 *Melanie* Born 1944 (United States). Two children born 1972 (Portsmouth, hospital) and 1974 (Grantham, hospital).

CO17 *Sheilagh* Born 1947 (Lancashire). Two children born 1970 (Reading, Royal Berkshire Hospital) and 1973 (Oxford, John Radcliffe Hospital).

Crowthorne

CR1 *Sylvia* Born 1933 (Eversley). Three children born 1957 (Weymouth, hospital), 1960 (Eversley, home) and 1962 (Crowthorne, home).

CR2 *Adele* Born 1927 (Brighton). Three children born 1958 (Crowthorne, home), 1961 (Crowthorne, home) and 1962 (Crowthorne, home).

CR3 *Flora* Born 1939 (Epsom). Two children born 1966 (Bracknell, hospital) and 1969 (Bracknell, hospital).

CR4 *Beatrice* Born 1937 (Worthing). Three children born 1968 (Enfield, hospital), 1971 (London, home) and (Crowthorne, home).

CR5 *Stella* Born 1945 (Cheshire). Three children born 1971 (Middlesex, hospital), 1973 (Wokingham, hospital) and 1975 (Crowthorne, home).

CR6 *Thelma* Born 1942 (East Molesey). One child born 1972 (Reading, Royal Berkshire Hospital).

CR7 *Bernice* Born 1958 (Essex). Two children born 1985 (Camberley, Frimley Park Hospital) and 1995 (Camberley, Frimley Park Hospital).

CR8 *Harriet* Born 1955 (Taplow). Two children (twins) born 1986 (Reading, Royal Berkshire Hospital).

CR9 *Geraldine* Born 1954 (Uxbridge). Two children born 1987 (Ascot, Heatherwood Hospital) and 1989 (Ascot, Heatherwood Hospital).

CR10 *Bev* Born 1954 (Feltham). Two children born 1987 (Chertsey, St Peter's Hospital) and 1990 (Chertsey, St Peter's Hospital).

CR11 *Elaine* 1936 (London). Two children born 1960 (Ashford, Middlesex, home) and 1961 (Sandhurst, home).

CR12 *Tilly* Born 1924 (Lossiemouth). Two children born 1953 (Edinburgh, hospital) and 1955 (Edinburgh, hospital).

CR13 *Dawn* Born 1950 (Wimbledon). Three children born 1979 (Reading, Royal Berkshire Hospital) and 1981 (twins) (Reading, Royal Berkshire Hospital).

CR14 *Bonnie* Born 1948 (London). Three children born 1978 (Camberley, Frimley Park Hospital), 1981 (Reading, Royal Berkshire Hospital), and 1987 (Reading, Royal Berkshire Hospital).

Ewelme

EW1 *Agnes* Born 1938 (London). Two children born 1965 (Wokingham, hospital) and 1968 (Wokingham, hospital).

EW2 *Diana* Born 1931 (Southport). Three children born 1958 (Oxford, hospital), 1959 (Oxford, hospital) and 1964 (Yemen, hospital).

EW3 *Ellen* Born 1947 (Tunbridge Wells). Six children born 1975 (Reading, Royal Berkshire Hospital), 1976 (Wallingford, Community Hospital), 1977 (Wallingford, Community Hospital), 1980 (Wallingford, Community Hospital), 1982 (Wallingford, Community Hospital) and 1985 (Wallingford, Community Hospital).

EW4 *Bethany* Born 1944 (Wallingford). Two children born 1969 (Wallingford, St George's Maternity Hospital) and 1971 (Wallingford, St George's Maternity Hospital).

EW5 *Queenie* Born 1919 (Eynsham). Two children born 1949 (Oxford, Radcliffe Infirmary) and 1950 (Henley, hospital).

EW6 *Lily* Born 1924 (Ipswich). Five children born 1946 (Ipswich, maternity home), 1947 (Ipswich, maternity home), 1956 (Ipswich, home), 1958 (Ipswich, home) and 1961 (Ipswich, home).

EW7 *Stephanie* Born 1938 (Sutton). Four children born 1962 (Munster, British Military Hospital), 1963 (Ewelme, home), 1965 (Ewelme, home) and 1972 (Ewelme, home).

EW8 *Tania* Born 1931 (Hastings). Four children born 1952 (Hastings, hospital), 1953 (Ewelme, home), 1954 (Ewelme, home) and 1962 (Ewelme, home).

EW9 *Sharon* Born 1944 (Prestatyn). Two children born 1972 (Reading, hospital) and 1974 (Reading, hospital).

EW10 *Mavis* Born 1930 (Crowmarsh). Three children born 1956 (Wallingford, St George's Maternity Hospital), 1960 (Wallingford, St George's Maternity Hospital) and 1967 (Wallingford, St George's

Maternity Hospital).

EW11 *Bertha* Born 1932 (Sutton Coldfield). Two children born 1961 (Reading, home) and 1962 (Reading, home).

EW12 *Viv* Born 1945 (Stourbridge). Two children born 1968 (Reading, Battle Hospital) and 1971 (Reading, Royal Berkshire Hospital).

EW13 *Sandra* Born 1950 (London). Three children born 1976 (Reading, Royal Berkshire Hospital), 1979 (Reading, Royal Berkshire Hospital) and 1982 (Reading, Royal Berkshire Hospital).

EW14 *Jean* Born 1959 (Moreton-in-Marsh). Two children born 1987 (Wallingford, Community Hospital) and 1990 (Wallingford, Community Hospital).

EW15 *Margaret* Born 1944 (Romford). Two children born 1969 (Tilehurst, home) and 1970 (Wokingham, home).

North Oxford and Summertown

NO1 *Claire* Born 1933 (London). Six children born 1960 (Oxford, home), 1961 (Oxford, home), 1963 (London, home), 1965 (London, home), 1969 (London, hospital) and 1972 (London, hospital).

NO2 *Sarah* Born 1912 (Liverpool). Four children born 1940 (Oxford, Radcliffe Infirmary), 1943 (Oxford, maternity home), 1948 (Oxford, maternity home) and 1950 (Oxford, maternity home).

NO3 *Yvonne* Born 1940 (Oxford). Four children born 1959 (Oxford, Radcliffe Infirmary), 1961 (Oxford, home), 1963 (Oxford, home) and 1977 (London, home).

NO4 *Molly* Born 1926 (London). Two children born 1952 (Durham, hospital) and 1955 (Oxford, home).

NO5 *Hayley* Born 1926 (Welwyn Garden City). Three children born 1956 (Royston, hospital), 1958 (Leeds, home) and 1959 (Dorking, hospital).

NO6 *Cassie* Born 1913 (Nottingham). Two children born 1946 (Oxford, Radcliffe Infirmary) and 1952 (Oxford, maternity home).

NO7 *Grace* Born 1937 (London). Two children born 1965 (Oxford, Radcliffe Infirmary) and 1967 (Oxford, Radcliffe Infirmary).

NO8 *Emily* Born 1938 (South Africa). Three children born 1963 (Oxford, home), 1964 (Oxford, home) and 1967 (Oxford, home).

NO9 *Juliet* Born 1919 (Southampton). Two children born 1945 (Oxford, Radcliffe Infirmary) and 1946 (Oxford, Radcliffe Infirmary).

NO10 *Marjorie* Born 1931 (Southampton). Four children born 1959 (Oxford, home), 1961 (Southampton, home), 1964 (Southampton, home) and 1966 (Southampton, home).

NO11 *Janice*   Born 1917 (Newport). Two children born 1943 (London, hospital) and 1945 (London, hospital).

NO12 *Rose*   Born 1932 (Yorkshire). Two children born 1959 (Oxford, home) and 1961 (Oxford, home).

NO13 *Anna*   Born 1941 (Oxford). Three children born 1967 (Oxford, Radcliffe Infirmary), 1971 (Oxford, Radcliffe Infirmary), 1973 (Oxford, John Radcliffe Hospital).

NO14 *Martha*   Born 1945 (Taunton). Three children born 1969 (Oxford, Churchill GP Unit), 1971 (Oxford, home) and 1973 (Oxford, John Radcliffe Hospital).

NO15 *Hermione*   Born 1948 (Leicester). Three children born 1976 (London, West London Hospital), 1979 (London, West London Hospital) and 1984 (High Wycombe, hospital).

NO16 *Carmel*   Born 1949 (Rochdale). Three children born 1977 (London, West London Hospital), 1982 (Oxford, John Radcliffe Hospital) and 1985 (Oxford, John Radcliffe Hospital).

NO17 *Jane*   Born 1942 (London). Three children born 1974 (Oxford, John Radcliffe Hospital), 1976 (Oxford, John Radcliffe Hospital) and 1978 (Oxford, John Radcliffe Hospital).

Oxford City

OX1 *Esther*   Born 1930 (Portsmouth). Two children born 1959 (Oxford, Radcliffe Infirmary) and 1963 (Oxford, Radcliffe Infirmary).

OX2 *Georgie*   Born 1936 (Surrey). Two children born 1961 (Oxford, Radcliffe Infirmary) and 1975 (Oxford, John Radcliffe Hospital).

OX3 *Nora*   Born 1915 (Canada). Four children born 1941 (Oxford, Radcliffe Infirmary), 1945 (Oxford, home), 1948 (Oxford, home) and 1953 (Oxford, home).

OX4 *Fanny*   Born 1929 (Oxford). Two children born 1966 (Oxford, Churchill Hospital) and 1967 (Oxford, Churchill GP Unit).

OX5 *Laura*   Born 1940 (Swindon). Two children born 1963 (Oxford, Radcliffe Infirmary) and 1965 (Oxford, Radcliffe Infirmary).

OX6 *Olive*   Born 1916 (Oxford). Two children born 1945 (Oxford, Radcliffe Infirmary) and 1950 (Oxford, Radcliffe Infirmary).

OX7 *Rachel*   Born 1930 (Ilford). Two children born 1957 (Oxford, Radcliffe Infirmary) and 1960 (Oxford, Radcliffe Infirmary).

OX8 *Michelle*   Born 1937 (Oxford). Three children born 1964 (Oxford, Radcliffe Infirmary), 1966 (Oxford, home) and 1969 (Oxford, home).

OX9 *Mabel*   Born 1920 (Croydon). Two children born 1940 (Croydon, hospital) and 1945 (Oxford, Ruskin College).

OX10 *Rebecca*   Born 1929 (Burton-on-Trent). Three children born 1951 (Oxford, Radcliffe Infirmary), 1954 (Oxford, maternity home) and 1961 (Oxford, maternity home).

OX11 *Megan*   Born 1944 (London). Two children born 1971 (Oxford, Churchill GP Unit) and 1973 (Oxford, Churchill GP Unit).

OX12 *Lindsay*   Born 1935 (Sudan). Two children born 1960 (Oxford, home) and 1962 (Oxford, home).

OX13 *Edna*   Born 1939 (Oxford). One child born 1966 (Oxford, Radcliffe Infirmary).

OX14 *Lynne*   Born 1946 (Cardiff). One child born 1973 (Canada, hospital).

OX15 *Kim*   Born 1948 (Nottinghamshire). Two children born 1976 (Oxford, John Radcliffe Hospital) and 1978 (Oxford, home).

Sandhurst

SA1 *Dot*   Born 1925 (Ipswich). Two children born 1947 (Wiltshire, home) and 1950 (Wiltshire, home).

SA2 *Eunice*   Born 1928 (West Sussex). Four children born 1950 (Carlisle, City General Hospital), 1951 (Windlesham, maternity home), 1956 (Reading, Battle Hospital), 1959 (Wokingham, home).

SA3 *Myrtle*   Born 1927 (Sri Lanka). Eight children born 1951 (Aldershot, military hospital), 1953 (Libya, military hospital), 1955 (Libya, military hospital), 1958 (Libya, military hospital), 1960 (Germany, military hospital), 1963 (twins) (Malaysia, military hospital), 1965 (Belfast, military hospital).

SA4 *Valerie*   Born 1947 (Kent). Three children born 1972 (Reading, Royal Berkshire Hospital), 1973 (Reading, Royal Berkshire Hospital), 1977 (Newbury, hospital).

SA5 *Liz*   Born 1946 (Lancashire). Three children born 1973 (Germany, military hospital), 1975 (Omagh, hospital) and 1980 (West Midlands, hospital).

SA6 *Lorraine*   Born 1950 (Wokingham). Three children born 1976 (Wallingford, Community Hospital), 1978 (Reading, Royal Berkshire Hospital) and 1983 (Reading, Royal Berkshire Hospital).

SA7 *Pam*   Born 1947 (Pembrokeshire). Two children born 1977 (Ashford, Middlesex, hospital) and 1979 (Camberley, Frimley Park Hospital).

SA8 *Gina*   Born 1951 (London). Two children born 1978 (Solihull, maternity hospital) and 1980 (Camberley, Frimley Park Hospital).

SA9 *Andrea*   Born 1952 (London). Three children born 1978 (Camberley, Frimley Park Hospital), 1981 (Camberley, Frimley Park Hospital) and 194 (Camberley, Frimley Park Hospital).

SA10 *Shirley*   Born 1952 (Huddersfield). Two children born 1978 (Camberley, Frimley Park Hospital) and 1983 (Buckinghamshire; adopted).
SA11 *Sonia*   Born 1949 (Ireland). Three children born 1979 (Dublin, hospital), 1980 (Dublin, hospital) and 1982 (Ascot, hospital).
SA12 *Katherine*   Born 1954 (Wolverhampton). Two children born 1983 (Camberley, Frimley Park Hospital) and 1986 (Camberley, Frimley Park Hospital).
SA13 *Jemma*   Born 1957 (Liverpool). Two children 1984 (Camberley, Frimley Park Hospital) and 1985 (Camberley, Frimley Park Hospital).
SA14 *Natalie*   Born 1955 (Bristol). Two children born 1983 (Camberley, Frimley Park Hospital) and 1985 (Camberley, Frimley Park Hospital).

Somerville College, Oxford

SO1 *Monika*   Born 1927 (Germany). One child born 1955 (Oxford, maternity home).
SO2 *Claudia*   Born 1944 (Yorkshire). Three children born 1970 (Oxford, Radcliffe Infirmary), 1972 (Australia, hospital), 1977 (New Zealand, hospital).
SO3 *Jill*   Born 1936 (Southampton). Two children born 1966 (Oxford, Radcliffe Infirmary) and 1970 (Oxford, Radcliffe Infirmary).
SO4 *Karen*   Born 1945 (Middlesex). Four children born 1967 (Oxford, Churchill Hospital), 1970 (Sussex, hospital), 1984 (Warwickshire, hospital) and 1985 (Warwickshire, hospital).
SO5 *Louisa*   Born 1939 (Latvia). Three children born 1968 (Oxford, Churchill GP Unit), 1972 (Oxford, Churchill GP Unit) and 1975 (Oxford, John Radcliffe Hospital).
SO6 *Camilla*   Born 1937 (Sheffield). Three children born 1961 (Oxford, Churchill Hospital), 1963 (Rugby, home) and 1965 (Rugby, home).
SO7 *Hannah*   Born 1924 (Romania). Three children born 1952 (Oxford, Churchill Hospital), 1955 (Oxford, Churchill Hospital) and 1956 (Oxford, Churchill Hospital).
SO8 *Phoebe*   Born 1921 (Northern Ireland). Five children born 1948 (Oxford, Radcliffe Infirmary), 1950 (Oxford, home), 1955 (Oxford, home), 1956 (Oxford, home) and 1957 (Oxford, home).
SO9 *Bella*   Born 1927 (Monaco). Two children born 1953 (Oxford, home) and 1955 (Oxford, home).
SO10 *Kelly*   Born 1935 (India). Two children born 1968 (Oxford, Radcliffe Infirmary) and 1970 (Manchester, Royal Infirmary).
SO11 *Ingrid*   Born 1932 (London). Two children born 1961 (Oxford, Churchill Hospital) and 1962 (Oxford, Churchill Hospital).

SO12 *Faith*   Born 1944 (United States). One child born 1971 (Oxford, Churchill GP Unit).

SO13 *Alexa*   Born 1952 (United States). One child born 1993 (Oxford, John Radcliffe Hospital).

SO14 *Tasha*   Born 1943 (Cornwall). Two children born 1972 (Oxford, John Radcliffe Hospital) and 1975 (Oxford, John Radcliffe Hospital).

SO15 *Tara*   Born 1954 (India). Two children born 1988 (Oxford, John Radcliffe Hospital) and 1990 (Oxford, John Radcliffe Hospital).

SO16 *April*   Born 1953 (Stockton-on-Tees). Three children born 1978 (Oxford, John Radcliffe Hospital GP Unit), 1981 (Oxford, John Radcliffe Hospital GP Unit) and 1986 (Oxford, John Radcliffe Hospital GP Unit).

Thame

TH1 *Donna*   Born 1946 (Farringdon). Two children born 1969 (Farringdon, home) and 1971 (Marlow, home).

TH2 *Linda*   Born 1947 (London). Three children born 1970 (Aylesbury, Royal Buckinghamshire Hospital), 1973 (Stoke Mandeville Hospital GP Unit) and 1978 (Stoke Mandeville Hospital GP Unit).

TH3 *Nina*   Born 1951 (Oxford). Two children born 1974 (Oxford, John Radcliffe Hospital) and 1978 (Oxford, John Radcliffe Hospital).

TH4 *Barbie*   Born 1947 (London). Two children born 1977 (Harrow, Norwick Park Hospital) and 1979 (Harrow, Norwick Park Hospital).

TH5 *Mary*   Born 1959 (Essex). Two children born 1982 (Kent, hospital) and 1984 (Kent, hospital).

TH6 *Josie*   Born 1950 (Redhill). Four children born 1985 (Oxford, John Radcliffe Hospital), 1989 (Oxford, John Radcliffe Hospital) and 1991 (twins) (Oxford, John Radcliffe Hospital).

TH7 *Alma*   Born 1950 (Nottingham). Two children born 1986 (twins) (Oxford, John Radcliffe Hospital).

TH8 *Aida*   Born 1936 (London). Two children born 1957 (Wimbledon, hospital), 1958 (Wimbledon, hospital) and 1972 (Oxford, John Radcliffe Hospital).

TH9 *Brenda*   Born 1946 (Amersham). Four children born 1963 (Buckinghamshire, home), 1966 (Buckinghamshire, home) 1966 (Towersey, home), 1969 (Towersey, home).

TH10 *Colleen*   Born 1943 (Oxford). Three children born 1964 (Oxford, Radcliffe Infirmary), 1966 (Oxford, Radcliffe Infirmary) and 1970 (Oxford, Churchill Hospital).

TH11 *Mildred*   Born 1944 (Towersey). Two children born 1965

(Aylesbury, Royal Buckinghamshire Hospital) and 1969 (Aylesbury, Royal Buckinghamshire Hospital).

TH12 *Sophie*   Born 1943 (Kent). Two children born 1968 (Portsmouth, hospital) and 1970 (Newport Pagnell, maternity hospital).

TH13 *Frances*   Born 1942 (Felstead). Two children born 1970 (Oxford, Churchill Hospital) and 1972 (Oxford, John Radcliffe Hospital).

TH14 *Carol*   Born 1962 (Cheltenham). Five children born 1979 (Oxford, John Radcliffe Hospital), 1980 (Oxford, John Radcliffe Hospital), 1982 (Oxford, John Radcliffe Hospital), 1984 (Oxford, John Radcliffe Hospital) and 1996 (Oxford, John Radcliffe Hospital).

Wychwood villages

WY1 *Joy*   Born 1923 (Birmingham). Two children born 1945 (Chipping Norton, hospital) and 1947 (Chipping Norton, hospital).

WY2 *Alice*   Born 1939 (Gloucestershire). Three children born 1964 (Chipping Norton, hospital), 1966 (Chipping Norton, hospital) and 1967 (Chipping Norton, hospital).

WY3 *Phyllis*   Born 1925 (Burton-on-Trent). Four children born 1946 (Chipping Norton, hospital), 1950 (Chipping Norton, hospital), 1952 (Chipping Norton, hospital) and 1956 (Chipping Norton, hospital).

WY4 *Maud*   Born 1921 (Churchill Heath). Two children born 1941 (Milton-under-Wychwood, home) and 1944 (Milton-under-Wychwood, home).

WY5 *Celia*   Born 1924 (Chipping Norton). Two children born 1952 (Chipping Norton, hospital) and 1955 (Chipping Norton, hospital).

WY6 *Maxine*   Born 1932 (Bolton). Three children born 1957 (Chipping Norton, hospital), 1959 (Chipping Norton, hospital) and 1962 (Chipping Norton, hospital).

WY7 *Bobbie*   Born 1921 (Wales). Two children born 1955 (Oxford, Radcliffe Infirmary) and 1959 (Oxford, Radcliffe Infirmary).

WY8 *Madge*   Born 1918 (Shipton-under-Wychwood). Five children born 1940 (Chipping Norton, hospital), 1941 (Chipping Norton, hospital), 1942 (Chipping Norton, hospital), 1943 (Milton-under-Wychwood, home) and 1948 (Chipping Norton, hospital).

WY9 *Daisy*   Born 1923 (Bradford). Two children born 1948 (Eynsham, home) and 1950 (Eynsham, home).

WY10 *Jackie*   Born 1933 (London). Two children (twins) born 1965 (Oxford, Radcliffe Infirmary).

WY11 *Susan*   Born 1940 (London). Two children born 1971 (Swindon, military hospital) and 1972 (Swindon, military hospital).

WY12 *Cynthia*   Born 1957 (Kettering). One child born 1993 (Oxford, John Radcliffe Hospital).

WY13 *Amy*   Born 1947 (Barnstable). One child born 1977 (Oxford, John Radcliffe Hospital).

WY14 *Kaye*   Born 1950 (London). Two children born 1981 (Oxford, John Radcliffe Hospital GP Unit) and 1984 (Wantage Community Hospital).

Select bibliography of published secondary sources

Abrams, Lynn, *Oral History Theory* (London: Routledge, 2010).

Aiston, Sarah, 'A maternal identity? The family lives of British women graduates pre- and post-1945', *History of Education*, 34 (2005), 407–26.

Alexander, Sally, *Becoming a Woman, and Other Essays in 19th and 20th Century Feminist History* (London: Virago, 1994).

Allan, Graham, *Kinship and Friendship in Modern Britain* (Oxford: Oxford University Press, 1996).

Arnup, Katherine, Andrée Lévesque and Ruth Roach Pierson (eds), *Delivering Motherhood: Maternal Ideologies and Practices in the 19th and 20th Centuries* (London: Routledge, 1990).

Badinter, Elizabeth, *The Myth of Motherhood: An Historical View of the Maternal Instinct* (London: Souvenir Press, 1981).

Bailey, Jenna, *Can Any Mother Help Me?* (London: Faber and Faber, 2007).

Beaumont, Caitriona, 'Housewives, workers and citizens: voluntary women's organisations and the campaign for women's rights in England and Wales during the post-war period', in Nick Crowson, Matthew Hilton and James McKay (eds), *NGOs in Contemporary Britain: Non-State Actors in Society and Politics since 1945* (Houndmills: Palgrave Macmillan, 2009), 59–76.

Beier, Lucinda McCray, '"We were green as grass": learning about sex and reproduction in three working-class Lancashire communities, 1900–1970', *Social History of Medicine*, 16 (2003), 461–80.

Beier, Lucinda McCray, 'Expertise and control: childbearing in three twentieth-century working-class Lancashire communities', *Bulletin of the History of Medicine*, 78 (2004), 379–409.

Beier, Lucinda McCray, *For Their Own Good: The Transformation of English Working-Class Health Culture, 1880–1970* (Columbus: The Ohio State University Press, 2008).

Bernard, Jessie, *The Future of Parenthood* (London: Calder and Boyars, 1975).

Birmingham Feminist History Group, 'Feminism as femininity in the nineteen-fifties?', *Feminist Review*, 3 (1979), 48–65.

Bourke, Joanna, *Working-Class Cultures in Britain 1890–1960: Gender, Class and Ethnicity* (London: Routledge, 1994).

Boyd, Carol, 'Mothers and daughters: a discussion of theory and research', *Journal of Marriage and the Family*, 51 (1989), 291–301.

Braithwaite, Brian, *Women's Magazines: The First 300 Years* (London: Peter Owen, 1995).

Brannen, Julia and Ann Nilsen, 'From fatherhood to fathering: transmission and change among British fathers in four-generation families', *Sociology*, 40 (2006), 335–52.

Bryan, Beverley, Stella Dadzie and Suzanne Scafe, *The Heart of the Race: Black Women's Lives in Britain* (London: Virago, 1985).

Clark, David (ed.), *Marriage, Domestic Life and Social Change: Writings for Jacqueline Burgoyne (1944–88)* (London: Routledge, 1991).

Connolly, Sara and Mary Gregory, 'Women and work since 1970', in Nicholas Crafts, Ian Gazley and Andrew Newell (eds), *Work and Pay in Twentieth-Century Britain* (Oxford: Oxford University Press, 2007), 142–77.

Cook, Hera, *The Long Sexual Revolution* (Oxford: Oxford University Press, 2004).

Dale, Jennifer and Peggy Foster, *Feminists and State Welfare* (London: Routledge, 1986).

Dally, Ann, *Inventing Motherhood: The Consequences of an Ideal* (New York: Schocken, 1983).

Davidoff, Leonore, Megan Doolittle, Janet Fink and Katherine Holden, *The Family Story: Blood, Contract and Intimacy, 1830–1960* (London and New York: Longman, 1999).

Davis, Angela, 'To what extent were women's experiences of maternity influenced by locality? Benson, Oxfordshire c. 1945–1970', *Family and Community History*, 8 (2005), 21–34.

Davis, Angela, 'Oral history and the creation of collective memories: women's experiences of motherhood in Oxfordshire c. 1945–1970', *University of Sussex Journal of Contemporary History*, 10 (2006), 1–10.

Davis, Angela, 'The ordinary good mother': women's construction of their identity as mothers, Oxfordshire c. 1945–1970', in Alyson Brown (ed.), *Historical Perspectives on Social Identities* (Newcastle: Cambridge Scholars Press, 2006), 114–28.

Davis, Angela, '"So it wasn't a brilliant education, not really I don't think": class, gender and locality: women's accounts of school in rural Oxfordshire, c. 1930–1960', *History of Education Researcher*, 78 (2006), 72–83.

Davis, Angela, '"Oh no, nothing, we didn't learn anything": sex education and the preparation of girls for motherhood, c. 1930–1970', *History of Education*, 37 (2008) 551–678.

Davis, Angela, 'A critical perspective on British social surveys and community studies and their accounts of married life c.1945–70', *Cultural and Social History*, 6 (2009), 47–64.

Davis, Angela, 'A revolution in maternity care? Women and the maternity services, Oxfordshire c. 1948–1974', *Social History of Medicine* (2011, doi: 10.1093/shm/hkq092).

Dawson, Graham, *Soldier Heroes: British Adventure, Empire, and the Imagining of Masculinities* (London: Routledge, 1994).

DiQuinzio, Patrice, *The Impossibility of Motherhood* (London: Routledge, 1999).

Doane, Janice and Devon Hodges, *From Klein to Kristeva: Psychoanalytic Feminism and the Search for the 'Good Enough' Mother* (Ann Arbor: University of Michigan Press, 1992).

Donnison, Jean, *Midwives and Medical Men: A History of the Struggle for the Control of Childbirth* (New Barnett: Historical Publications, 1988).

Dyhouse, Carol, 'Graduates, mothers and graduate mothers: family investment in higher education in twentieth-century England', *Gender and Education*, 14 (2002), 325–36.

Ehrenreich, Barbara and Deirdre English, *For Her Own Good: 150 Years of the Experts' Advice to Women* (London: Pluto Press, 1978).

Ferguson, Marjory, *Forever Feminine: Women's Magazines and the Cult of Femininity* (London: Heinemann, 1983).

Finch, Janet, 'The deceit of self help: preschool playgroups and working class mothers', *Journal of Social Policy*, 13 (1984), 1–20.

Fisher, Kate, '"She was quite satisfied with the arrangements I made": gender and birth control in Britain 1920–1950', *Past and Present*, 169 (2000), 161–93.

Fisher, Kate, *Birth Control, Sex and Marriage in Britain, 1918–1960* (Oxford: Oxford University Press, 2006).

Fredman, Sandra, *Women and the Law* (Oxford: Oxford University Press, 1997).

Garcia, Jo, Robert Kilpatrick and Martin Richards (eds), *The Politics of Maternity Care* (Oxford: Clarendon Press, 1990).

Geiger, Susan, 'Women's life histories', *Signs*, 11 (1986), 334–51.

Giles, Judy, 'Narratives of gender, class, and modernity in women's memories of mid-twentieth-century Britain, *Signs*, 28 (2002), 21–41.

Gillis, John R., *For Better, For Worse: British Marriages, 1600 to the Present* (New York: Oxford University Press, 1985).

Gijswijt-Hofstra, Marijke and Hilary Marland (eds), *Cultures of Child Health in Britain and the Netherlands in the Twentieth Century* (Amsterdam and New York: Rodpoi, 2003).

Glenn, Evelyn Nakano, Grace Chung and Linda Rennie Forcey (eds), *Mothering: Ideology, Experience and Agency* (London: Routledge, 1994).

Gluck, Sherna Berger and Daphne Patai (eds), *Women's Words: The Feminist Practice of Oral History* (New York and London: Routledge, Chapman and Hall, 1991).

Goldthorpe, J.E., *Family Life in Western Societies: A Historical Sociology of Family Relationships in Britain and North America* (Cambridge: Cambridge University Press, 1987).

Hall, Lesley A., 'In ignorance and in knowledge: reflections on the history of sex education in Britain', in Lutz Sauerteig and Roger Davidson (eds), *Shaping Sexual Knowledge: A Cultural History of Sex Education in Twentieth Century Europe* (London: Routledge, 2009), 19–36.

Halsey, A.H. with J. Webb (eds), *Twentieth-Century British Social Trends* (Houndmills: Macmillan, 2000).

Hanson, Clare, *A Cultural History of Pregnancy: Pregnancy, Medicine and Culture, 1750–2000* (Houndmills: Palgrave Macmillan, 2004).

Hardyment, Christina, *Dream Babies: Childcare Advice from John Locke to Gina Ford* (London: Frances Lincoln Limited, 2007).

Hirsch, Marianne, *The Mother/Daughter Plot: Narrative, Psychoanalysis, Feminism* (Bloomington and Indiana: Indiana University Press, 1989).

Holloway, Gerry, *Women and Work in Britain since 1840* (London and New York: Routledge, 2005).

Howkins, Alun, *The Death of Rural England* (London: Routledge, 2003).

Jackson, Mark (ed.), *Health and the Modern Home* (London: Routledge, 2007).

Jewish Women in London Group, *Generations of Memories: Voices of Jewish Women* (London: The Women's Press, 1989).

Jones, Helen, *Health and Society in Twentieth-Century Britain* (London: Longman, 1994).

Jones, Margaret and Rodney Lowe, *From Beveridge to Blair: The First Fifty Years of Britain's Welfare State, 1948–98* (Manchester: Manchester University Press, 2002).

Katbamna, Savita, *'Race' and Childbirth* (Buckingham: University of Buckingham Press, 2000).

Kiernan, Kathleen, Jane Lewis and Hilary Land, *Lone Motherhood in Twentieth-Century Britain: From Footnote to Front Page* (Oxford: Oxford University Press, 1998).

Kitzinger, Sheila, *The Politics of Birth* (London: Elsevier, 2005).

Koven, Seth and Sonya Michel (eds), *Mothers of a New World* (London: Routledge, 1993).

Langhamer, Claire, *Women's Leisure in England 1920–1960* (Manchester: Manchester University Press, 2000).

Langhamer, Claire, 'The meanings of home in postwar Britain', *Journal of Contemporary History*, 40 (2005), 341–62.

Langhamer, Claire, 'Love and courtship in mid-twentieth-century England', *Historical Journal*, 50 (2007), 173–96.

Leap, Nicky and Billie Hunter, *The Midwife's Tale: An Oral History from Handywoman to Professional Midwife* (London: Scarlet Press, 1993).

Lennon, Mary, Marie McAdam and Joanne O'Brien, *Across the Water: Irish Women's Lives in Britain* (London: Virago, 1988).

Lewis, Jane, *The Politics of Motherhood* (London: Croom Helm, 1980).

Lewis, Jane, *Women in Britain since 1945* (Oxford: Blackwell, 1992).

Lewis, Jane, *The End of Marriage?* (Cheltenham: Edward Elgar Publishing, 2001).

Marks, Lara, "'The luckless waifs and strays of humanity": Irish and Jewish immigrant unwed mothers in London, 1870–1939', *Twentieth Century British History*, 3 (1992), 113–37.

Marland, Hilary and Anne Marie Rafferty (eds), *Midwives, Society and Childbirth: Debates and Controversies in the Modern Period* (London: Routledge, 1997).

McCormick, Leanne, *Regulating Sexuality: Women in Twentieth-Century Northern Ireland* (Manchester: Manchester University Press, 2009).

McKibbin, Ross, *Classes and Cultures: England 1918–1951* (Oxford: Oxford University Press, 1998).

McRae, Susan (ed.), *Changing Britain: Families and Households in the 1990s* (Oxford: Oxford University Press, 1999).

Millar, Jane and Tess Ridge, *Families, Poverty, Work and Care: A Review of the*

Literature on Lone Parents and Low-Income Couple Families With Children (Department of Work and Pensions Research Report No. 153) (Leeds: Corporate Document Services, 2001).

Misztal, Barbara, *Theories of Social Remembering* (Maidenhead: Open University Press, 2003).

Oakley, Ann, *The Captured Womb: A History of the Medical Care of Pregnant Women* (Oxford: Basil Blackwell, 1984).

Oakley, Ann, *Essays on Women, Medicine and Health* (Edinburgh: Edinburgh University Press, 1993).

Parfit, Jessie, *The Health of a City: Oxford 1770–1974* (Oxford: The Amate Press, 1987).

Peretz, Elizabeth, 'The costs of modern motherhood to low income families in interwar Britain', in Valerie Fildes, Lara Marks and Hilary Marland (eds), *Women and Children First: International Maternal and Child Welfare 1870–1945* (London: Routledge, 1992), 257–80.

Peretz, Elizabeth, 'Infant welfare in inter-war Oxford', in Richard C. Whiting (ed.), *Oxford: Studies in the History of a University Town since 1800* (Manchester: Manchester University Press, 1993), 131–45.

Perks, Robert and Alistair Thomson (eds), *The Oral History Reader* (London: Routledge, 1998).

Pilcher, Jane, 'School sex education in England 1870–2000', *Sex Education*, 5 (2005), 153–70.

Portelli, Alessandro, *The Death of Luigi Trastulli and Other Stories: Form and Meaning in Oral History* (Albany: State University of New York Press, 1991).

Purvis, June, 'Domestic subjects since 1870', in Ivor Goodson (ed.), *Social Histories of the Secondary Curriculum: Subjects for Study* (Lewes: Falmer Press, 1985), 145–76.

Rhodes, Philip, *A Short History of Clinical Midwifery* (Hale: Books for Midwives Press, 1995).

Riley, Denise, *War in the Nursery: Theories of Child and Mother* (London: Virago, 1983).

Roberts, Elizabeth, *A Woman's Place: An Oral History of Working-Class Women, 1890–1940* (Oxford: Blackwell, 1984).

Roberts, Elizabeth, *Women and Families: An Oral History, 1940–1970* (Oxford: Blackwell, 1995).

Rose, Jacqueline, 'Femininity and its discontents', *Feminist Review*, 14 (1983), 7–21.

Ross, Ellen, 'Survival networks: women's neighbourhood sharing in London before the First World War', *History Workshop Journal*, 15 (1983), 4–27.

Ross, Ellen, *Love and Toil: Motherhood in Outcast London 1870–1918* (New York, Oxford University Press, 1993).

Ross, Ellen, 'New thoughts on the oldest vocation: mothers and motherhood in recent feminist scholarship', *Signs*, 20 (1995), 397–413.

Rowbotham, Sheila, 'To be or not to be: the dilemmas of mothering', *Feminist Review*, 31 (1989), 82–93.

Samuel, Raphael (ed.), *Village Life and Labour* (London: Routledge and Kegan Paul, 1975).

Scott, Joan W., 'Fantasy echo: history and the construction of identity', *Critical Inquiry*, 27 (2001), 284–304.

Shaw, Alison, *Kinship and Continuity: Pakistani Families in Britain* (London: Routledge, 2000).

Smith, Graham, 'Protest is better for infants: motherhood, health and welfare in a woman's town, c. 1911–1931', *Oral History*, 23 (1995), 63–70.

Spencer, Stephanie, 'Reflections on the site of struggle: girls' experience of secondary education in the late 1950s', *History of Education*, 33 (2004), 437–49.

Spencer, Stephanie, *Gender, Work and Education in Britain in the 1950s* (Basingstoke: Palgrave Macmillan, 2005).

Steedman, Carolyn, *Landscape of a Good Woman: The Story of Two Lives* (London: Virago, 1986).

Stone, Lawrence, *Road to Divorce: England 1530–1987* (Oxford: Oxford University Press, 1990).

Summerfield, Penny, *Reconstructing Women's Wartime Lives* (Manchester: Manchester University Press, 1998).

Summerfield, Penny, 'Culture and composure: creating narratives of the gendered self in oral history interviews', *Cultural and Social History*, 1 (2004), 65–93.

Tew, Marjorie, *Safer Childbirth? A Critical History of Maternity Care* (London: Chapman and Hall, 1995).

Thane, Pat, 'Women since 1945', in Paul Johnson (ed.), *20th Century Britain: Economic, Social, and Cultural Change* (Longman: London, 1994), 392–410.

Thane, Pat, 'Girton graduates: earning and learning, 1920s–1980s', *Women's History Review*, 13 (2004), 349–58.

Thomson, Rachel, 'Moral rhetoric and public health pragmatism: the recent politics of sex education', *Feminist Review*, 48 (1994), 40–60.

Tilly, Louise and Joan Scott, *Women, Work and Family* (London and New York: Methuen, 1987).

Todd, Selina, *Young Women, Work and Family in England 1918–1950* (Oxford: Oxford University Press, 2005).

Tosh, John, *A Man's Place: Masculinity and the Middle-Class Home in Victorian England* (New Haven and London: Yale University Press, 1999).

Umansky, Lauri, *Motherhood Reconceived: Feminism and the Legacies of the Sixties* (London: New York University Press, 1996).

Urwin, Cathy, 'Constructing motherhood: a persuasion of normal development', in Carolyn Steedman, Cathy Urwin and Valerie Walkerdine, *Language, Gender and Childhood* (London: Routledge and Kegan Paul, 1985), 164–202.

Verdon, Nicola, '"The modern countrywoman": farm women, domesticity and social change in interwar Britain', *History Workshop Journal*, 70 (2010), 86–107.

Vincent, Carol, Stephen J. Ball and Soile Pietikainen, 'Metropolitan mothers:

mothers, mothering and paid work', *Women's Studies International Forum*, 27 (2004), 571–87.

Watkin, Brian, *Documents on Health and Social Services: 1834 to the Present Day* (London: Methuen, 1975).

Webster, Wendy, *Imagining Home: Gender, 'Race' and National Identity, 1945–64* (London: UCL Press, 1998).

Whetham, Edith H., *The Agrarian History of England and Wales: Volume VIII, 1914–1939* (Cambridge: Cambridge University Press, 1978).

White, Cynthia L., *Women's Magazines 1693–1968* (London: Michael Joseph, 1970).

Williams, A. Susan, *Women and Childbirth in the Twentieth Century: A History of the National Birthday Trust Fund 1928–93* (Stroud: Sutton, 1997).

Wilson, Amrit, *Finding a Voice: Asian Women in Britain* (London: Virago, 1978).

Wilson, Dolly Smith, 'A new look at the affluent worker: the good working mother in post-war Britain', *Twentieth Century British History*, 17 (2006), 206–29.

Wilson, Elizabeth, *Women and the Welfare State* (London: Tavistock, 1997).

Winship, Janice, *Inside Women's Magazines* (London: Pandora, 1987).

Wolpe, AnnMarie 'Sex in schools: back to the future', *Feminist Review*, 27 (1987), 37–47.

Zweiniger-Bargielowska, Ina (ed.), *Women in Twentieth-Century Britain* (Harlow: Pearson Education Limited, 2001).

Index

.